Between Literalness and Freedom

To Joel

Publications of the Finnish Exegetical Society
Edited by Jaakko Hyttinen

Cover design by Tapio Arhola

ISSN 0356-2786
ISBN 951-9217-30-4
ISBN 3-525-53549-X

Nord Print Oy 1999

PUBLICATIONS OF THE FINNISH EXEGETICAL SOCIETY 75

SEPPO SIPILÄ

BETWEEN LITERALNESS AND FREEDOM

Translation technique in the Septuagint of Joshua and Judges regarding the clause connections introduced by ו and כי

The Finnish Exegetical Society in Helsinki
Vandenhoeck & Ruprecht in Göttingen
1999

Τῷ ἀναγινωσκόντῳ ὁ γράφων χαίρειν

A dissertation is always the tip of the iceberg, the visible part of a long process of working and thinking, of love and hate, of passion and despair. In my case this process started more than ten years ago, when I was considering a suitable subject for my master's thesis in Old Testament studies. At the suggestion of Professor Raija Sollamo I started to work with the Septuagint translation of the book of Joshua. I am still working with this book and this translation.

The process has continued smoothly thanks to the possibility of working in the Department of Biblical Studies in Helsinki. I have been extremely blessed to have Raija Sollamo as my supervisor. Her constant encouragement probably saved my sanity. I am also proud to have a very helpful colleague in Anssi Voitila, whose vision and skills I deeply admire. Professor Anneli Aejmelaeus, without whom this study would not be possible, has also been very helpful during all these years. Her advice and suggestions clarified many things. Professor Ilmari Soisalon-Soininen, despite having retired, has been constantly interested in my work and offered many fine suggestions. Due to his influence the present work also includes material from Judges.

I have had the honour to discuss my work with many scholars and colleagues, mainly in connection with papers presented at the meetings of the International Organization of the Septuagint and Cognate Studies. Professor Timo Veijola and the members of the seminar for post-graduate studies in Old Testament have been kind enough to read parts of my work despite its speciality. I can now gladly thank all of them for their support, interest and encouragement. At the same time I feel a certain pressure and duty to live up to their expectations.

The Department of Biblical Studies, the Finnish Academy, and the Research Unit for Early Jewish and Christian Culture and Literature, one of the Centres of Excellence at the University of Helsinki, have offered me constant financial support to enable me to work full-time, some thing for which one cannot be thankful enough.

Michael Cox, Lic. Theol. went through the drafts and tried to stop me from making errors in English. For the errors, however, I alone am to blame. I also wish to thank the Finnish Exegetical Society for including my book in its series of publications.

I dedicate this work to my son Joel, who in spite of his disability has always shown a keen interest in my doings. He is the one who demands that I use the computer!

ἔρρωσο

Abstract

Between Literalness and Freedom. Translation technique in the Septuagint of Joshua and Judges regarding the clause connections introduced by ו and כי.

In this doctoral thesis a study is made of every occurrence of the clause-initial conjunctions ו and כי in the books of Joshua and Judges, and of their renderings in the LXX. The corpus includes 2293 ו-initial clauses and 216 כי-initial clauses. These were divided into sub-groups reflecting the translator's point of view and the difference between the conjunction system of Hebrew and Greek, since the translators did not handle every ו or כי in a similar fashion.

The translation techniques employed in the LXX of the given books are described in the light of the Greek renderings of the Hebrew conjunctions, using the methodology developed by Ilmari Soisalon-Soininen and successfully employed by the Helsinki school of LXX studies, most notably by Soisalon-Soininen himself and by his pupils Anneli Aejmelaeus and Raija Sollamo.

The main factors influencing the translation techniques are found to be narrow segmentation, the limitations and requirements imposed by the Hebrew and Greek languages, and the individual characteristics of the translators.

The LXX of Judges is more literal than the LXX of Joshua, the difference being clarified when the translations of Joshua and Judges are compared with those of the Pentateuch. This is further compared with the results of other studies describing the translation techniques of the given books. Literalness implies atypical Greek because of the high number of simple co-ordinated clauses and the low number of embedded constructions such as *participium coniunctum* and *genetivus absolutus*. In spite of the literalness of their translations the translators were able occasionally to take into account the special character of the Hebrew expression and produce renderings displaying imagination and a clear understanding of the possibilities of the Greek language.

Table of contents

1 Introduction

1.1 Context of the study

The present study concentrates on two books of the Septuagint, Joshua and Judges, and their translation technique. Many studies on the translation technique of the books of the Pentateuch have appeared, but studies on Joshua or on Judges in particular are few in number, creating a need for a study of the translation technique of Joshua and Judges.[1] These two books, when put together, make an interesting couple. The contents of the books clearly belong together, but the translations are dissimilar due to the different translation techniques.

The dissimilarity of the translation techniques of Joshua and Judges may be deduced from existing studies, as will soon become evident. In my study I shall examine the differences more closely by discussing the translation technique of these books in detail. I shall try to answer the question why the translations are as they are.

Existing studies on the translation technique of the Greek Joshua and Judges can be divided into two groups: studies describing the translation technique of particular grammatical phenomena in the LXX as a whole, and studies describing the translation technique of the LXX of Joshua or Judges from a broader perspective.

Already at the beginning of the century *Thackeray* classified the books of the LXX into four different groups reflecting the translation technique employed and the stylistic impression various books gave him.[2] The first three groups are good, indifferent and literal or

---

[1]   Cf. den Hertog 1996, 160 and recently van der Meer 1998: "Overall studies on the translation technique employed by the Greek translator of Joshua are still relatively modest."

[2]   Thackeray 1909, 13. For the method whereby Thackeray produces his classification see Sollamo 1975, 775.

unintelligent translations, the fourth group being paraphrases. In Thackeray's classification Joshua represents a good translation[3], but Judges a bad one. Since the classification is based on Thackeray's own subjective impression of the translation, discussion regarding the classification was unavoidable and, indeed, the classification has been the subject of various comments.

Some translation-technical studies published recently deal with the whole of the LXX, Joshua and Judges included. Thackeray's classification may thus be set within a wider perspective.

Study of the position of the enclitic personal pronouns in the LXX makes it possible for *Wifstrand* to arrange the Septuagintal books into two different groups. Books where the position of the pronoun in Greek (nearly) always follows the Hebrew word order belong in one group. Books where the position of the pronoun could be changed according to classical Greek usage belong in the other group.

The LXX of Joshua and Judges turns out to be very similar, since in these books the translators hardly ever changed the position of the pronoun.[4] After making his classification Wifstrand turns to Thackeray's older classification, which in his opinion is valid only if taken rather broadly. Even in the best translations of the LXX the parent text greatly influenced the translation. So great is the influence that Wifstrand does not count even the best parts of the LXX as representative of good contemporary *Koiné*.[5]

Soisalon-Soininen discusses in minute detail the infinitive and its use by the various translators of the LXX in his study *Die Infinitive in der Septuaginta*.[6] The study allows him to compare various translators and set them in relation to each other.

Soisalon-Soininen classifies the books of the LXX in descending order according to various criteria and counts the mean of the

[3]   Thackeray (1909, 13) speaks about "Joshua (part)", but unfortunately offers no explanation for the ambiguous expression "(part)". Does he mean that his classification fits the book only partly, or that he based his judgement only on a limited sample of the book, or that the translation is only partly good Greek?

[4]   Wifstrand 1950, 45-49 gives the full listing of the books of the LXX.

[5]   Wifstrand 1950, 67.

[6]   The work is cited here as Soisalon-Soininen 1965.

relative positions of various books.[7] Joshua belongs in the first third of the freest translations, with the mean value of 6.3. Judges, on the other hand, belongs in the last third with a mean of 17.7.

In her study *Sollamo* examines every occurrence of the semi-prepositions in the Hebrew Old Testament and observes the way they are rendered in the LXX. She bases her calculations and the translation-technical discussion on the renderings of the common semiprepositions only.[8] The renderings are classified as free, literal, and slavish,[9] but Sollamo offers no discussion as to how the status of an equivalent is defined in this classification.

Sollamo's conclusions regarding the translation technique are based on three criteria.[10] She calculates a ratio for free renderings of the semipreposition by comparing the number of free renderings to the total number of renderings in a book of the LXX.[11] The ratio for slavish renderings is calculated accordingly. Finally, Sollamo uses the stereotyping tendency as a criterion. By the stereotyping tendency she means the ratio of the most common single Greek equivalent for a semipreposition against the total number of renderings.[12]

Sollamo then arranges the Septuagintal books into four groups according to the position they occupy when different criteria are used.[13] Joshua (the mean of the relative position is 10.0) belongs in the second group, but Judges (the mean is 22.6) turned out to be among the most slavish renderings in the LXX.

Aejmelaeus' studies on the translation technique of Hebrew conjunctions in the LXX form the basis of my study, and I shall introduce them when discussing the methodological issues involved.[14] Here the occurrence of כי at the beginning of a causal clause provides information about the translations of Joshua and Judges.[15] For

---

[7] Soisalon-Soininen 1965, 176-190.
[8] See Sollamo 1979, 280.
[9] Sollamo 1979, 280 note 1.
[10] Sollamo 1979, 281-283.
[11] Sollamo 1979, 280.
[12] Sollamo 1979, 283.
[13] Sollamo 1979, 284-286.
[14] See pp. 10-12.
[15] The study is "OTI *causale* in Septuagintal Greek." *La Septuaginta en la investigación contemporánea* (V Congreso de la IOSCS) Ed. por N.

the causal כִּי the translators of the LXX usually employed two equivalents, namely ὅτι or γάρ. Aejmelaeus shows that the use of ὅτι instead of γάρ describes the translation techniques in the Septuagint.[16]

She discusses in detail the translation technique of the books of the Pentateuch but adds brief comments about the other books as well. According to her analysis Joshua appears to be situated between the first two and latter three books of the Pentateuch. In Genesis and Exodus γάρ is used more often than ὅτι in renderings of the causal כִּי, but in the other books of the Pentateuch ὅτι is more common. In Joshua ὅτι is used equally as often as γάρ. In Judges, on the other hand, ὅτι is the normal rendering for כִּי.[17]

The studies concerning the whole LXX thus show that the translation technique employed in Joshua differs from that employed in Judges. The picture can further be enriched by describing studies that concentrate on the individual translation techniques of either Joshua or Judges. Of these two, the translation technique of Joshua has received more attention than that of Judges.

The earliest publication referring to the translation technique of Joshua is *Hollenberg*'s study *Der Charakter der alexandrinischen Übersetzung des Buches Josua und ihr textkritischer Werth*, published in 1876. Hollenberg's main interest is the textual criticism of the book. He is, however, aware that the translation technique needs to be taken into account when one seeks to use the LXX in the textual criticism of the Old Testament. His description of the translation technique of Joshua is based on selected *examples* reflecting the translator's renderings. Hollenberg notes that occasionally the translator deviated from the wording of the parent text when allowing for genuine Greek idiom.[18] Thus, Hollenberg argues that the translator understood the Hebrew and followed its meaning. He also

---

Fernández Marcos. Textos y estudios "Cardenal Cisneros" 34. Madrid 1985, 115-132 (= Aejmelaeus 1993, 17-36).

[16] Aejmelaeus 1993, 26.

[17] Aejmelaeus 1993, 26-27.

[18] Hollenberg 1876, 5.

claims that the translator's religious attitude towards the text prevented him from changing the content.[19] A useful overview of the translation technique of Joshua was published by Sollamo in a short Finnish article in 1987.[20] Sollamo describes mainly the aforementioned studies by Thackeray, Soisalon-Soininen, herself, and Aejmelaeus and gives some examples to illustrate the translation technique employed. Sollamo's overview also includes observations not found in the studies. These are related to the use of the apodotic καί and the renderings of the Hebrew possessive suffixes. She does not collect the cases of the apodotic καί and the renderings of the Hebrew possessive suffix exhaustively, but limits her discussion to selected examples.

Sollamo concludes that the translator was inconsistent as far as the renderings of the Hebrew ו at the beginning of apodosis are concerned, because "occasionally the apodosis is opened with καί (e.g. Josh 2:5, 4:1, 5:1) but in other places the conjunction is missing (e.g. 1:1, 3:2, 5:13, 6:20)," as she states. Sollamo explains that the use of the apodotic καί was a result of narrow segmentation.[21] She also observes that the translator "often" left the possessive suffix without a visible counterpart or employed an article instead, acting like other free translators. The more common and literal way of translating the Hebrew possessive suffix in the LXX is to employ the genitive of a personal pronoun.[22]

Sollamo's conclusion is firmly based on the studies and examples she describes. According to her, the translator of Joshua was relatively free but not particularly free. The translation is not among the freest, but it does not belong among the most literal translations either.[23]

---

[19] Hollenberg 1876, 9.
[20] "Joosuan kirjan Septuaginta-käännöksen luonteesta." [= On the character of the Septuagint version of the Book of Joshua] published in the journal *Teologinen Aikakauskirja* 92 (1987), 191-198. She describes her overview by saying: "[N]ämä esimerkit ja tutkimukset riittävät antamaan yleiskuvan Joosuan kirjan kääntäjän noudattamasta käännöstekniikasta." *ibid*, 196.
[21] Sollamo 1987, 195.
[22] Sollamo 1987, 196. She does not have any accurate statistic for the renderings of the suffix, though.
[23] Sollamo 1987, 196.

The translation technique of Joshua has recently been discussed in a number of studies. Joshua has become a very popular subject in Septuagintal studies over the last two decades. Many doctoral dissertations have been defended or are under preparation.[24] These include Leonard Greenspoon's *Textual Studies in the Book of Joshua*, Lea Mazor's *The Septuagint Translation of the Book of Joshua*[25] and Cornelius den Hertog's *Studien zur griechischen Übersetzung des Buches Josua*.

Although none of these studies directly addresses the translation technique of Joshua, they nevertheless describe it. *Mazor*, for instance, argues that the translation is "situated midway between extreme literalness and fully free translation."[26] This is due to the translator's effort to produce a meaningful text of a high style. The translator used rich vocabulary and varied the equivalents for single words and phrases. However, Mazor also sees cases of inconsistency. These, she argues, might show that the translator did not pay sufficient attention to the translation process.[27]

The translation technique of Joshua has also been studied by *den Hertog*. He commences by saying that translation-technical analysis has only just begun in Joshua.[28] He argues that the translator of Joshua attempted to achieve syntactical clarity.[29] The conclusion is based on the use of the Greek article with proper nouns. Also, den Hertog claims that the translator was very competent in the execution of his task.[30] This is seen if one studies the renderings of the

---

[24] I shall only mention Birgit Lucassen, Michaël van der Meer, Paul Sodke, and Cor de Vos, who are preparing dissertations on the LXX of Joshua. Many of the studies do not discuss translation technique but concentrate on the textual history of Joshua, and especially the complex relationship between the LXX and the MT in Joshua.

[25] Mazor's thesis (1994a) includes a chapter relating to translation technique. The work was not, however, at my disposal. My knowledge of the work is based on the abstract published as an article in the Bulletin of IOSCS (= Mazor 1994b).

[26] Mazor 1994b, 33.

[27] Mazor 1994b, 32.

[28] Den Hertog 1996, 160. To support the claim den Hertog refers to three studies: Hollenberg 1876; Tov 1978, and Sipilä 1995.

[29] Den Hertog 1996, 164.

[30] Den Hertog 1996, 172.

status constructus. Usually the translator simply used the genitive to render the *status constructus*. Occasionally he used another way to render the construction, such as the dative.[31]

From my point of view the most important part of den Hertog's discussion about the translation technique in the LXX of Joshua concentrates on the linkage of clauses. This linkage he studies by addressing the use of the *participium coniunctum* and the main and subordinate clauses in the Greek text. According to den Hertog, the participle construction is mainly used according to Greek idiom and only seldom did the translator use the conjunction καί to link the participle and the predicate of the main clause.[32] With reference to the clause constructions den Hertog concentrates on the temporal clauses commencing with ἐπεί, ἡνίκα, ὅταν, and ὡς.[33] He notes that the translator of Joshua seldom changed the parataxis in Hebrew to hypotaxis in Greek.[34] His conclusion is correct, but since den Hertog does not include all the paratactic clauses in Hebrew in the discussion, his material does not really support his conclusion.[35] He also argues that the material shows that the translator used narrow segmentation.[36] To be sure, the renderings of the temporal clauses themselves do not show this, but the use of the apodotic καί.[37]

Moatti-Fine explains the translation technique used by the translator of Joshua by proposing that the translator used as his aid the translations of the Pentateuch. By studying the use of some rare

---

[31] Den Hertog 1996, 165-172. I find it difficult to follow den Hertog's argument. The problem is that he does not say how often the translator used the genitive in cases where another way of rendering the Hebrew construction was also used. Also, den Hertog does not say how many cases of the Hebrew construction he has taken into consideration and how often the genitive actually is the rendering of the construction.

[32] Den Hertog 1996, 176.

[33] Den Hertog 1996, 177-180.

[34] Den Hertog 1996, 179.

[35] I am not even sure that his reference to my publications (den Hertog 1996, 180 note 28) shows this either. Only now, when the material is under discussion in its entirety can such a claim be verified — and it will be.

[36] Den Hertog 1996, 180.

[37] Since den Hertog seems to be aware of this, one wonders why he does not study the use of apodotic καί directly, but the renderings of subordinate clauses.

words and expressions Moatti-Fine suggests that the translator used the model and help provided by the translations of the Pentateuch. The words in question are φυγαδευτήριον, θυσιαστήριον, ἀνάθεμα, and the expression is ὁ ἀγχιστεύων τὸ αἷμα.[38]

The best study concentrating on the translation technique of Judges is a part of Soisalon-Soininen's work on the textual history of the Greek Judges. Soisalon-Soininen concludes that Judges is the weakest of the LXX translations.[39] The translator followed the clause construction and the idiom of the *Vorlage* very closely.[40] Soisalon-Soininen's conclusion is based on comprehensive data including, among other things, the renderings of ו and כי.[41] Instead of presenting a detailed discussion of all renderings of ו and כי, Soisalon-Soininen limits himself to describing the general lines and observes that καί was the most common rendering of ו and ὅτι of כי. Occasionally the translator employed other renderings too, but their

---

[38] Moatti-Fine 1995, 321. Her introduction to the French translation of the LXX of Joshua includes a short discussion about the language and translation technique of the book (Moatti-Fine 1996, 66-67). The language the translator used can be classified as translation language (*traduction-décalque*). This is reflected, for instance, in the word order, the constant use of parataxis and asyndetic infinitive constructions. On the other hand, the translation includes examples of stylistic Greek constructions. By taking together all these elements Moatti-Fine classifies the translation of Joshua among other "literal" translations, such as the translations of Numbers and Deuteronomy.

[39] Soisalon-Soininen 1951, 60: "Man geht kaum fehl, wenn man Jdc. für die seinem Sprachgebrauch nach *schwächste* Übersetzung der ganzen LXX hält" [italics mine]. On the other hand, he recognizes a limited "tendency" towards freer translation in Judges.

[40] The literal character of the translation of Judges is also discussed by Paul Harlé in his French translation of the LXX of Judges, though fairly briefly. Harlé's interest lies in the lexicalization and not in the syntactical issues involved. He nevertheless describes the translation of Judges as literal and notes that the literalness is a special feature of the translation. He then explains that there is a difference between the LXX of Judges and the LXX of the Hexateuch based on the literalness of the translation. In Judges Harlé sees a tendency to literalness, but in the Hexateuch the translators tried to express the idea of the parent text and not just copy the Hebrew wording; Harlé 1999, 35.

[41] Soisalon-Soininen 1951, 31-58.

importance is mainly left outside the discussion.[42] In this study I shall present a more detailed and thoroughgoing analysis of the renderings of ו and כי in Judges.

The discussion described can be summarized by saying that studies on the translation technique in Joshua and Judges are relatively few in number and that they provide us with an incomplete picture. Thus there is a need for a fresh study and my aim is to meet this need.

1.2 Methodological considerations

The understanding of the manner in which the translators of the LXX once worked is very important for any scientific approach to the LXX. We need to know how they produced the Greek text. The manner of the translators' operation or the translation process is called, somewhat misleadingly, translation technique. Although the word "technique" appears in the term, no specific *technique* is to be assumed when studying translation technique. The term itself is neutral and does not include the idea of fixed rules of translation.

It should not come as a surprise to anyone that methodologically I wish to follow the scholars working on the LXX in Helsinki. The founder of the LXX study in Helsinki, Soisalon-Soininen, developed a special way typical of himself and his pupils in the treatment of translation technique, including some very fundamental methodological suppositions.

The point of departure when studying translation technique is the parent text. Without the parent text the study of the translation cannot address any questions relating to the translation process. Because the translator decided how he considered the parent text and issues related to it, the basic questions of translation technique are how the Hebrew words, phrases, and clauses were rendered in the

---

[42] Soisalon-Soininen 1951, 38-40.

LXX, what the Greek equivalents were, and how the translators used them?[43]

Some words, idioms, or items of Hebrew were easy to translate, since there happened to be only one obvious way of rendering the particular word or phrase. The translations of these words or phrases do not add anything to our understanding of the translation technique. Only those Hebrew words or phrases that were not self-evident to translate form the meaningful point of departure when we try to understand the translation process. If the translator had a choice, if it was possible to render the word or phrase in more than one way, the renderings the translator actually employed may tell us something about his translation technique. Especially important are idioms that were "difficult" to translate if one wished to produce idiomatic Greek. In cases where the first equivalent that comes to mind is either wrong or produces unidiomatic Greek, we may detect the translator's manner of working, his translation technique. Thus, the separation of significant instances for translation technique from insignificant ones is fundamental for the analysis. The classification of instances as significant or insignificant is, of course, a modern operation undertaken during the study of translation technique. We do not know if the translators analysed the problems during the translation process at all. Neither do we know if they ever considered different ways of rendering a Hebrew word or phrase. We have their translations and must base our conclusions solely on the Greek text they produced.

Similar to the identification of the meaningful instances in the translation is the proper grouping of the cases under investigation. An important rule lays it down that *only comparable items can be compared*. Consequently, when studying translation technique the Hebrew phenomena under study must be organized in such a way that only those phenomena where the translator meets similar conditions can be dealt with together. This leads us to categorize the material in a specific way where the requirements of both Hebrew and Greek are allowed.

In the present study the point of departure for studying translation technique will be the two most common Hebrew conjunctions — ו

---

[43] See especially Soisalon-Soininen 1963, 226-227.

and כִּי. In her studies Anneli Aejmelaeus shows the usefulness of ו
and כִּי for the study of the translation technique of the LXX. My
study is closely related to her studies and is comprehensible only in
relation to them.

The conjunction ו and its translations are studied in her thesis
Parataxis in the Septuagint[44]. This study is limited to the Pentateuch
and, thus, does not overlap with mine. It nevertheless provides the
necessary background and media for a wider comparison of the
translations.[45]

For the study of the parataxis Aejmelaeus went through every ו-
initial clause in the Hebrew Pentateuch and divided them into three
different groups.

The largest group includes ordinary co-ordinate clauses.[46] The
Hebrew ו in this clause is customarily rendered by καί in the Greek
Pentateuch, though the ratio for καί differs from book to book. The
other main equivalents for ו in ordinary co-ordinate clauses are δέ
and the *participium coniunctum* construction. The ratios for the different equivalents employed as well as the contexts in which they
appear in the Greek made it possible to argue that the individual
books of the Pentateuch were rendered by individual translators. The
translators of Genesis and Exodus used Greek more fluently than did
the other translators of the Pentateuch.[47]

The Hebrew ו may also introduce an apodosis. These must be
separated from ordinary co-ordinate clauses, because καί is hardly
suitable at the beginning of an apodosis. The translators of the
Pentateuch, nevertheless, also employed καί with apodoses.[48] There
is, however, a difference between the books of the Pentateuch. In
Leviticus, Numbers and Deuteronomy καί appears more often than
in Genesis or Exodus, but the division is not as sharp as with the
translations of ו with ordinary co-ordinate clauses.[49]

---

[44] I shall refer to her work as Aejmelaeus 1982.
[45] For a description of Aejmelaeus' study (Aejmelaeus 1982), see further pp. 22-23.
[46] Aejmelaeus 1982, 10-125.
[47] Aejmelaeus 1982, 124.
[48] Aejmelaeus 1982, 126-147.
[49] Aejmelaeus 1982, 146-147.

The third group of ו-initial clauses include clauses where the co-ordinator appears with another conjunction, such as כי or אם.[50] These clauses are interesting because the translators perhaps took the other conjunction into account when rendering ו. Aejmelaeus' conclusion is that the translations of the Pentateuch, all of them, correspond to normal Greek practice in the treatment of ו in connection with a subordinator. Especially noteworthy is the frequent use of δέ as an equivalent for ו in these instances.[51]

Based on the study, Aejmelaeus concludes that Genesis and especially Exodus represent a good, stylistic translation if compared with Leviticus, Numbers and Deuteronomy. The difference between these two groups is very clear in her analyses, clearer than in any other study on the translation technique of the Pentateuch or the LXX before her. That her conclusion concerning the difference in the Pentateuch is not limited only to the handling of the parataxis was later demonstrated by Sollamo in a study on the repetition of the possessive pronouns in the Pentateuch.[52]

Methodologically speaking, Aejmelaeus clearly demonstrates the importance and benefit of meaningful grouping of the material. All the ו-initial clauses should not be treated simultaneously, but the material should be divided on the basis of the translators' point of view and the difference between the conjunction systems of Hebrew and Greek. Other scholars must simply follow the path laid down by her.

For the translation technique of כי no such complete discussion as for ו exists. Aejmelaeus published a study on the use of כי in Hebrew,[53] and two studies on the translations of כי in the LXX.[54]

---

[50] Aejmelaeus 1982, 148-155.

[51] Aejmelaeus 1982, 155.

[52] Sollamo 1995 esp. pp.82-83.

[53] "Function and Interpretation of כי in Hebrew" JBL 105, 193-209 (= Aejmelaeus 1993, 166-185). Cf. Bandstra 1982.

[54] "OTI causale in Septuagintal Greek" La Septuaginta en la investigación contemporánea (V Congreso de la IOSCS) Ed. por N. Fernández Marcos. Textos y estudios "Cardenal Cisneros" 34. Madrid 1985, 115-132 (= Aejmelaeus 1993, 17-36) and "OTI recitativum in Septuagintal Greek" Studien zur Septuaginta – Robert Hanhart zu Ehren. Hrsg. von D. Fraenkel und U. Quast. MSU 20. Göttingen 1990, 74-82 (= Aejmelaeus 1993, 37-48).

Aejmelaeus sees a limited number of functions for כי in Hebrew. If the כי clause precedes its main clause it normally states the circumstance pertaining to the main clause, and accordingly Aejmelaeus suggests the name 'circumstantial כי clause' for a כי clause of that type.[55] The כי clause following the main clause very often bears causal force, on the other hand, but the causality is understood very broadly including many nuances such as cause, reason, motivation, and explanation.[56] The causal function is not, however, the only possible function but a כי clause following its main clause may well be an object clause or sometimes it may express a positive alternative after a negative clause.[57] These four functions of כי neatly explain various instances where it is employed in the Hebrew.

The two studies on the translation technique concern the renderings of the causal כי clauses and the use of the ὅτι recitativum in the LXX. The content of the former study has already been explained.[58] The latter study concerning the ὅτι recitativum is based on the fact that the Hebrew כי hardly functions as a marker of direct speech. There are, however, occasional instances in the LXX where ὅτι is naturally interpreted as ὅτι recitativum. There are good reasons for the infrequency of ὅτι recitativum in the LXX. A clear Hebrew counterpart for it does not exist and the subject-matter of the Hebrew and the rarity of direct speech make it unnecessary to use ὅτι recitativum. Its use is thus connected to a free translation technique, which is not a very frequent phenomenon. In some parts of the LXX stylistic sensitivity also limited its use.[59]

It is difficult to describe the translation technique of an individual book without making comparisons. Expressions such as "literal" or "free" will remain ambiguous without the relevant background. If all the translations of the LXX are described as literal, which is correct, it is hard to speak about freedom in a meaningful way. The only possible way of illustrating the background of the translation tech-

---

[55] Aejmelaeus 1993, 170-171.
[56] Aejmelaeus 1993, 174 and 177.
[57] Aejmelaeus 1993, 174-176.
[58] See pp. 3-4 above.
[59] Aejmelaeus 1993, 37-48. For the reasons for the infrequency see *ibid.*, 48.

nique available for the present study is to compare the translations of Joshua and Judges with other translations of the LXX. Since Aejmelaeus' studies offer available material from the Pentateuch, the Pentateuch will be used in comparison.

The benefit of studying the translation of Hebrew conjunctions is clear. By making such a study it is possible to find an answer to the questions how often the translators used a standard equivalent for a Hebrew conjunction and how often they employed another rendering. The answers to these questions are naturally important in themselves, but they also have a great deal to tell regarding the translation technique used by an individual translator.[60] The statistical results, if used in an appropriate way, describe the literalness of the translator. Naturally, one does not limit the study to statistical description, but by making a translation-technical study one may asking why the result is what it is.[61]

1.3 Linguistic considerations

I feel a need to clarify my treatment of the conjunctions on a theoretical level. This does not mean that I will follow any particular linguistic framework in my study. Since I am not studying the general way of using the conjunctions, I need not follow any framework, but I can operate on a more general level. Conjunctions and the way they link clauses have been the subject of many linguistic studies. Clearly, the conjunctions mark a relationship or a syntactical function. The nature of a conjunction as a marker of a special relationship or function ties the conjunction and its context together. This is the consensus,[62] but should the function of a conjunction be addressed more closely, different opinions about the function emerge. It is not clear how the conjunction and the context function together. Fortunately, I need not solve this problem. For the present analysis

---

[60] Aejmelaeus 1993, 53.

[61] Aejmelaeus 1993, 55.

[62] See also Aejmelaeus 1993, 51, who points out that the interpretation of a passage depends on the content of clauses and on the linking conjunction.

only the knowledge that one should not separate the conjunction from the context suffices.

The problem of the interplay with the conjunction and the context may be addressed as the question whether a conjunction has a *meaning*. In recent studies it has been claimed that conjunctions do not have any meaning of their own. The meaning, if one may speak about such, comes from the context alone.[63] Here some scholars see a clear difference between conjunctions and other classes of words. Contrary to them, Korhonen argues that we should not treat conjunctions differently from any other words in the language.[64] I find Korhonen's description of co-ordinators as a functional element helpful. Korhonen explains that co-ordinators mark "relational features" (in my terminology logical relationship) and thus they seem to convey some information.[65] This can be seen if the conjunction that links two clauses is changed but the other elements of the expression are left untouched.[66]

On the practical level this means that while conjunctions must be interpreted in the context, they themselves affect the context in which they are used. The lesson is that it is not enough to observe the conjunctions alone, but one has to study them in their context.[67]

---

[63] For co-ordinate conjunctions see Aejmelaeus 1982, 35. She bases her judgement on a special linguistic theory called Functional Grammar. The dependence may also be turned the other way round, as is done by Lang, who claims that a co-ordinated clause depends semantically on the conjunction; Lang 1977, 26-27. Cf. also Haumann 1997, 43.

[64] Korhonen 1993, 27. Korhonen uses the Government and Binding framework in her study and is dependent on such scholars as Munn and Abney.

[65] Korhonen 1993, 27; see also Givón 1990, 847-851.

[66] Consider e.g. the following two expressions:
(i) John is poor, *but* he is happy.
(ii) John is poor *and* (he is) happy.
The switching of the conjunction either adds a degree of unexpecedness (i) or omits it (ii). As Greenbaum-Quirk 1990, 268 explain, the first expression may be replaced by "John is poor, *and yet* he is happy." This only shows that the user of a language like English may employ different strategies to mark the logical relationship that he or she desires to express.

[67] The importance of the context for the translation is also underlined by Aejmelaeus 1993, 18.

Remembering that the conjunctions differ in their usage might be helpful. Whereas one conjunction may mark a very specific function, another may mark the similar function on a more general level. Thus, the English co-ordinate conjunction *but* marks a contrast. The conjunction *and*, on the other hand, may be used in a context where a contrast is present, but *and* does not express contrast as such. *And* is used to mark a more general relation between clauses than is *but*.[68] I argue the same with respect to καί and δέ as well as to γάρ and ὅτι.

Because the Hebrew ו is a co-ordinate conjunction, discussion of the difference between co-ordination and subordination is necessary. Traditionally the division between these two has been thought to be a clear one. Nowadays, many linguists will point out the ambiguity of the terminology. It has become problematic to define co-ordination and subordination in a way that these two do not overlap.[69] Aejmelaeus points out that Hebrew, especially, did not make a distinction between co-ordination and subordination.[70] Still, I prefer to use the traditional nomenclature. If there are some practical problems with determining how to distinguish co-ordination from subordination, the terms are still useful in describing the translation.

The Hebrew conjunction ו will be discussed first and כי thereafter. Finally, I will collect the main results of the analysis and discuss the relevance of my results. The discussion of a conjunction will be divided into certain sections. The division is based on the following rule: only comparable items should be compared. After the division is made, I will ask which Greek equivalents were used in rendering the Hebrew conjunction, how often the equivalents were used, and what was the consequence of using an equivalent. Also, I shall address the question what was the possible reason for the use of an equivalent.

---

[68] Greenbaum-Quirk 1990, 266-269.
[69] E.g. Kortmann 1997, 57 notes: "[I]t is simply impossible to come up with a valid bundle of hard-and-fast criteria which distinguish subordinate from co-ordinate clauses, either across languages or even for many individual languages."
[70] Aejmelaeus 1993, 170.

1.4 Textual problems involved in the analysis

The basic interest in the recent studies on Joshua and Judges is not translation-technical, but text critical or text historical. For Joshua this has been the most important question for at least a century. The complex relationship between the Greek and the Hebrew texts still awaits a minute thoroughgoing study.[71] The importance of the textual history in Joshua arises from the fact that the LXX differs considerably from the MT. The LXX is shorter than the MT and the position of certain sections differs between the Greek and the Hebrew. This raises a problem for the present study, and for those studies addressing textual history. How should we treat the sections of the Hebrew text which do not appear in the Greek or sections appearing in the Greek without a counterpart in the Hebrew? Since I am not here studying textual criticism or textual history, I have simply left out the difficult sections of the text and will concentrate on those sections where the difficulty does not arise.[72]

An illustrative example of the sections left out in this study is a long section from the 20th chapter of Joshua. Verses 4-5 and a large portion of verse 6 appear only in Hebrew. It has been proposed that the reason for this lies in the textual history of the book. The plus in the MT was simply added to the Hebrew text and did not appear in the older text used by the translator of Joshua.[73]

---

[71] Cf. Noort 1998, 59: "Die Übersicht zeigt, daß die Frage der Textgeschichte des Buches Josua noch längst nicht gelöst ist." For a promising start in this field see Bieberstein 1995.

[72] The basic reason for the difference between the MT and the LXX seems to go back to the Hebrew *Vorlage* of the LXX. Very probably the *Vorlage* represents a textual tradition deviating from the MT and older than the MT; see Tov 1997, 245.

[73] Rofé 1985, 142-143. See also e.g. Nelson 1997, 226-228, where the LXX and the MT are placed side-by-side in English translations. Interestingly a major difference between the MT and the LXX is not always noted. E.g. Fritz in his commentary (1994, 202) simply passes over the difference, but mentions that in verse 3 the MT contains the gloss בבלי דעת absent from the LXX.

In other passages, I will simply suppose that the Hebrew *Vorlage* used by the translators of Joshua and Judges was almost identical with the present MT as published in the standard edition, i.e. BHS. I will deviate from the basic supposition only if there is a difference in the content of the passage between the LXX and the MT. In these cases I shall comment on the deviation when discussing the individual instances.

After describing my methodological point of departure regarding the MT and the *Vorlage* of the LXX, I need to clarify the ambiguous term, the Septuagint. In this study the Septuagint, and the abbreviation LXX, refer to the oldest form of the translation, the so-called Old Greek. I will suppose that the best printed editions are fairly close to the Old Greek.

For the LXX of Joshua we have two possible editions, that of Margolis and that of Rahlfs.[74] I aim to strike a balance between the two. Fortunately the editions are very similar and are based on a similar understanding of the textual history of the Greek Joshua. I shall constantly deviate from the editions only in spellings of the proper names in Joshua. Because of the complexity of the names, I shall employ the spelling of the Codex Vaticanus (B) as given by the edition of Brooke and McLean.

For the LXX of Judges, Rahlfs edited two different texts, the A and the B. Soisalon-Soininen's study on the textual history of the Greek Judges still offers solid ground for the textual criticism of the LXX of Judges.[75] Only in one point have later studies changed the picture drawn by him. Barthélemy and Bodine have shown that the B text represents the so-called *kaige* group.[76] Rahlfs' A text, on the other hand, is an eclectic text based on the Hexaplaric, Lucianic and later Byzantine witnesses, just as Soisalon-Soininen concludes. In my work I shall follow the A text for Judges as my main text.

---

[74] The difference between these editions is the main theme of den Hertog's dissertation; den Hertog 1996.

[75] Soisalon-Soininen 1951. The most important addition to his grouping of the MSS. is the linking of the B text and the *kaige* group together; see Bodine 1980. Now the combination of Soisalon-Soininen and Bodine seems to be the consensus; see Trebolle-Barrera 1992.

[76] For *kaige* in Judges see especially Bodine 1980,11-45. The basis for the *kaige* group is laid down in Barthélemy's famous *Les devanciers d'Aquila*, which idetifies the B text of Judges as a member of the group; *ibid.*, 47.

1.5 Terminology defined

Clause, the almost metaphysical entity, will be used in this study in a general way. A clause is a passage including one (and only one) predicate which may be separated from the other passages by a conjunction.[77]

Genuine Greek will refer to the Greek language and texts composed in Greek that are not translations from another language. Thus, the LXX does not reflect genuine Greek but translation Greek. Often the term refers in my discussions to natural Greek usage at the time the LXX was composed, i.e. the Hellenistic and early Roman era.

Studies on the translation technique, style, and correctness of the Greek are naturally closely related. As I shall describe the translation technique and discuss the result, i.e. the translation itself, some references to the quality of Greek are unavoidable. My study will not focus on the language, but on the translation technique. Therefore, I will not offer any fresh analysis of genuine Hellenistic or Post-Classical Greek. The linguistic information necessary for my purpose is gathered from existing grammars and studies on which I will simply rely.[78] The most valuable information is given by Aejmelaeus,[79] but other studies also turned out to be useful. In order to gain insight into the language and problems related to it I went through the Hellenistic private letters listed by Buzón in his study on the

---

[77] Cf. Aejmelaeus 1982, 9.

[78] The most important grammars used in my study are Kühner's and Gerth's grammar of Classical Greek (= Kühner-Gerth), Mayser's grammar of the Greek papyri (= Mayser) and Blass's, Debrunner's and Rehkopf's grammar of New Testament Greek (= Blass-Debrunner-Rehkopf 1984). From other grammars and studies I will here mention only Denniston's study on the Greek particles (= Denniston 1954). Other titles are listed in the bibliography.

[79] See Aejmelaeus 1982, 6-7 and 1993, 23-24 for a description of the material collected for her analyses.

language of letters in Ptolemaic papyri.[80] By doing this I could only note that the picture Aejmelaeus and others draw is reliable for my purposes.

Free, literal, and — occasionally — *slavish* are the adjectives gene-rally used to describe the translations of the LXX. It is especially customary to use the opposition 'literal' versus 'free'. On a theoreti-cal level the most important study on literalness is no doubt that by James Barr.[81] There is a difference between one literal rendering and another. For instance, let us consider the following example from Judg 19:29-30:

וַיְשַׁלְּחֶהָ בְּכָל גְּבוּל יִשְׂרָאֵל: וְהָיָה כָל הָרֹאֶה וְאָמַר לֹא נִהְיְתָה וְלֹא

נִרְאָתָה כָּזֹאת לְמִיּוֹם עֲלוֹת בְּנֵי יִשְׂרָאֵל מֵאֶרֶץ מִצְרַיִם – καὶ ἐξαπέστειλεν αὐτὰς εἰς πάσας τὰς Ἰσραήλ. καὶ ἐγένετο πᾶς ὁ ὁρῶν
ἔλεγεν· οὔτε ἐγενήθη οὔτε ὤφθη οὕτως ἀπὸ τῆς ἡμέρας
ἀναβάσεως υἱῶν Ἰσραὴλ ἐξ Αἰγύπτου

Clearly we would call the conjunction καί a literal rendering of the Hebrew ו and the expression καὶ ἐγένετο of the Hebrew וְהָיָה. At the same time there is a difference between these two literal render-ings. καί fits the Greek context and the construction is clear, but καὶ ἐγένετο disturbs the reader, since the clause construction is unclear.

I suggest, therefore, that we make a distinction between suitable literary renderings and unsuitable literary renderings and speak about three categories: slavish, literal, and free.[82] A *free* rendering is a rendering that on some level departs from the surface of the Hebrew parent text. I shall employ the term *slavish* rendering for those Greek equivalents that reflect the surface construction of the Hebrew text very closely, and are at the same time disturbing or even unsuitable in their context. Finally, renderings reflecting the Hebrew idiom closely may be called *literal* renderings, if they suit the Greek context.

[80] Buzón 1984, 1-4.
[81] His *The Typology of Literalism in ancient biblical translations* (= Barr 1979) has become a standard work in LXX studies.
[82] Cf. Sollamo 1979, where the renderings of different Hebrew semiprepo-sitions are divided into these three categories; for a brief description of the categorization see *ibid*, 30.

2 The renderings of the clause initial Hebrew ‫ו‬

2.1 The use of ‫ו‬ in Hebrew

The use of the conjunction ‫ו‬ in Hebrew is extensive.[1] In general terms ‫ו‬ is the co-ordinative conjunction in Hebrew. It is used to indicate a simple co-ordination between two clauses or parts of a clause. By the term *simple co-ordination* the usual kind of co-ordination is meant, where clauses that are parallel in meaning, function and form are linked together.[2]

It is claimed that the use of ‫ו‬ is not restricted to linking co-ordinated clauses. Grammarians often list various other instances where ‫ו‬ is used, such as the beginning of causal, circumstantial, comparative, consecutive, and final clauses.[3] Thus, ‫ו‬ is a very flexible medium in Hebrew clause linkage.

When in recent years a growing interest has been shown among linguists in the phenomenon of co-ordination, it has been noticed that the distinction between co-ordination and subordination is a very

---

[1] Joüon-Muraoka § 177a: "Generally Hebrew shows a very marked tendency towards the syndetic construction (with Waw)."

[2] Cf. Joüon-Muraoka § 115a, where the main function of ‫ו‬ is described as "simple *et*".

[3] See GesK § 154, which is the source of my list. Joüon-Muraoka (§ 115a) recognizes the various "semantic values" of ‫ו‬ by dividing the function of ‫ו‬ into two. ‫ו‬ either expresses pure juxtaposition (= "simple" ‫ו‬) or succesion-consecution-purpose (= "energic" ‫ו‬). Later on (§ 177) the grammar provides discussion about the use of ‫ו‬ in functions where we would use an adverbial clause. Clines 1995, 596-598 provides a list of 15 different usages of ‫ו‬. Cf. also BDB that recognizes five basic usages: ‫ו‬ as a coordinating conjunction, ‫ו‬ consecutive, ‫ו‬ with a volitive verb form, ‫ו‬ expressing a inference or consequence at the beginning of a speech and ‫ו‬ introducing an apodosis. For ‫ו‬ with a volitive verb form see Muraoka 1997, 240.

complex matter.[4] Traditionally drawing a clear line between the two was an almost self-evident affair, but now many scholars have questioned the distinction altogether. It seems that co-ordination and subordination overlap in many languages. In Hebrew this is also the case, because it does not make any grammatical distinction between co-ordination and subordination[5].

How should one translate the Hebrew conjunction ו into Greek? What would be a proper equivalent for the Hebrew conjunction?

Aejmelaeus, in her innovative study on the treatment of parataxis in the LXX of the Pentateuch, dealt with the question in a painstaking manner. Her study offers the most important model for a study concerning the renderings of the Hebrew ו. She showed that the appropriate treatment of the Hebrew ו in Greek, indeed, depends on the context in which ו appears. The translator needs to take into account not only the conjunction itself but the context in which the conjunction is used.

If ו stands at the beginning of an ordinary main clause, the translators may use all kinds of Greek co-ordinative constructions to render it. Among these is the conjunction καί, but this is not always the best way to render ו.

If ו stands at the beginning of an apodosis,[6] the best way to treat it would be to leave it without any counterpart at all in the translation, but the conjunction δέ could be used, according to the standard Greek grammars. Thus, here the Greek does not support the use of καί. Also, in cases where the preceding element is a temporal expression, an infinitive construction or a part of the clause itself (*casus pendens*), the structure comes very close to an apodosis and can be called such.[7] In these cases no co-ordinating conjunction is required in Greek.

The Hebrew co-ordinate conjunction may naturally appear at the beginning of a subordinate clause. Subordinate clauses with co-ordination should be divided into two rather different groups. The

---

[4]   Cf. e.g. Kortmann 1997, 57.
[5]   See e.g. Aejmelaeus 1993, 170.
[6]   By the term *apodosis* is meant a main clause that is preceded by a subordinate clause or clauses.
[7]   Thus eg. Aejmelaeus 1982, 126.

first group includes chains of co-ordinated subordinate clauses. In many cases the subordinate conjunction is not repeated with every subordinate clause in the chain, but the co-ordinate conjunction ו stands alone at the beginning of the clause. The *second* group includes cases where the subordinate clause starts a period containing a subordinate clause(s) and an apodosis (e.g. Num 27:9 ואם אין לו בת ונתתם את נחלתו לאחיו). Since genuine Greek does not favour καί in cases like this, such cases make the special demand that the translators take Greek usage into account.[8]

Aejmelaeus' study shows clear differences between the translators of the Septuagint in their treatment of the Hebrew ו. The translators of Genesis and Exodus more often than the other translators of the Pentateuch produced natural Greek expressions and idiomatic style. The translators were individuals, and their personal input can be seen even in such a small detail as the treatment of the conjunction ו.

For the study of translation technique the Hebrew conjunction ו evidently needs to be divided into certain subgroups or categories. This is the most crucial lesson to be learnt from Aejmelaeus' study. Cases where the conjunction ו begins an ordinary main clause form one of these subgroups. In these cases the LXX translators could use, if they chose to do so, the conjunction καί and quite a variety of other Greek conjunctions or constructions. If the clause is opened by a certain formula in Hebrew, the normal co-ordination in rendering the clause is not enough. The translator has to consider the special character of the formula. The third group of instances is formed by cases where ו begins an apodosis or a clause structure that resembles an apodosis and there καί was not the proper rendering for ו. In cases where the Hebrew ו begins a co-ordinated subordinate clause, the translators could usually use only one alternative, the conjunction καί. This is because normally two subordinated clauses of the same type are co-ordinated with καί.

In this study the material concerning the translation of ו is divided accordingly into four parts: ordinary main clauses, clauses with a formula, apodoses, and subordinate clauses. Each of these types of ו initial Hebrew clause forms an independent chapter in the following discussion. The chapters are composed in a similar way. The discus-

---

[8]   Aejmelaeus 1982, 148.

sion will be opened by a short outline of the use of the Hebrew conjunction ו in the particular position. Then the Greek renderings of ו will be presented and discussed. Finally, the translation-technical details will be summarised.

2.2 The Hebrew conjunction ו at the beginning of an ordinary main clause

From the Books of Joshua and Judges 2293 ordinary main clauses beginning with the Hebrew conjunction ו will be discussed here.[9] The term 'main clause' refers in this chapter to an ordinary main clause if nothing else is indicated. In my study the term 'ordinary main clause' does not include those main clauses that are opened with the formulas ויהי, והיה והנה, or ועתה. This is the difference between my study and Aejmelaeus' study. She included the formulas in the category 'ordinary main clause'. The clause initial ו conjunctions have been rendered by many different Greek conjunctions or constructions. Some renderings do not express logical co-ordination but, indeed, logical subordination. This shows the translators' ability to make use of free renderings. The following discussion is organized by the Greek equivalents used in rendering the Hebrew ו. Each of the Greek equivalents will be studied in separate chapters beginning with the most common co-ordinating conjunctions καί and δέ.

2.2.1 καί

In the LXX of Joshua and Judges καί is used altogether 2167 times to render an ordinary main clause with initial Hebrew ו. Of the cases under discussion 716 come from Joshua and 1451 from Judges. καί is the normal equivalent of the Hebrew conjunction ו. The frequent

---

[9] Joshua 808 clauses and Judges 1485 clauses.

use of καί in the LXX was recognized long ago.[10] Its suitability in
rendering the Hebrew ﬠ was also recognized early on.[11]

The logical relationship covered by ﬠ at the beginning of a main
clause may be described as a *simple co-ordination*. The term refers
to co-ordination where the co-ordinated elements are simply set side
by side. The Greek conjunction καί is used in basically the same
way. Because καί has been used in a context that seems to have a
logical relation other than a simple co-ordination, Aejmelaeus discusses at length the possibility that the Greek καί could be a marker
or an indicator of some logical relationship other than a simple co-
ordination. Her answer is negative. She does not believe that καί
could in fact express any logical relationship between two clauses by
itself, but writes that "a co-ordinator like καί is not capable of
conveying any meaning independent of the context, let alone entirely
different meanings at different times." The use of a co-ordinating
conjunction like καί in an adversative or any other logical relation,
means to her only that "this relation is in fact left un-specified." The
writer did not wish to specify the relation.[12]

In fact the phenomenon that a simple co-ordinating conjunction
can be used between clauses that have some logical relationship is
not totally unknown in English either. The following examples will
illustrate this:[13]

> He heard an explosion *and* he phoned the police (CONSEQUENCE or
> RESULT)
> She tried hard *and* she failed (CONCESSION)
> Give me some money *and* I'll do the shopping (CONDITION)

In the following discussion about the use of καί the examples
illustrate the various contexts and logical relationships that appear in
my material. The most obvious cases where καί is employed include
cases where the logical relationship between co-ordinated clauses is

---

[10] See e.g. Frankel 1841, 162 and Conybeare-Stock 1905 § 40.
[11] See e.g. Thackeray 1909, 54-55.
[12] Aejmelaeus 1982, 14. Compare Lang 1977, 70-71. Lang uses the German
term "gilt zugleich" for simple co-ordination and says: "[D]ie Bedeutung von
und enthält die Anweisung: 'Betrachte die in SB$_1$ und SB$_2$ repräsentierten
Sachverhalte als ZUGLEICH GELTEND im Hinblick auf GEI!'" See also
Muraoka 1997, 229-240 who discusses the Hebrew ﬠ.
[13] The examples are taken from Greenbaum-Quirk 1980, 266-267.

simple co-ordination, as I call it. The Hebrew ו in question and its Greek counterpart καί are underlined in each of the examples.

Josh 3:6

וישאו את ארון הברית וילכו לפני העם – καὶ ἦραν οἱ ἱερεῖς τὴν κιβωτὸν τῆς διαθήκης Κυρίου <u>καὶ</u> ἐπορεύοντο ἔμπροσθεν τοῦ λαοῦ

Josh 24:29-30

וימת יהושע בן נון עבד יהוה בן מאה ועשר שנים ³⁰ ויקברו אתו בגבול נחלתו – καὶ ἀπέθανεν Ἰησοῦς υἱὸς Ναυὴ δοῦλος Κυρίου ἑκατὸν δέκα ἐτῶν ³⁰ <u>καὶ</u> ἔθαψαν αὐτὸν πρὸς τοῖς ὁρίοις τοῦ κλήρου αὐτοῦ

Judg 10:6

ויעזבו את יהוה ולא עבדוהו – καὶ ἐγκατέλιπον τὸν Κύριον <u>καὶ</u> οὐκ ἐδούλευσαν αὐτῷ

Judg 13:24

ותלד האשה בן ותקרא את שמו שמשון – καὶ ἔτεκεν ἡ γυνὴ υἱὸν <u>καὶ</u> ἐκάλεσεν τὸ ὄνομα αὐτοῦ Σαμψών

The *adversative relationship* between co-ordinated clauses in Hebrew is easy to recognize. On the other hand, it may be that often the opposition causing one to see the adversative relation is not quite relevant to the context or the opposition comes from a wider context than the two co-ordinated clauses in question. It is often claimed that the Greek καί could be an adversative conjunction having the meaning "but".[14] This kind of use of the conjunction καί has led many to use a special term for καί in an adversative context, namely καί *adversativum*. But the use of the conjunction καί in an adversative context does not mean that καί could express an adversative relationship. On the contrary, the adversative "meaning" of the expression comes from the context, from the clauses that the conjunction happens to co-ordinate, but the special relationship is left unspecified in the use of the conjunction. In other words, καί

---

[14] See. e.g. Kühner-Gerth II:2 § 152.4.

does not mark the adversative relationship, but the relationship is left unmarked.[15]

Saying that καί in these cases is faulty or unidiomatic would be wrong. It is not, but one could use an alternative rendering as well. Occasionally the use of the Greek conjunction δέ or ἀλλά would perhaps have been more suitable or even obvious. Later I shall deal with cases where the conjunction δέ or the conjunction ἀλλά are used as a rendering of a main clause with initial Hebrew ו.[16]

Josh 8:22-23

וַיַּכּוּ אוֹתָם עַד בִּלְתִּי הִשְׁאִיר לוֹ שָׂרִיד וּפָלִיט 23 וְאֶת מֶלֶךְ הָעַי

תָּפְשׂוּ חָי – καὶ ἐπάταξαν ἕως τοῦ μὴ καταλειφθῆναι αὐτῶν σεσωσμένον καὶ διαπεφευγότα. ²³ καὶ τὸν βασιλέα τῆς Γαὶ συνέλαβον ζῶντα

Josh 24:4

וָאֶתֵּן לְעֵשָׂו אֶת הַר שֵׂעִיר לָרֶשֶׁת אוֹתוֹ וְיַעֲקֹב וּבָנָיו יָרְדוּ מִצְרָיִם

– καὶ ἔδωκα τῷ Ἠσαὺ τὸ ὄρος τὸ Σηεὶρ κληρονομῆσαι αὐτό. καὶ Ἰακὼβ καὶ οἱ υἱοὶ αὐτοῦ κατέβησαν εἰς Αἴγυπτον

Judg 6:10

וָאֹמְרָה לָכֶם אֲנִי יְהוָה אֱלֹהֵיכֶם לֹא תִירְאוּ אֶת אֱלֹהֵי הָאֱמֹרִי אֲשֶׁר

אַתֶּם יוֹשְׁבִים בְּאַרְצָם וְלֹא שְׁמַעְתֶּם בְּקוֹלִי – καὶ εἶπα ὑμῖν Ἐγὼ Κύριος ὁ θεὸς ὑμῶν, οὐ φοβηθήσεσθε τοὺς θεοὺς τοῦ Ἀμορραίου, ἐν οἷς ὑμεῖς ἐνοικεῖτε ἐν τῇ γῇ αὐτῶν· καὶ οὐκ εἰσηκούσατε τῆς φωνῆς μου

Judg 8:20

וַיֹּאמֶר לְיֶתֶר בְּכוֹרוֹ קוּם הֲרֹג אוֹתָם וְלֹא שָׁלַף הַנַּעַר חַרְבּוֹ כִּי יָרֵא

כִּי עוֹדֶנּוּ נָעַר – καὶ εἶπεν τῷ Ἰέθερ τῷ πρωτοτόκῳ αὐτοῦ Ἀναστὰς ἀπόκτεινον αὐτούς· καὶ οὐκ ἔσπασεν τὸ παιδάριον αὐτοῦ τὴν μάχαιραν αὐτοῦ, ὅτι ἐφοβήθη, ὅτι ἦν νεώτερος

---

[15] Aejmelaeus 1982, 14-15.

[16] For δέ as a rendering of the Hebrew ו, see pp. 35-43 and for ἀλλά, see pp. 51-53.

Judg 11:27

וְאָנֹכִי לֹא חָטָאתִי לָךְ וְאַתָּה עֹשֶׂה אִתִּי רָעָה לְהִלָּחֶם בִּי – καὶ ἐγὼ οὐχ ἥμαρτόν σοι, καὶ σὺ ποιεῖς μετ᾽ ἐμοῦ πονηρίαν τοῦ πολεμῆσαι ἐν ἐμοί

Judg 13:3

הִנֵּה נָא אַתְּ עֲקָרָה וְלֹא יָלַדְתְּ וְהָרִית וְיָלַדְתְּ בֵּן – ἰδοὺ δὴ σὺ στεῖρα καὶ οὐ τέτοκας· καὶ ἐν γαστρὶ ἕξεις[17] καὶ τέξῃ υἱόν

The adversative cases are not the only special type of co-ordinated clause in the Hebrew text. Occasionally one meets a *consecutive* relationship. In these cases the succeeding clause naturally expresses an action that is clearly based on the action expressed by the preceding clause and that depends on it. Parallel cases can be found in classical Greek also and based on them, a special usage of καί, the so-called καί *consecutivum* is said to exist.[18] Here, of course, a parallel claim is made as with the so-called καί *adversativum*. We need not see any special consecutive usage of καί, but it only needs to be said that in consecutive cases, the logical relation is not directly expressed.[19]

Josh 2:21-22

וַתְּשַׁלְּחֵם ...[20] [22] וַיֵּלְכוּ וַיָּבֹאוּ הָהָרָה – καὶ ἐξαπέστειλεν αὐτούς. [22] καὶ ἐπορεύθησαν καὶ ἦλθοσαν εἰς τὴν ὀρεινήν

Josh 3:6

וַיֹּאמֶר יְהוֹשֻׁעַ אֶל הַכֹּהֲנִים לֵאמֹר שְׂאוּ אֶת אֲרוֹן הַבְּרִית ... וַיִּשְׂאוּ אֶת אֲרוֹן – καὶ εἶπεν Ἰησοῦς τοῖς ἱερεῦσιν Ἄρατε τὴν κιβωτὸν τῆς διαθήκης Κυρίου ... καὶ ἦραν οἱ ἱερεῖς τὴν κιβωτόν

---

[17] MSS Beijqrsuza₂ and 𝔄 ℭ 𝔈 read a clause καὶ συλλήμψῃ instead of καὶ ἐν γαστρὶ ἕξεις.

[18] See Kühner-Gerth II:2 § 521.5. E.g. Abel 1927 § 78b.2 lists examples in the New Testament.

[19] Aejmelaeus 1982, 16.

[20] The MT includes a large plus here omitted from the example. It is difficult to say if the shorter text of the LXX is due to corruption. There is a good chance that there is a homoioteleuton here. See Margolis 1931, 31 and Boling 1982, 143.

Josh 7:5

וירדפום לפני השער עד השברים ויכום במורד וַיִּמַּס לבב העם
למים וַיְהִי – καὶ κατεδίωξαν αὐτοὺς ἀπὸ τῆς πύλης καὶ
συνέτριψαν αὐτοὺς ἐπὶ τοῦ καταφεροῦς· <u>καὶ</u> ἐπτοήθη ἡ καρδία
τοῦ λαοῦ καὶ ἐγένετο ὥσπερ ὕδωρ

Josh 7:25-26[21]

וירגמו אתו כל ישראל אבן ... ²⁶ ויקימו עליו גל אבנים גדול ...
אפו מחרון יהוה וַיָּשָׁב – καὶ ἐλιθοβόλησαν αὐτὸν λίθοις πᾶς
Ἰσραήλ. ²⁶ καὶ ἐπέστησαν αὐτῷ σωρὸν λίθων μέγαν· <u>καὶ</u>
ἐπαύσατο Κύριος τοῦ θυμοῦ τῆς ὀργῆς

Judg 2:14

אותם וישסו שסים ביד וַיִּתְּנֵם בישראל יהוה אף וייחר – καὶ
ὠργίσθη θυμῷ Κύριος τῷ Ἰσραὴλ <u>καὶ</u> παρέδωκεν αὐτοὺς ἐν
χειρὶ προνομευόντων, καὶ ἐπρονόμευσαν αὐτοὺς

Judg 8:21

ויאמר זבח וצלמנע קום אתה ופגע בנו כי כאיש גבורתו וַיָּקָם
צלמנע ואת זבח את ויהרג גדעון – καὶ εἶπεν Ζέβεε καὶ
Σαλμανά Ἀνάστα δὴ σὺ καὶ ἀπάντησον ἡμῖν ὅτι ὡς ἀνὴρ ἡ
δύναμις αὐτοῦ. <u>καὶ</u> ἀνέστη Γεδεὼν καὶ ἀνεῖλεν τὸν Ζέβεε καὶ
τὸν Σαλμανά

Judg 14:6

בידו אין ומאומה הגדי כשסע וַיְשַׁסְּעֵהוּ יהוה רוח עליו ותצלח –
καὶ κατηύθυνεν ἐπ᾽ αὐτὸν πνεῦμα Κυρίου, <u>καὶ</u> διέσπασεν
αὐτόν, ὡσεὶ διασπάσαι ἔριφον αἰγῶν, καὶ οὐδὲν ἦν ἐν τῇ χειρὶ
αὐτοῦ.

Judg 19:28

האיש ויקם החמור על וַיִּקָּחֶהָ ענה ואין ונלכה קומי אליה ויאמר
– καὶ εἶπεν πρὸς αὐτὴν Ἀνάστηθι καὶ ἀπέλθωμεν· καὶ οὐκ
ἀπεκρίθη αὐτῷ, ἀλλὰ τεθνήκει. <u>καὶ</u> ἀνέλαβεν αὐτὴν ἐπὶ τὸ
ὑποζύγιον καὶ ἀνέστη ὁ ἀνήρ

---

²¹ The MT is longer here. I have omitted the plusses in the MT from the
example.

Note the LXX plus providing an explanation as to why the concubine did not answer a word.[22]

Although Greek has many conjunctions and structures to express consequence, the translators of Joshua and Judges did not use them in connection with Hebrew co-ordinate clauses. According to Aejmelaeus, the same applies to the Pentateuch also.[23] She argued that there are two main reasons for the avoidance of consecutive renderings when the co-ordination was at hand. The Greek usage of co-ordinative conjunctions was enough. There was no special demand for anything other than the use of co-ordination in Greek. On the other hand, Aejmelaeus pointed out that some cases where a modern critic would expect a consecutive rendering were rendered by other subordinate constructions such as conditional, temporal or causal constructions. Examples of these are rare, but we shall see that the translators of Joshua and Judges were also capable of using subordination instead of co-ordination.

There are cases in Hebrew where one could claim that the co-ordination is attached to an expression of purpose. This is not totally unknown in Greek either. For instance, in papyrus UPZ 1.78 a command and its result are co-ordinated:

πρόσμινον {= πρόσμεινον} βραχὺ <u>καὶ</u> ἄξω σε πρὸς τὸν δαίμονα Κνηφιν [ἵν]α [προ]σκυνήσῃς [α]ὐτόν *Wait a second <u>and</u> I will lead you to the god Knephin in order that you may worship him*

Judg 13:15

נֶעְצְרָה נָּא אוֹתָךְ וְנַעֲשֶׂה לְפָנֶיךָ גְּדִי עִזִּים – βιασώμεθα δή σε <u>καὶ</u> ποιήσομεν[24] ἐνώπιόν σου ἔριφον αἰγῶν

---

[22] Schreiner 1957, 69 proposes that there was a gloss in the *Vorlage* of the LXX. See also Harlé 1999, 246. According to BHK, the wording of the gloss is כי מתה. Note that MSS Bdefijkqrsuza₂ use the conjunction ὅτι at the beginning of the plus.

[23] Aejmelaeus 1982, 16.

[24] MSS Aehiklrstvwza₂ and 𝕴 read ποιήσομεν. Other witnesses read ποιήσωμεν ie. the subjunctive. For the use of the subjunctive in the final clauses in the LXX of the Pentateuch see Aejmelaeus 1982, 19-20.

Judg 14:13

וַנִשְׁמָעֶנָּה חִידָתְךָ חוּדָה לּוֹ וַיֹּאמְרוּ – καὶ εἶπαν αὐτῷ Προβαλοῦ
τὸ πρόβλημά σου, <u>καὶ</u> ἀκουσόμεθα[25] αὐτοῦ

Judg 20:13

וּנְבַעֲרָה וַנְמִיתֵם בַּגִּבְעָה אֲשֶׁר בְלִיַעַל בְּנֵי הָאֲנָשִׁים אֶת תְּנוּ וְעַתָּה
מִיִשְׂרָאֵל רָעָה – καὶ νῦν δότε τοὺς ἄνδρας τοὺς ἀσεβεῖς τοὺς ἐν
Γαβαὰ τοὺς υἱοὺς Βελιάλ, <u>καὶ</u> θανατώσομεν αὐτοὺς καὶ
ἐξαροῦμεν κακίαν ἐξ Ἰσραήλ

Judg 20:18

בֵּאלֹהִים וַיִּשְׁאֲלוּ אֶל בֵּית וַיַּעֲלוּ וַיָּקֻמוּ – καὶ ἀνέστησαν καὶ
ἀνέβησαν εἰς Βαιθὴλ <u>καὶ</u> ἐπηρώτησαν[26] ἐν τῷ θεῷ

Judg 21:17

מִיִּשְׂרָאֵל שֵׁבֶט יִמָּחֶה וְלֹא לְבִנְיָמִן פְּלֵיטָה יְרֻשַּׁת – κληρονομία
διασεσωσμένη τῷ Βενιαμείν, <u>καὶ</u> οὐ μὴ ἐξαλειφθῇ φυλὴ ἐξ
Ἰσραήλ·

It is useful to note that in certain cases the translator could express
the logical relation by using other media than the conjunction. For
instance in Judg 13:15, 14:13, and 20:13 the translator used the
future in an instructive context. The use of the tense here suggests
that the action is supposed to be the result of the command that
precedes it.[27] Similar use of the conjunction καί and the future tense
is known from classical Greek literature as well.[28]

The cases listed above form only a selection. Someone else might
compose a different collection, but that is not the main point here. I
find it only of slight interest to try to classify every link between co-
ordinated clauses in Hebrew. Instead, I think that Aejmelaeus has
convincingly shown that the Greek conjunction καί is not only a

---

[25] MSS b'dgiklnwx read ἀκουσώμεθα.

[26] MSS Bq read ἠρώτησαν.

[27] Voitila in his Licenciate thesis lists many instances from the Pentateuch
where a similar phenomenon occurs (Voitila 1995, 168-169).

[28] For the classical usage see Kühner-Gerth II:2 § 521.5. For the post-classical
texts see Blass-Debrunner-Rehkopf § 442.2c and Mayser II:3 § 12.II.4.

possible rendering in these and related cases, but that it is also very suitable.

Conclusions

The Greek conjunction καί has been used extremely often to render the Hebrew ו at the beginning of an ordinary main clause. In Joshua this happens in 88.6% of cases where ו opens a new main clause. In Judges the ratio is even higher, namely 97.6%.

Stylistically καί is used too often in the LXX if the genuine Greek language is taken into account. In standard post-classical Greek prose the most often used (coordinating) conjunction is δέ, but not in the LXX, nor in the translations of Joshua and Judges in particular.[29]

This raises the question whether the extensive use of καί is improper in Greek. Should one regard it merely as a Hebraism, a syntactical feature copied from the Hebrew syntax by the translators? Trenkner, in her study *Le style KAI dans le récit attique oral*, argued that the heavy use of καί belongs to a certain style in Greek.[30] The style can be identified, according to her, from many different genres of Greek literature.[31] She mentions orators like Andocides as well as Lysias, Hyperides and Demosthenes. She found this style employed by historians, philosophers and comedy writers. The style is used within narration, in various descriptions and in sacred writings. In the last group belong the LXX and the NT. Trenkner said quite explicitly:

> D'un autre côté, le style parlé attique éclaire le problème du style biblique, par l'analogie de ses structures avec ce dernier. Le style biblique s'avère style grec.[32]

---

[29] For the statistics concerning the use of καί and δέ in Greek see Aejmelaeus 1982, 43.

[30] E.g. Ruijgh 1971, 163 made use of Trenkner's theory without any critical comments. Aejmelaeus 1982, 31-32 takes a different attitude towards Trenkner's study; see esp. *ibid*, 32 footnote 2.

[31] Trenkner 1960, 2-5.

[32] Trenkner 1960, 59.

The style is basically simple, oral, and narrative and the use of καί is naturally extensive.[33] Trenkner collected statistics to show how the various conjunctions are used within the style. In most of the sections of documents mentioned in her statistics the ratio of καί is higher than the ratio of δέ or any other means of linking clauses.[34] Then it is possible that καί is the most frequently used conjunction to link clauses in some Greek documents or parts of them. This fact does not suffice to show that the use of καί as a common equivalent for the Hebrew ו is not a Hebraism in the LXX.

Trenkner was able to show that in certain sections of Greek documents καί is a major conjunction used to link clauses. For the discussion about the question concerning the use of καί in the LXX this is not, however, enough. The present question is, may a certain conjunction be used *regardless of the context* as the almost sole tool for putting together clause sequence. For this I think, Trenkner's theory does not provide any help.[35] The result in the LXX is tolerable Greek in the microcontext but paratactic and monotonous style in the wider context. Hence, we may speak of a stylistic Hebraism here as Aejmelaeus does.[36]

In her thesis Aejmelaeus concluded that the use of καί to render a clause initial ו is based on three reasons.[37] *Firstly*, she said that καί has the widest applicability of all the equivalents used in the LXX. By this she meant that καί resembles the Hebrew ו in many respects. Both may connect words, phrases and clauses in almost any context. καί as well as ו is a simple co-ordinator; they do not restrict the logical relationship between the clauses they connect. This, I think, explains very well the high ratio of καί. In fact, I believe that this is

[33] Trenkner 1960, 28-29.
[34] Trenkner 1960, 8 Table 1. The only writer who used δέ more often than καί was Andocides. Trenkner gave exact references to the works represented in the table on pages 6-8.
[35] An interesting parallel discussion about the use of Trenkner's theory is linked with a trilingual inscription found in Xanthus. Henri Metzger tried to use Trenkner's theory to explain the heavy use of καί in the Xanthus inscription (see Metzger 1979, 41-42). Without any doubt, however, the use of καί should be explained as due to the influence of Lycian; see Blomqvist 1982, 17-19.
[36] Aejmelaeus 1982, 31-32.
[37] Aejmelaeus 1982, 29-30.

the most powerful explanation Aejmelaeus offers. *Secondly*, she referred to studies where a narrow segmentation connected with the translator's manner of operation is supposed.[38] If the translators did not take into too much account the (preceding) context, it was quite natural for them to choose equivalents that are very close to the function of the Hebrew ו. Clearly, the use of free renderings often denotes an awareness of the context. It is not enough to know the context, but one needs to analyse the logical relationship between clauses linked with ו to be able to provide a suitable free rendering. When using καί as an equivalent, the translator did not need to analyse the relationship.

One may doubt the possibilities to generalize Aejmelaeus' argumentation on this point. She, as well as the rest of the people working among the Helsinki group, supposes that the translators of the LXX did not use any worked-out policy or method for translating. Therefore she may explain that the narrow segmentation makes it easier to use καί. This surely is the case in the Pentateuch and in Joshua. But the translator of Judges seems to pose some difficulties. His translation is so literal that one begins to think that he indeed chose to work in a literal fashion. If the narrow segmentation was after all a result of a policy to strive for literal translation in Judges, Aejmelaeus' argument cannot be used in connection with the translation of Judges. Then one must argue in a much simpler way, namely claiming that the result depends on a tendency towards literalness.[39] We must return to this issue later on.

Thirdly, Aejmelaeus claimed that the word order plays some part here. It was noted in earlier studies that the LXX translators hardly ever abandon the Hebrew word order.[40] καί was very suitable if one

---

[38] Aejmelaeus mentions the studies of Soisalon-Soininen, Sollamo and Barr. Eg. Soisalon-Soininen 1987, 29 wrote concerning the translation technique of the LXX: "Diese Arbeitsweise setzt voraus, daß die Übersetzer keine sehr großen Einheiten auf einmal vor sich hatten. Sie haben einen etwas kürzeren oder längeren Teil des Satzes gelesen, übersetzt und niedergeschrieben und sind dann zur folgenden Einheit übergangen." Soisalon-Soininen spoke notably about parts of a clause as narrow segments.

[39] A number of scholars suppose that the translators had an active policy to guide them in their work. See eg. Jellicoe 1968, 314-318. Compare also Olofsson 1990, 10-11.

[40] Aejmelaeus mentioned the studies of Wifstrand, Soisalon-Soininen and Barr. In his thesis Soisalon-Soininen wrote: "Der Übersetzer des Jdc. ist beinahe

wanted to retain the word order, since the other frequently used rendering δέ cannot take the clause initial position. A general technical evaluation like this cannot *alone* explain the heavy use of καί. When explaining the procedures of the LXX translators of Joshua and Judges, a *fourth explanation* for the extensive use of καί may exist. Possibly the translators of Joshua and Judges followed a model provided by the Pentateuch. In the Pentateuch καί was the most frequently used equivalent for the Hebrew 1 and if the translators of Joshua and Judges knew the Greek Pentateuch they probably noticed how often καί was used.

The Pentateuch is not only a possible source for the translators. The present study may also make use of it and compare the translation of Joshua and Judges with the books of the Pentateuch. This is, of course, possible because Aejmelaeus has studied the renderings of the Hebrew 1 in the Pentateuch. The books of the Pentateuch can be divided into two groups depending on the ratio of καί. The first two books, Genesis and Exodus, belong in one group and the rest of the books, Leviticus, Numbers and Deuteronomy, in another group. In the first group the ratio of καί is smaller than 75% but in the second group it is larger than 80%.[41] Thus, both Joshua and Judges are closer to the second group, i.e. Leviticus, Numbers and Deuteronomy. The ratio for Joshua is approximately equally as large as the ratios for Leviticus and Numbers, but the ratio for Judges is much larger than the ratio for any of the books of the Pentateuch.

2.2.2 δέ

The Greek conjunction δέ is also an equivalent for the ordinary main clause initiative Hebrew 1, but it is not used as often as καί. In Joshua δέ occurs 39 times but in Judges only 14 times. In Greek the conjunction δέ is said to have a twofold usage: it is an adversative

---

immer bemüht gewesen, die postpositionalen Konjunktionen zu vermeiden, und hat es vorgezogen, sich an solche zu halten, die sich der hebräischen Wortfolge leichter anpassen lassen"; Soisalon-Soininen 1951, 36.
[41] Aejmelaeus 1982, 13.

conjunction with a copulative function as well.[42] The distinction between adversative and copulative cases is not without subjectivity, since there are many cases where the contrast between co-ordinated clauses is only very weak. Despite the subjective aspect the examples in the following discussion are arranged into adversative cases and copulative cases. The last-named group includes all the cases where the logical relationship between co-ordinated clauses is *not* clearly adversative.

The *adversative cases* are easy to find among the instances where δέ is used.

Josh 1:14

נשיכם טפכם ומקניכם ישבו בארץ אשר נתן לכם משה בעבר הירדן – וָאַתֶּם תעברו חמשים לפני אחיכם – αἱ γυναῖκες ὑμῶν καὶ τὰ παιδία ὑμῶν καὶ τὰ κτήνη ὑμῶν κατοικείτωσαν ἐν τῇ γῇ ῇ ἔδωκεν ὑμῖν· ὑμεῖς δὲ διαβήσεσθε εὔζωνοι πρότεροι τῶν ἀδελφῶν ὑμῶν

Josh 17:13

ויתנו את הכנעני למס וָהוֹרֵשׁ לא הורישו – καὶ ἐποίησαν τοὺς Χαναναίους ὑπηκόους, ἐξολεθρεῦσαι δὲ αὐτοὺς οὐκ ἐξωλέθ-ρευσαν

Judg 1:25

ויכו את העיר לפי חרב וָאֶת האיש ואת כל משפחתו שלחו – καὶ ἐπάταξαν τὴν πόλιν ἐν στόματι ῥομφαίας, τὸν δὲ ἄνδρα καὶ τὴν συγγένειαν αὐτοῦ ἐξαπέστειλαν

Judg 15:13

ונתנוך בידם וָהֵמֵת לא נמיתך – καὶ παραδώσομέν σε εἰς χεῖρας αὐτῶν, θανάτῳ δὲ οὐ θανατώσομέν σε

---

[42] The basic references are listed in Aejmelaeus 1982, 34 note 1. There is a slight misprint in her text. She claims that Blass-Debrunner-Rehkopf "include δέ in the group of adversative conjunctions only." This means that the grammar treats the conjunction δέ under the title *Adversative Konjunktionen*, but the grammar clearly states that it has the twofold usage (§ 447.1).

Josh 9:22

למה רמיתם אתנו לאמר רחוקים אנחנו מכם מאד וַאתם בקרבנו
ישבים – διὰ τί παρελογίσασθέ με λέγοντες Μακρὰν ἀπὸ σοῦ
ἐσμεν σφόδρα, ὑμεῖς δὲ ἐγχώριοί ἐστε τῶν κατοικούντων ἐν
ἡμῖν;

Here a concessive relationship is present.[43] It is no wonder that the
translator could use δέ in this kind of instance, since the adversative
relationship comes close to the concessive relationship.[44]

The *copulative cases* are rarer than the adversative ones and the
material is more heterogeneous. This being the case, listing all the
cases counted as copulative is most helpful.

Josh 2:18

את תקות חוט השני הזה תקשרי בחלון אשר הורדתנו בו וַאת
אביך ואת כל בית אביך תאספי אליך ... – τὸ σπαρτίον τὸ κόκ-
κινον τοῦτο ἐκδήσεις εἰς τὴν θυρίδα, δι᾿ ἧς κατεβίβασας ἡμᾶς
δι᾿ αὐτῆς, τὸν δὲ πατέρα σου ... καὶ πάντα τὸν οἶκον τοῦ πατρός
σου συνάξεις πρὸς σεαυτὴν

The topic of the instructions is changed.

Josh 3:14

ויהי בנסע העם מאהליהם לעבר את הירדן וַהכהנים נשאי הארון
הברית לפני העם – καὶ ἀπῆρεν ὁ λαὸς ἐκ τῶν σκηνωμάτων
αὐτῶν διαβῆναι τὸν Ἰορδάνην, οἱ δὲ ἱερεῖς ἦροσαν τὴν κιβωτὸν
τῆς διαθήκης Κυρίου[45] πρότεροι τοῦ λαοῦ

Now, the narrative seems to continue without disturbance. Only the
subject changes from the people to the priests.

---

[43] Similar cases in the Pentateuch are listed by Aejmelaeus 1982, 39. Especially
Gen 26:27, where a מדוע clause is followed by a ו clause, comes very close
to the Josh case in question.

[44] See e.g. Bandstra 1982, 149.

[45] MSS Bqx and 𝔈, 𝔏, 𝔖ᵐ omit κυρίου (= Margolis), see den Hertog 1996,
44.

Josh 3:14-15

והכהנים נשאי הארון הברית לפני העם ¹⁵ וכבוא נשאי הארון עד
המים בקצה נטבלו הארון נשאי הכהנים ורגלי הירדן – οἱ δὲ
ἱερεῖς ἤροσαν τὴν κιβωτὸν τῆς διαθήκης Κυρίου πρότεροι τοῦ
λαοῦ. ¹⁵ ὡς δὲ εἰσεπορεύοντο οἱ ἱερεῖς οἱ αἴροντες τὴν κιβωτὸν
τῆς διαθήκης ἐπὶ τὸν Ἰορδάνην καὶ οἱ πόδες τῶν ἱερέων τῶν
αἰρόντων τὴν κιβωτὸν τῆς διαθήκης Κυρίου ἐβάφησαν εἰς μέρος
τοῦ ὕδατος

The narrator focuses the reader's attention on what happens by the
river. The previous passage is a description of the marching order.

Josh 8:3

וישלחם החיל גבורי איש אלף שלשים יהושע ויבחר – לילה
ἐπέλεξεν δὲ Ἰησοῦς τριάκοντα χιλιάδας ἀνδρῶν δυνατοὺς ἐν
ἰσχύι, καὶ ἀπέστειλεν αὐτοὺς νυκτός

Now, the clause starts a new section in the narrative.[46]

Josh 13:22-23

חלליהם אל בחרב ישראל בני הרגו הקוסם בעור בן בלעם ואת
ראובן בני גבול ויהי ²³ – καὶ τὸν Βαλαὰμ τὸν τοῦ Βεὼρ τὸν
μάντιν ἀπέκτειναν ἐν τῇ τροπῇ[47] ²³ ἐγένετο δὲ τὰ ὅρια Ῥουβήν

The narrative turns into a new topic.

Josh 15:20-21

העזים ויהיו ²¹ למשפחתם יהודה בני מטה נחלת זאת – αὕτη ἡ
κληρονομία φυλῆς υἱῶν Ἰούδα. ²¹ ἐγενήθησαν δὲ [αἱ][48] πόλεις
αὐτῶν

The description of the possessions of the tribe of Judah seems to
continue, but verse 21 introduces a town list.[49]

Josh 21:11-12

יהודה בהר חברון היא הענוק אבי ארבע קרית את להם ויתנו
לכלב נתנו חצריה ואת העיר שדא ואת ¹² סביבתיה מגרשה ואת

---

[46]   For other similar cases, see eg. Josh 13:24, 17:14 and 23:3.

[47]   The majority of MSS read here ῥοπῇ (= Rahlfs), but Margolis follows MSS
abh^by^a and Compl and reads τροπῇ, which is probably the OG; see den
Hertog 1996, 98-99 and Moatti-Fine 1996, 170.

[48]   MSS BGabcfhqrx omit the article (= Margolis); cf. den Hertog 1996, 47.

[49]   Cf. Margolis 1931, 292 and Moatti-Fine 1996, 184.

בֶּן יִפֻנֶּה בְּאֶחֻזָתוֹ – καὶ ἔδωκεν αὐτοῖς τὴν Καραθαρβὸκ μητρό-
πολιν τῶν Ἐνάκ, αὕτη ἐστὶν Χεβρών, ἐν τῷ ὄρει Ἰούδα. τὰ δὲ
περισπόρια κύκλῳ αὐτῆς [12] καὶ τοὺς ἀγροὺς τῆς πόλεως καὶ τὰς
κώμας αὐτῆς ἔδωκεν Ἰησοῦς τοῖς υἱοῖς Χαλὲβ υἱοῦ Ἰεφοννὴ ἐν
κατασχέσει·
The translator wanted to place the border between clauses at this
point. Many modern translations start the new clause at the beginning of verse 12. Probably the use of δέ is influenced by the
desire to mark the border between clauses clearly. The use of καί
would make the border less obvious here.

Judg 1:23

וַיָּתִירוּ בֵית יוֹסֵף בְּבֵית אֵל וְשֵׁם הָעִיר לְפָנִים לוּז – καὶ παρενέ-
βαλον οἶκος Ἰσραὴλ[50] κατὰ Βαιθήλ· τὸ δὲ ὄνομα τῆς πόλεως ἦν
ἔμπροσθεν Λουζά.
Compare also Judg 1:10, 1:11, Josh 14:15 and 15:15. The Hebrew
construction ... וְשֵׁם ... לְפָנִים does not occur elsewhere in the OT.
All the cases are translated in the same way.

Judg 7:8

וְאֵת כָּל אִישׁ יִשְׂרָאֵל שִׁלַּח אִישׁ לְאֹהָלָיו וּבִשְׁלֹשׁ מֵאוֹת הָאִישׁ הֶחֱזִיק
וּמַחֲנֵה מִדְיָן הָיָה לוֹ מִתַּחַת בָּעֵמֶק – καὶ πάντα ἄνδρα Ἰσραὴλ
ἐξαπέστειλεν ἄνδρα εἰς τὸ σκήνωμα αὐτοῦ, τῶν δὲ τριακοσίων
ἀνδρῶν ἐκράτησεν. ἡ δὲ παρεμβολὴ Μαδιὰμ ἦν ὑποκάτωθεν
αὐτοῦ ἐν τῇ κοιλάδι.
Attention is shifted from Gibeon's troops to the position of the camp
of Midian.

Judg 8:5

תְּנוּ נָא כִכְּרוֹת לֶחֶם לָעָם אֲשֶׁר בְּרַגְלִי כִּי עֲיֵפִים הֵם וְאָנֹכִי רֹדֵף
אַחֲרֵי זֶבַח וְצַלְמֻנָּע מַלְכֵי מִדְיָן – δότε δὴ ἄρτους τῷ λαῷ τῷ μετ'
ἐμοῦ, ὅτι πεινῶσιν, ἐγὼ δὲ διώκω ὀπίσω Ζέβεε καὶ Σαλμανὰ
βασιλέων Μαδιάμ
Here the causal relationship comes into question.

---

[50] For the variation Joseph (MT) - Israel (LXX), see Harlé 1999, 81.

Judg 8:11

וַיִּךְ – אֵת הַמַּחֲנֶה וְהַמַּחֲנֶה הָיָה בֹטֵחַ καὶ ἐπάταξεν τὴν παρεμ-
βολήν, ἡ δὲ παρεμβολὴ ἦν πεποιθυῖα

There is a temporal relation between the clauses in this instance.

Judg 11:35

אֲהָהּ בִּתִּי הַכְרֵעַ הִכְרַעְתִּנִי וְאַתְּ הָיִית בְּעֹכְרָי וְאָנֹכִי פָּצִיתִי פִי אֶל־
יְהוָה וְלֹא אוּכַל לָשׁוּב – οἴμμοι, θύγατέρ μου, ἐμπεποδοστάτηκάς
με, εἰς σκῶλον ἐγένου ἐν ὀφθαλμοῖς μου, ἐγὼ δὲ[51] ἤνοιξα τὸ
στόμα μου περὶ σοῦ πρὸς Κύριον καὶ οὐ δυνήσομαι ἀποστρέψαι

In this case the relationship is causal.[52]

Judg 16:26-27

וַיֹּאמֶר שִׁמְשׁוֹן אֶל־הַנַּעַר הַמַּחֲזִיק בְּיָדוֹ הַנִּיחָה אוֹתִי וַהֲמִשֵׁנִי אֵת
הָעַמֻּדִים אֲשֶׁר הַבַּיִת נָכוֹן עֲלֵיהֶם וְאֶשָּׁעֵן עֲלֵיהֶם [27] וַהֲבַּיִת מָלֵא
הָאֲנָשִׁים וְהַנָּשִׁים – καὶ εἶπεν Σαμψὼν πρὸς τὸ παιδάριον τὸν
χειραγωγοῦντα αὐτόν Ἐπανάπαυσόν με δὴ καὶ ποίησον ψηλα-
φῆσαί με ἐπὶ τοὺς στύλους, ἐφ' ὧν ὁ οἶκος ἐπεστήρικται ἐπ'
αὐτῶν, καὶ ἐπιστηρίσομαι ἐπ' αὐτούς· ὁ δὲ παῖς ἐποίησεν
οὕτως. [27] ὁ δὲ οἶκος ἦν πλήρης ἀνδρῶν καὶ γυναικῶν

The case includes a shift from Samson's request to the description
of the members of the party.

Conclusions

Thus, occasionally it is not easy to say if the logical relationship
between co-ordinate clauses is really adversative. It is perhaps
helpful to think that the use of δέ forms a continuum between a
strong adversative relation and a pure connection.[53] In many
instances included under copulative cases one may note some
change. For instance, in Judg 8:11 the object of the preceding clause
(הַמַּחֲנֶה) becomes the subject of the following clause. Cases like this
may be interpreted as bearing a weak adversative connection if one

---

[51] MSS AMNabcdghklnoptvwxyb₂ and 𝕮 𝔈 𝔍 𝔖 read the conjunction δέ. The
rest of the MSS read καί.
[52] For similar cases in the Pentateuch see Aejmelaeus 1982, 39.
[53] Compare Denniston 1954, 162.

chooses to do so. Not always, however, is the change relevant in the context.

According to Aejmelaeus, among others, there needs to be some kind of dissimilarity between the co-ordinated items, if δέ is used.[54] Also, one may employ καί instead of δέ, but perhaps not always *vice versa*.[55] By contrast in genuine Greek the use of δέ depends on the nuance the writer wishes to emphasize. If the difference between clauses is underlined, δέ is used, but if the continuity is the main point καί comes into question.[56] These considerations explain well the use of δέ in various contexts in the LXX of Joshua and Judges.

The use of δέ in my material also differs from that of genuine Greek. In normal Greek prose δέ is used far more often than in the LXX of Joshua and Judges. The reasons for the limited use of δέ must be discussed next.

The most obvious reason for the limited use of δέ is the heavy use of καί described earlier. It seems that if the translators did not notice any particular reason to mark the dissimilarity, they did not use δέ, but rather καί, the normal equivalent for ‎ו‎.

Because δέ is not as neutral as καί, the use of δέ is more limited than the use of καί, but at the same time the use of δέ is more open than the use of ἀλλά. Perhaps the more limited function influenced the translators.[57]

---

[54] Aejmelaeus 1982, 35. See also Ruijgh 1971 § 127-133 and Sickling 1993, 11-12. Sickling's explanation of δέ as a marker of "the beginning of a new section" should be understood rather generally, I think. A new section here does not mean a new paragraph.

[55] Aejmelaeus refers to Denniston 1954, xlvii-xlviii when discussing the difference between καί and δέ. Denniston says that "there is a certain tendency,..., to use δέ, rather than καί, for connecting sentences", but explains the tendency very briefly by making an analogy with English writers' tendency to avoid the conjunction *and* at the beginning of a sentence.

[56] Therefore it is impractical to try to isolate cases where δέ could have been used from those where δέ should not have been used. This is not done by Aejmelaeus and I have not done so, although the fact that δέ cannot always replace καί seems to require one to make the separation.

[57] This is also stressed by Aejmelaeus 1982, 43.

The narrow segmentation made it difficult to recognize the discontinuity. If the content of the two co-ordinate clauses was not clear to the translator, he probably did not realize the possibility of using δέ. Thus, translation technique affected the limited use of δέ.

Perhaps the word order also played some role here. δέ is never the first word in the clause as is the Hebrew ו. When using δέ, the translator was forced to change the word order of the parent text.[58]

In Joshua cases where δέ is used to render an ordinary main clause initiative ו form 4.8% of all cases. In Judges the ratio is much smaller, only 0.9%. If these figures are compared with the equal figures in the Pentateuch one notices that in Genesis and in Exodus the ratio is higher, but in the rest of the books of the Pentateuch the figures stand in between those for Joshua and Judges.[59] The difference between Genesis and Exodus as compared with the rest of the afore-mentioned books is larger than between the other books. Therefore one could conclude that Joshua and Judges are closer to the last three books of the Pentateuch than to the first two. However, figures do not entirely count here. One should also take into account various contexts where the conjunction δέ is used by the translator to assign full right to the various translators.

In the Pentateuch the translators used the conjunction δέ in basically two ways. In Genesis and Exodus δέ is often used in copulative cases, but in Leviticus, Numbers and Deuteronomy copulative cases are very rare.

More important than the frequency of δέ in the latter books is the context in which it is used. The conjunction δέ is never used at the beginning of a clause starting with a verb in Hebrew in Leviticus, Numbers, or Deuteronomy.[60] Aejmelaeus was therefore able to classify translators' handling of the conjunction δέ into two different categories. In Genesis and Exodus δέ was used in an idiomatic way. For the translators of Leviticus, Numbers, and Deuteronomy δέ occurred only if the context of the passage was "felt to require" a

---

[58] Accordingly Aejmelaeus 1982, 43.
[59] For the statistics for the Pentateuch see Aejmelaeus 1982, 36.
[60] For the sake of clarity: in genuine Greek it is fully possible to use δέ at the beginning of a clause in which the predicate is the first word.

conjunction other than καί, as Aejmelaeus put it.[61] If this kind of division is taken into account, Joshua seems to be close to Genesis and Exodus. After all, there are some passages in Joshua where δέ is used to render ו at the beginning of the clause starting with a verb in Hebrew (see eg. Josh 8:3 above).[62] On the other hand, no such cases exist in Judges and therefore Judges resembles Leviticus, Numbers and Deuteronomy.

Excursus: Text critical variants in the book of Judges

TABLE 1 Cases where δέ is used in Judges

```
        ABKNMZabcdefghijklmnopqrstuvwxyza₂b₂d₂
 1:10 -     x
 1:23 -
 1:25 +
 1:33 +
 6:39 +     x                  x xxx x      x
 6:40 +     x           x  x  x x xxx x     xx
 7:8  +     x           xx xx   x xxx x     xx    x
 7:8  -     x           xx xx   x xxx x     xx
 7:10 +     x           xx xx   x xxx x     x     x
 8:5  -     x           xx xx   x xxx x     xx
 8:11 -     x              x    x xx   x
11:35 -     x           xx xx x   xxx x     xx
15:13 +     x           xx xx     xxx x     xx
16:27 +     x           xxx xxxx xx xxx x x xx
```

The table gives every instance in Judges where δέ is used to render a clause initiative Hebrew ו. In the first column the reference is given. In the second column + indicates that the Hebrew ו is used in an adversative context and - that the context is not adversative. In the other columns the letter x indicates that the given MS reads in the particular instance the Greek conjunction καί instead of δέ.

Because of the complex nature of the textual history of Judges, it is interesting to study how the different MSS deviate in the use of the conjunction δέ. As stated in the chapter above, there are only 14 instances where δέ is used at the beginning of a main clause.

---

[61] Aejmelaeus 1982, 42-43. The expression "was felt to require" is rather ambiguous, and it is difficult to know what exactly Aejmelaeus meant by it.

[62] Other cases are Josh 15:21 and 17:14.

TABLE 2 Cases where a variant reading δέ is found in Judges

```
               ABKNMZabcdefghijklmnopqrstuvwxyza₂b₂d₂
01:11 -        x        xxx  x x x x xxx x      xx
04:08 +                 x
04:21 -                x     x x        x
07:25 -                 x
07:25 -          x
08:01 -          x
08:30 -                x     x x        x
09:15 -                             x
09:20 +        x        xxxx xx xxxxxxxxxxxx    x
09:20 -                 x
09:44 -                x     x xx       x
11:01 -          x
11:17 -                x  x    x xxx    x xx
11:27 -                x  x    x xxx    x x
11:36 ±        x        xx xx       xxx x     x
13:01 -          x
13:16 ±          x
13:23(+)               x     x x        x
19:16 +                           x x       x
20:38 -          x     x     x xx       x
20:39 -          x     x     x xx       x
```

The table gives every instance in Judges where δέ appears as a variant for καί in rendering a clause initiative Hebrew ו. In the first column the reference is given. In the second column + indicates that the Hebrew ו is used in an adversative context and - that the context is not adversative. In the other columns the letter x indicates that the given MS reads in the particular instance the Greek conjunction δέ instead of καί.

In most of the cases where the MSS offer an alternative to the conjunction δέ, the alternative is καί.[63] This happens in 11 instances. Interestingly, the variant reading is found mostly in MSS Befijoqrsuz. These MSS belong to the so-called *kaige* group in Judges, except MS o, which has a mixed type of text. Especially often the deviation is found in MSS Befjqsz, which form the subgroup *BI*.[64]

Compared with these cases, there are also cases where the conjunction καί has a variant δέ in some MSS. There are 21 such cases in Judges.

The MSS where the variant reading δέ often occurs are dglnow. Mostly these MSS belong to the subgroup *AII₁*, i.e. they are *Lucianic* MSS. There are also two MSS which contain a mixed type of text, i.e. MS d and o, and these two contain the variant quite often. The material is heterogeneous and there are

---

[63] Only sporadically may some other variants exist, but they are not of great significance here.

[64] The variant occurs in B 11 times, e 7 times, f 8 times, j 7 times, q 10 times, s 9 times and z 9 times.

only nine cases where the variant occurs in practically every MS of the group
AII₁. The MS d has the variant very often and there are four cases where d is
the only MS to have the variant. In six cases where the variant is shared with
the MSS of the group *AII₁*, d does not have it. These figures show how
independent the MS d is concerning the handling of the clause initial καί.
Interestingly, the context does not seem to affect the occurence of a variant
reading. The variant could be used both in adversative and non-adversative
contexts.

It should not surprise the reader that the Lucianic texts tend to change the
clause initial καί into δέ. This phenomenon closely follows the habit of
improving the Greek readability of the text typical of the Lucianic activity. The
kaige group is known to have the tendency to change the Greek text to bring
it closer to the Hebrew and especially to the MT. Therefore, one may
understand that *kaige* MSS also change δέ into καί, which is the most
frequently used rendering for the Hebrew ו. The sporadic nature of these
changes reveals itself when one compares the figures of the variants to the total
number of cases where καί is used to render the clause initiative Hebrew ו. The
changes are rare.

Thus I conclude that Rahlfs' A text is skilfully edited and I have followed this
text regularly.[65]

2.2.3 *οὐδέ*

The negative word οὐδέ is used four times in Joshua to render a
main clause initiative Hebrew ו. Three times ו is connected to the
negative word לא and once to אין. οὐδέ never occurs in the LXX of
Judges in renderings of the main clause initiative Hebrew ו.[66] In
Greek the use of οὐδέ is limited to such contexts where another
negative clause precedes the οὐδέ clause in question. The limitation
is valid both in Classical Greek and in *Koiné*.[67] Because of the
limitation, it is natural that cases in Joshua are quite rare.

---

[65] There are four cases where one might question Rahlfs' choice. In Judg 1:11,
9:20, 11:36 and 19:16 the OG perhaps read δέ instead of καί.

[66] For οὐδε in between various parts of a clause see, however, Judg 1:27, 1:33,
2:2 and 14:6.

[67] See Aejmelaeus 1982, 48 and the literature mentioned there.

Below all the cases are listed.

Josh 1:5

לא ארפך ולא אעזבך – καὶ οὐκ ἐγκαταλείψω σε οὐδὲ ὑπερ-
όψομαί σε

Josh 6:1

אין יוצא ואין בא – καὶ οὐθεὶς[68] ἐξεπορεύετο ἐξ αὐτῆς οὐδὲ
εἰσεπορεύετο

Josh 23:7

ובשם אלהיהם לא תזכירו ... ולא תעבדום ולא תשתחוו להם –καὶ
τὰ ὀνόματα τῶν θεῶν αὐτῶν οὐκ ὀνομασθήσεται ἐν ὑμῖν, οὐδὲ
μὴ προσκυνήσητε αὐτοῖς οὐδὲ μὴ λατρεύσητε αὐτοῖς
The negative word οὐδέ is used twice in this instance as part of a
strong negation οὐ μή.[69] I have left out the plus in the MT from the
example to make it clearer.

As the cases show, the negative word οὐδέ is used in Joshua
according to Greek idiom. The translator of Joshua always used
οὐδέ at the beginning of the negative co-ordinated clause preceded
by another negative clause with the negation οὐ. He did not use
expressions such as καί οὐ at all. The same applies to the use of
μηδέ if the preceding negation is μή.[70] This shows that the translator
was aware of the context or that he knew, when translating a
negative clause, whether there was another negative clause in the
preceding context. An interesting notion may be observed. All the
four cases are direct speech.

---

[68] οὐθείς is a later form of the negative word οὐδείς. The change in the orthography is based on changes in pronunciation in the post-classical period. For
similar changes in dentals see Mayser I:1 § 33.3. In the LXX both forms
οὐθείς and οὐδείς are used. In Josh consider e.g. verses 8:17 and 10:8. In
these verses the MS B reads the negative word with the letter θ but the rest
of the MSS use δ.

[69] For the negation οὐ μή see Kühner-Gerth II:2 § 514.8 and Blass-Debrunner-
Rehkopf §365, esp. note 1.

[70] See the discussion on μηδέ, pp. 47-48.

2.2.4 μηδέ

The negative word οὐδέ and the negative word μηδέ have many
things in common in Greek. The limitation with οὐδέ governs μηδέ
as well: μηδέ may occur only at the beginning of a clause preceded
by another negative clause. The other limitation concerning the use
of μηδέ is linked with the context. As well as μή, μηδέ too is used
in prohibitions with the subjunctive. It is used four times in Joshua.[71]
Three times the prohibition is expressed in Hebrew by ואל and in
these instances the prohibition belongs to the expression "do not be
frightened or dismayed."

Josh 1:9

הלוא צויתיך חזק ואמץ אל תערץ ואל תחת – ἰδού[72]
ἐνετέταλμαί σοι. ἴσχυε καὶ ἀνδρίζου, μὴ δειλιάσῃς μηδὲ
φοβηθῇς

Josh 8:1

ויאמר יהוה אל יהושע אל תירא ואל תחת – καὶ εἶπεν Κύριος
πρὸς Ἰησοῦν Μὴ φοβηθῇς μηδὲ δειλιάσῃς

Josh 10:25

ויאמר אליהם יהושע אל תיראו ואל תחתו – καὶ εἶπεν πρὸς αὐτοὺς Ἰησοῦς Μὴ φοβηθῆτε αὐτοὺς μηδὲ δειλιάσητε

Once the prohibition is expressed in the Hebrew by the negative
word ולא with *yiqtol*.

Josh 6:10

ואת העם צוה יהושע לאמר לא תריעו ולא תשמיעו את קולכם
– τῷ δὲ λαῷ ἐνετείλατο Ἰησοῦς λέγων Μὴ βοᾶτε, μηδὲ ἀκουσάτω μηθεὶς ὑμῶν τὴν φωνήν
The translation of this case here does not differ too much from the
three other translations above, but there is a difference in Hebrew.
In Hebrew the negative word אל is used only in prohibitions and

---

[71] In the LXX of Judges μηδέ never occurs.
[72] Compare Josh 22:20, where the Hebrew הלוא is rendered καὶ ἰδού.

similar expressions, but לֹא is seldom used in prohibitions.[73] When לֹא is used in prohibitions, the negative word לֹא makes them more strict than the negative word אַל. The translator did not indicate the difference when choosing which negative word to use. On the other hand, he strengthened the Greek expression by using the imperative (βοᾶτε and ἀκουσάτω) instead of the subjunctive. The second negative imperative is also strengthened by μηθείς, an excellent free rendering.

The term *prohibition* is used here *only* with negative commands. In the Pentateuch μηδέ is used with expressions that are not prohibitions as such.[74] But in Joshua this is not true. Every instance in Joshua belongs to prohibitions. Aejmelaeus discussed the possibility that occasionally καὶ μή could have been used instead of μηδέ or καὶ οὐ instead of οὐδέ . Indeed she found some passages in the Pentateuch where this is the case.[75] In Joshua such cases cannot be found. On the contrary, the translator used μηδέ as well as οὐδέ in *every* possible case. In prohibitions the Hebrew negative word may vary, while in Greek the only possibility is μή (and of course μηδέ). In Hebrew, as well as in Greek, the context sets the limits to the use of the negative word. In Hebrew, for instance, prohibitions are usually expressed with אַל and the jussive mode but seldom with לֹא and the *yiqtol*. In the translation of Joshua the negative words μή and μηδέ always start prohibitions. οὐ and οὐδέ appear in negative expressions of other types, i.e. if the Greek verb form is the indicative or the negation is οὐ μή.

---

[73] Joüon-Muraoka § 160.
[74] Aejmelaeus 1982, 48.
[75] Aejmelaeus 1982, 52.

2.2.5 οὔτε

The Greek negative word οὔτε as used by the translator of Judges belongs to a disjunctive construction οὔτε – οὔτε, "neither – nor".[76] There is only one such construction in Judges.[77]

Judg 19:30

לא נהיתה וֿלֿאֿ נראתה כזאת למיום עלות בני ישראל מארץ
מצרים עד היום הזה – οὔτε ἐγενήθη οὔτε ὤφθη οὕτως ἀπὸ τῆς ἡμέρας ἀναβάσεως υἱῶν Ἰσραὴλ ἐξ Αἰγύπτου ἕως τῆς ἡμέρας ταύτης

From the translation-technical point of view the use of οὔτε requires an awareness of the context. This explains why οὔτε seldom appears in the LXX. Because the translator of Judges used the construction οὔτε – οὔτε he must have realized that there were two disjunctive negative clauses in the *Vorlage*. Here we have encountered a good idiomatic rendering by a literal translator.

2.2.6 εἴτε

The Greek connective εἴτε may be used to form a similar construction as οὔτε except that the former is positive.[78] The disjunctive construction εἴτε – εἴτε shows that the writer does not wish to indicate which of the choices is to be preferred.

---

[76] For a description of the use of disjunctive οὔτε – οὔτε construction see Kühner-Gerth II:2 § 535.1, Denniston 1954, 505-511, and Ruijgh 1971 § 182. According to Denniston, οὔτε – οὔτε is common to all periods and styles of Greek literature. For its use in the NT see Blass-Debrunner-Rehkopf § 445. For the use in papyri Mayser II:3 § 165.7.I.1 says: "Beispiele sind überaus zahlreich."

[77] The construction does not appear in the Pentateuch, see Aejmelaeus 1982, 54. In the LXX of Joshua οὔτε is not used at all.

[78] For the use of εἴτε in Greek see Kühner-Gerth II:2 § 593 and Ruijgh 1971 § 179. For an example that comes close to the example in Josh see Philo *Spec.* 3.24.3.

Josh 24:15

בחרו לכם היום את מי תעבדון אִם את אלהים אשר עבדו
אבותיכם ... וְאִם את אלהי האמרי – ἕλεσθε[79] ὑμῖν ἑαυτοῖς
σήμερον τίνι λατρεύσητε εἴτε τοῖς θεοῖς τῶν πατέρων ὑμῶν ...
εἴτε τοῖς θεοῖς τῶν ᾿Αμορραίων

From the Hebrew disjunctive construction (וְאִם – אִם) the translator
produced a corresponding Greek construction.[80] As is the case with
the construction οὔτε – οὔτε, the use of the construction εἴτε – εἴτε
requires an awareness of the context.

2.2.7 οὖν

The Greek conjunction οὖν is used to mark a consecutive or inferential relation.[81] In the earliest phases of the Greek language οὖν functions mainly as an adverb (certainly, in fact), but in the post-classical
period it is one of the most frequently used particles.[82] οὖν has a
more limited function than καί or δέ and therefore one could argue
that its use shows considerable freedom on the translators' part.[83]
Just like the conjunction δέ, οὖν is not used as the first word of the
clause.

οὖν never appears in Judges as a rendering of the main clause
initiative Hebrew ו, but in Joshua it is used three times.[84] Twice the
Hebrew clause begins with ועתה. Once οὖν is not connected with a
formula in Hebrew. The formulas will be treated in a separate

---

[79] MS B with many other witnesses reads ἐκλέξασθε (= Margolis), a reading
also found in α´ and θ´. For the evaluation of the variant see Greenspoon
1983, 111, den Hertog 1996, 32, and Moatti-Fine 1996, 234.

[80] According to Aejmelaeus 1982, 54 the construction εἴτε – εἴτε is used as the
appropriate rendering for the Hebrew וְאִם – אִם in the LXX.

[81] Denniston 1954, 425.

[82] See Mayser II:3 § 164.19, Blass-Debrunner-Rehkopf § 451. For the
Pentateuch see Aejmelaeus 1982, 56-60.

[83] Aejmelaeus 1982, 56.

[84] See, however, Judg 1:7 (a כאשר clause) and Judg 16:10 (כ + inf.).

chapter in this study, therefore only the instance not connected with the formula is discussed here.[85]

Josh 23:5-6

וירשתם את ארצם כאשר דבר יהוה אלהיכם לכם ⁶ <u>ו</u>חזקתם מאד
לשמר ולעשות את כל הכתוב בספר תורת משה – καὶ
κατακληρονομήσατε τὴν γῆν αὐτῶν καθὰ ἐλάλησεν Κύριος ὁ
θεὸς ὑμῶν ὑμῖν. ⁶κατισχύσατε <u>οὖν</u> σφόδρα φυλάσσειν καὶ
ποιεῖν πάντα τὰ γεγραμμένα ἐν τῷ βιβλίῳ τοῦ νόμου Μωυσῆ
In this instance one may understand the translator's judgement that the first clause in verse 6 expresses a consequence, yet the clause itself does not employ any clear marker of the consecutive relation.[86]

In the Pentateuch the use of οὖν generally reflects freedom of translation in a given book. In Genesis it is used 21 times to render the Hebrew ו in connection with "ordinary parataxis", as Aejmelaeus puts it, and in Exodus 14 times, but in Numbers only once. The translations of Leviticus and Deuteronomy do not use οὖν at all.[87] In Joshua, one might argue, the situation comes close to the more literal translations of the Pentateuch, since the cases are rare. The translation of Judges shows similarities with Leviticus and Deuteronomy. In Joshua, and in most of the cases in the Pentateuch, οὖν is used in direct discourse.

2.2.8 ἀλλά

The conjunction ἀλλά has a very restricted function in Greek. It is strongly adversative and it is often used in cases where an affirmative clause is connected with a negative clause.[88] Not always is the negative clause present, but occasionally ἀλλά may be used

---

[85] For the renderings of the formula ועתה see pp. 102-107.
[86] A consecutive expression is also employed by many modern translations, such as NRSV, NEB or NJB.
[87] Aejmelaeus 1982, 56. The case in Num is connected with the formula ועתה (Num 24:11).
[88] Kühner-Gerth II:2 § 534.2, Aejmelaeus 1982, 61.

in cases where the first clause sets limitations to the second clause or in cases where a concessive relation is present.[89] Other situations might also come into question. Especially worthy of mention are cases where there is a shift to a new topic.[90]

There are only two cases of ἀλλά used in Joshua as a rendering for the main clause initiative Hebrew ו.[91] The same phenomenon, the rare use of ἀλλά, is present in the Pentateuch,[92] and, one may add, in the entire LXX.

Josh 6:17-18

רק רחב הזונה תחיה היא וכל אשר אתה בבית כי החבאתה את המלאכים אשר שלחנו ¹⁸ ורק אתם שמרו מן החרם – πλὴν ʿΡαὰβ τὴν πόρνην περιποιήσασθε αὐτὴν καὶ ὅσα ἐστὶν ἐν τῷ οἴκῳ αὐτῆς ¹⁸ ἀλλὰ ὑμεῖς φυλάξασθε σφόδρα ἀπὸ τοῦ ἀναθέματος

Josh 22:23-24

לבנות לנו מזבח לשוב מאחרי יהוה ואם להעלות עליו עולה ומנחה ואם לעשות עליו זבחי שלמים יהוה הוא יבקש ²⁴ ואם לא מדאגה מדבר עשינו את זאת – καὶ εἰ ᾠκοδομήσαμεν αὐτοῖς βωμὸν ὥστε ἀποστῆναι ἀπὸ Κυρίου τοῦ θεοῦ ἡμῶν, ὥστε ἀναβιβάσαι ἐπ᾽ αὐτὸν θυσίαν ὁλοκαυτωμάτων ἢ ὥστε ποιῆσαι ἐπ᾽ αὐτοῦ θυσίαν σωτηρίου, Κύριος ἐκζητήσει. ²⁴ ἀλλ᾽ ἕνεκεν εὐλαβείας ῥήματος ἐποιήσαμεν τοῦτο

In Joshua the use of ἀλλά is linked with expressions that themselves mark the adversative relation (ורק in 6:18 and ואם לא in 22:24).

---

[89] Kühner-Gerth II:2 § 534.3.
[90] Kühner-Gerth II:2 § 534.8 specifies the shift by saying that either the new topic in the text is in some respect contrary to the preceding topic (quite often a confirmative adverb μήν is added) or the shift suddenly breaks the direct discourse.
[91] In general ἀλλά is used by the translator of Joshua 17 times and by the translator of Judges 8 times.
[92] For the Pentateuch see Aejmelaeus 1982, 61: there are six cases in Genesis, three in Exodus, two in Leviticus, four in Numbers and three in Deuteronomy.

The cases meet the normal Greek use of ἀλλά. It is used to express a sudden shift in the direct discourse.[93]

The rare use of the conjunction ἀλλά is best explained by the fact that its use in Greek is highly specified. The translator had to take the context of the clause into account, if he used ἀλλά. Those alternatives that required less attention to the context would more easily have occurred to him.

2.2.9 ἵνα

The Greek conjunction ἵνα starts a final clause. As a rule, the verb form of the final subordinate clause depends on the verb form used in the main clause.[94] In the Classical language if the predicate in the main clause was in the past tense, the optative was used in the subordinate clause. Otherwise, the subjunctive was used. In the Post-classical period the use of the optative disappears and the subjunctive is used with ἵνα even in cases where the main clause includes a verb in the past tense.[95] There appears to be one case both in Joshua and in Judges where the conjunction ἵνα is used to render a main clause initiative Hebrew ו.[96]

Josh 20:9

אלה היו ערי המועדה ... לנוס שמה כל מכה נפש בשגגה ולא
ימות ביד גאל הדם – αὗται αἱ πόλεις αἱ ἐπίκλητοι ... κατα-
φυγεῖν ἐκεῖ παντὶ παίοντι ψυχὴν ἀκουσίως, ἵνα μὴ ἀποθάνῃ ἐν
χειρὶ ἀγχιστεύοντος τὸ αἷμα

Judg 19:22

ויאמרו אל האיש בעל הבית הזקן לאמר הוצא את האיש אשר
בא אל ביתך ונדענו – καὶ εἶπαν πρὸς τὸν ἄνδρα τὸν κύριον τῆς

---

[93] A number of ἀλλά clauses will be discussed later in a chapter concentrating on the rendering of כי expressing a positive alternative on pp. 189-192.

[94] Kühner-Gerth II:2 § 553.2-4.

[95] See. e.g. Blass-Debrunner-Rehkopf § 369.1.

[96] Otherwise ἵνα is used 15 times in the LXX of Joshua and 11 times in the LXX of Judges.

οἰκίας τὸν πρεσβύτην λέγοντες Ἐξάγαγε τὸν ἄνδρα τὸν εἰσ-
ελθόντα εἰς τὴν οἰκίαν σου, ἵνα γνῶμεν αὐτόν.

The final interpretation works well in the cases presented. The verb
forms in both of the cases follow general Greek practice. The cases
show that the translators were able to work with the context while
translating. In the Pentateuch the final cases occur more often than
in Joshua or Judges.[97]

2.2.10 ὅτι

Judg 18:7

ואין מכלים דבר בארץ יורש עצר וַרחקים המה מצדנים – καὶ
μὴ δυναμένους λαλῆσαι ῥῆμα, ὅτι μακράν εἰσιν ἀπὸ Σιδῶνος
The example includes a well-known *crux*[98] and the Greek rendering
of it is perhaps due to the difficulty to understand the Hebrew.[99]

The translator of Judges uses in this instance a causal subordinate
clause to render the Hebrew parataxis.[100] The solution is very clever
and shows that even a literal translator can use a suitable and free
rendering if he chooses to do so. Interestingly enough, the translators
of the Pentateuch do not very often use the ὅτι *causale* to render the
Hebrew parataxis. Aejmelaeus lists only one case (Num 9:23).[101]

2.2.11 γάρ

Judg 19:14

ויעברו וילכו וַתבא להם השמש אצל הגבעה – καὶ παρῆλθον καὶ
ἀπῆλθον· ἔδυ γὰρ ὁ ἥλιος ἐχόμενα τῆς Γαβαά

---

[97] The total number of cases in the Pentateuch is, according to Aejmelaeus, 47
(Aejmelaeus 1982, 68). The number also includes cases where the Greek
conjunction ὅπως is used to translate the main clause initiative Hebrew ו.
Such cases do not occur in Joshua or Judges. In Joshua ὅπως is used only
three times (4:24, 11:20 and 23:7). In Judges ὅπως is not used at all. None
of these cases belong to the present discussion.

[98] See especially Macintosh 1985, 68-77.

[99] See Schreiner 1957, 107-108.

[100] For renderings of the causal כי see pp. 142-168.

[101] Aejmelaeus 1982, 82.

The Greek conjunction γάρ is used in a clause giving a cause or an explanation. As is the case with so many other Greek conjunctions, γάρ is never the first word of the clause. In the Pentateuch Aejmelaeus lists eleven cases where γάρ is used to render the Hebrew ו.[102] Though γάρ is a frequently used conjunction in all periods of the Greek language,[103] it is used rather seldom to render Hebrew parataxis in the LXX.[104] The translator of Joshua never uses it to that purpose and there is only one such case in Judges.

2.2.12 *διὰ τοῦτο*

Judg 2:4-5

וישאו העם את קולם ויבכו ⁵ויקראו שם המקום ההוא בכים – καὶ ἐπῆρεν ὁ λαὸς τὴν φωνὴν αὐτῶν καὶ ἔκλαυσαν. ⁵ διὰ τοῦτο ἐκλήθη τὸ ὄνομα τοῦ τόπου ἐκείνου Κλαυθμών

The causal interpretation of the Hebrew text in this case is clear though free.[105] Interestingly, neither the Pentateuch nor Joshua contain such cases. There are in these books several causal constructions used to render Hebrew parataxis, but never did the translators of the Pentateuch and Joshua use διὰ τοῦτο.

2.2.13 *Relative pronoun*

Josh 2:1

ויבאו בית אשה זונה ושמה רחב – καὶ εἰσήλθοσαν εἰς οἰκίαν γυναικὸς πόρνης ᾗ ὄνομα Ῥαάβ

Aejmelaeus 1982, 64.
Denniston 1954, 58-60; Mayser II:3 § 164.4; Blomqvist 1969, 134-135 and 138-139; Blass-Debrunner-Rehkopf § 452.
For γάρ as a rendering of the causal כי see pp. 153-158.
Many modern translations adopt a similar interpretation as well; compare eg. NRSV and NEB.

The translator of Joshua uses in this instance the Greek relative clause to render the Hebrew parataxis. Without any doubt the choice is a good one and the language is stylistically correct. Here the use of a relative clause to render parataxis is not odd, because a nominal relative clause comes very close to the Hebrew co-ordinate clause in function.

In the Pentateuch the use of the relative clause to render Hebrew parataxis is limited almost entirely to Genesis.[106] Many cases in Genesis are close to the present case in Joshua, since they too give a person's name.[107]

2.2.14 *Participium coniunctum*

A typical Greek text often uses a special construction that bears the Latin name *participium coniunctum*.[108] In classical Greek the *part.coni.* could be used to express many different logical relationships between two expressions, such as temporal, modal, causal, concessive, conditional and final. In her study Aejmelaeus pointed out that in the LXX we meet another type of *part.coni.* unknown from the classical usage. In this special type of *part.coni.* two successive verbs belong closely together describing the same activity or aspects of the same activity. Such expressions are typical of Hebrew, and Aejmelaeus called this kind of *part.coni.* the pleonastic *part. coni.*[109]

---

[106] Aejmelaeus 1982, 73-74. There are 15 cases in Gen, two in Ex (2:1 and 10:25), and one in Num (6:12).

[107] Aejmelaeus 1982, 73 mentions seven cases: Gen 16:1, 22:24, 24:29, 25:1, 38:1, 38:2, and 38:6.

[108] There is a difference between the *participium coniunctum* and the *genetivus absolutus*. The former is used if the subject of the participle is the same as the subject or the object of the clause in which the participle construction is embedded. The latter is used if the subject of the participle is neither the subject nor the object of the clause (Kühner-Gerth II:2 § 485.3). For some exceptions to this general rule see Kühner-Gerth II:2 § 485.3 Anmerk 4.

[109] Aejmelaeus 1982, 90. For Hebrew see e.g. Brockelmann 1956, 133 and the so-called *Enumerative Redeweise*.

The use of the construction in rendering the Hebrew co-ordinate clauses is an inventive one. While the embedded constructions increase in number, the paratactical nature of the translation decreases. At the same time the use of the *part.coni.* introduces a more natural Greek idiom. In the LXX the construction is used in various contexts, but most commonly it is used to render the Hebrew parataxis.[110]

In the LXX of Joshua the *part. coni.* construction is used 29 times to render a co-ordinate main clause. In the translation of Judges only six cases occur.

In the following some examples of the use of the *part. coni.* are listed. The participle and the predicate of the main clause are underlined in every example. The examples represent (a) temporal, (b) modal and (c) pleonastic cases and in the discussion they are arranged in these three groups, depending on the logical relationship between the participle expression and the main clause.

(a) *Temporal cases* amount to a third of the cases.[111]

Josh 5:13

וַיֵּלֶךְ יְהוֹשֻׁעַ אֵלָיו וַיֹּאמֶר לוֹ – καὶ προσελθὼν Ἰησοῦς εἶπεν αὐτῷ

Josh 22:30

וַיִּשְׁמַע פִּינְחָס הַכֹּהֵן וּנְשִׂיאֵי ... אֶת הַדְּבָרִים ... וַיִּיטַב בְּעֵינֵיהֶם – καὶ ἀκούσας Φεινεὲς ὁ ἱερεὺς καὶ πάντες οἱ ἄρχοντες ... τοὺς λόγους ... καὶ ἤρεσεν αὐτοῖς

The subject of the participle differs from the subject of the main clause here, but since the logical subjects are the same, the Greek construction is correct.[112] The translator, however, used the conjunction καί between the participle and its main verb.

---

[110] Aejmelaeus 1982a, 386-389. Aejmelaeus listed a number of Hebrew equivalents for the Greek *part.coni.* Among others are Hebrew paronomasis with the *inf.abs.*, the Hebrew idiom לֵאמֹר, the Hebrew structure בְּ + *inf. c.*, asyndetic verb pairs, Hebrew participles, and co-ordinated clauses.

[111] For examples of the temporal cases of the *part.coni.* in the Pentateuch see Aejmelaeus 1982, 98-100.

[112] See Kühner-Gerth II:2 § 493.1.

Josh 24:9

וישׁלח ויקרא לבלעם בן בעור לקלל אתכם – καὶ ἀποστείλας ἐκάλεσεν τὸν Βαλαὰμ ἀράσασθαι ὑμῖν

While the translator composed a correct construction, he ended up using an idiom not normally used in Greek. A more natural expression would be to use a finite form of the verb ἀποστέλλω with a nominal form of the verb καλέω.[113] Probably, the translator used a rare expression because the normal idiom would have resulted in an expression with two subsequent infinitives (καλέσαι ... ἀράσασθαι).

(b) *Modal cases* form as large a group of cases as do temporal cases.[114]

Josh 4:2-3

קחו לכם מן העם שנים עשׂר אנשׁים אישׁ אחד אישׁ אחד משׁבט ³וצוו אותם לאמר – παραλαβὼν ἄνδρας ἀπὸ τοῦ λαοῦ ἕνα ἀφ’ ἑκάστης φυλῆς, ³ σύνταξον αὐτοῖς

Josh 10:38-39

³⁹ וילכדה עליה וילחם – καὶ περικαθίσαντες αὐτὴν ³⁹ ἔλαβον αὐτήν

Judg 9:9

החדלתי את דשׁני ... והלכתי לנוע על העצים – ἀφεῖσα τὴν πιότητά μου,... πορευθῶ ἄρχειν τῶν ξύλων;

Verses Judg 9:11 and 9:13 contain similar translations.

---

[113] See Aejmelaeus 1982, 96 and the literature she mentioned. She also referred to seven cases where the participle of the verb ἀποστέλλω has been used; eg. Gen 31:4. The cases reflect the modal usage of the construction. Cf. however, Herodotus III.122.3 μαθὼν ὧν ταῦτά μιν διανοεύμενον ὁ Ὀροίτης πέμψας ἀγγελίην ἔλεγε τάδε· Ὀροίτης Πολυκράτει ὧδε λέγει. It seems then possible to use the participle as the translator did, at least occasionally, in genuine Greek.

[114] Examples of the modal cases of the *part.coni.* in the Pentateuch were mentioned by Aejmelaeus 1982, 94-97.

Judg 11:14-15

ויאמר לו ¹⁵ וישלח מלאכים אל מלך בני עמון – καὶ <u>ἀπέστειλεν</u>
Ἰεφθάε ἀγγέλους πρὸς τὸν βασιλέα υἱῶν Ἀμμὼν ¹⁵ <u>λέγων</u>
This case may be seen as final also. Unlike most of the cases with
the *part.coni.*, here the participle follows the main verb. Cf. also
Josh 9:24, a pleonastic case of the *part.coni.* in the following.

(c) The third group of examples includes *pleonastic cases*.[115] These
cases are very interesting, since, as Aejmelaeus has shown, the
pleonastic use of the *part.coni.* is one of the idiosyncrasies of the
LXX. Therefore, I shall list every case of the pleonastic use here.

Josh 2:4

ותקח האשה את שני האנשים ותצפנו – καὶ <u>λαβοῦσα</u> ἡ γυνὴ τοὺς
ἄνδρας <u>ἔκρυψεν</u> αὐτούς

Josh 18:4

ויקמו ויתהלכו בארץ – καὶ <u>ἀναστάντες</u> <u>διελθέτωσαν</u> τὴν γῆν

Josh 22:4

ועתה פנו ולכו לכם לאהליכם – νῦν οὖν <u>ἀποστραφέντες</u>
<u>ἀπέλθατε</u> εἰς τοὺς οἴκους ὑμῶν

Judg 19:6

ויאמר אבי הנערה אל האיש הואל נא ולין – καὶ εἶπεν ὁ πατὴρ
τῆς νεάνιδος πρὸς τὸν ἄνδρα <u>Ἀρξάμενος</u> <u>αὐλίσθητι</u>
Here one might note that while the construction is correct genuine
Greek usage does not support expressions like this.

Judg 19:17

וישא עיניו וירא את האיש הארח ברחב העיר – καὶ <u>ἀναβλέψας</u>
τοῖς ὀφθαλμοῖς <u>εἶδεν</u> τὸν ἄνδρα τὸν ὁδοιπόρον ἐν τῇ πλατείᾳ
τῆς πόλεως

Josh 9:24

ויענו את יהושע ויאמרו – καὶ <u>ἀπεκρίθησαν</u> τῷ Ἰησοῖ <u>λέγοντες</u>

---

[115] Examples of the pleonastic cases of the *part.coni.* in the Pentateuch were
listed by Aejmelaeus 1982, 90-94.

Normally the equivalent of the Greek participle of the verb λέγω is the infinitive לאמר. Exceptionally in this case the participle counts for *wayyiqtol* ויאמרו in Hebrew. There is, however, hardly any reason to suppose a Hebrew *Vorlage* different from the MT.[116] Cf. Judg 11:14-15 below.

Conclusions

In my material the *part.coni.* cases divide themselves into three different groups that are approximately equally large. One third of the cases are best interpreted as temporal. Another third of the cases are modal and the rest of the cases could be interpreted as pleonastic. The borderline between modal and pleonastic cases is not self-evident, as Aejmelaeus points out,[117] but the large-scale grouping of various types of the *part.coni.* holds true.

TABLE 3 Different functions of the *part.coni.* in Joshua and Judges

	Josh	Judg
Temporal	11	0
Modal	8	4
Pleonastic	10	2

Aejmelaeus mentioned some verbs that often occur in cases where the Hebrew parataxis is rendered by the *part.coni.*[118] One may find the same verbs in connection with the *part.coni.* in Joshua and Judges, too, but not all of them. On the other hand, some common Hebrew verbs not listed by Aejmelaeus occur in Joshua and Judges

---

[116] According to Aejmelaeus it is very difficult to draw any conclusions from cases like this where the participle of the verb λέγω is used; Aejmelaeus 1982a, 387. She based her insight on Soisalon-Soininen's more extensive study on the subject; Soisalon-Soininen 1965, 68-75.

[117] Aejmelaeus 1982, 90.

[118] Aejmelaeus 1982, 89.

rather often when the translators used the *part.coni.* to render the Hebrew parataxis. Such verbs as הלך (4), שמע (3) and שוב (2) may be mentioned, yet one must note that they come into the picture only in Joshua. In Judges חדל hithp. (3) is the most common verb when the translator uses the *part. coni.* to render Hebrew parataxis, though all the cases are in the ninth chapter (cf. example Judg 9:9). There is a clear difference between Joshua and Judges when it comes to the Hebrew verbs rendered by the *part.coni.* There are only two Hebrew verbs (אמר and נשא) that occur in both of the books in cases in question. Since the number of cases where the *part.coni.* is used is rather small in my material, it is difficult to say whether certain verbs in fact attracted the use of the *part.coni.* as is the case in the Pentateuch, according to Aejmelaeus.

The ratio of the *part.coni.* to the total number of translations of the ז initial Hebrew main clauses is very low in Joshua, only 3%. In Judges the ratio of the *part.coni.* is as low as 0.4%. This is striking, since the frequent use of the *part.coni.* is typical of Greek. Despite its rarity in the material, the *part. coni.* was a natural choice for the translators. It fits very well in many places, because it expresses many different types of logical relationship. In the LXX the *part. coni.* is even used to link clauses that form a pleonastic expression.

Because cases where the *part.coni.* is used are quite rare in Joshua and in Judges, one must see them as occasional good perceptions on the translator's part. Usually, the translations of Joshua and Judges are very monotonous and repeat almost every Hebrew conjunction ז with the Greek καί. The rarity of the *part.coni.* becomes understandable when one realizes that its use requires an active knowledge of the context in which the co-ordinate clause happens to appear. In Aejmelaeus' words its use reflects the translators' "ability to master larger units than a couple of words."[119]

The translators did not always use the *part.coni.* without problems. When they began a clause by using the *part. coni.* they should *not* have given any equivalent for the Hebrew ז between clauses linked with the participle construction. This did not always happen and the result is an unidiomatic or even incorrect expression

---

[119] Aejmelaeus 1982, 108.

(cf. Josh 22:30).[120] Cases like these will be dealt later in connection with the apodotic καί.[121] That there are some problems in the use of the *part.coni.* indicates that sometimes the translators were unaware of the context and its requirements.

Does the length of the Hebrew clause have any effect on the translation? One might think that longer constructions were more difficult to handle than shorter ones. Indeed, such a claim may be made if one studies the correctness of the constructions. Longer constructions are more often problematic than shorter ones. In cases where the Hebrew counterpart of *part.coni.* in Joshua contains less than four words, the translator uses the construction correctly, but in cases where the clause is longer problems appear. Not only does the subject of the participle occasionally differ from the subject of the main clause (Josh 22:30), but there are cases where the conjunction καί is used between the *part.coni.* and the main clause. It must, however, be admitted that the translator does not produce problematic language in every case where the clause is longer than four words. In two cases where the clause is longer than ten words, the translator manages to formulate an acceptable expression (Josh 4:2 and 4:4). In Judges the translator *always* omits the conjunction between the participial construction and its main clause. This means that even a literal translator may nevertheless succeed in producing idiomatic language.

In comparison with the translations in the Pentateuch one may note that the LXX of Joshua resembles the books of the Pentateuch when it comes to the use of the *part.coni.*, but the LXX of Judges is dramatically different. In the Pentateuch the average ratio of the use of the *part.coni.* is 4.9%. The ratio for Joshua (3.4%) is almost the same, but the ratio for Judges (0.4%) is much lower, indicating a more literal translation. This is probably due to the narrower segmentation used by the translator of Judges. It is noteworthy, nevertheless, that when the translator of Judges decided to use the *part.coni.* he mastered the context well. Unlike in the Pentateuch and in Joshua there is *not* a single case of καί between the participle and the main clause predicate in the LXX of Judges. The closest

---

[120] The example is dealt with on p. 57.
[121] See pp. 127-129.

counterpart to the LXX of Joshua among the books of the Pentateuch is Numbers, if the statistics are to be followed.[122]

Special cases

In three cases the Greek text is difficult to interpret and accordingly the grouping of the material becomes problematic.

Josh 9:4

– וילכו ויצטירו ויקחו שקים בלים לחמוריהם ... ⁵ ונעלות בלות
καὶ ἐλθόντες ἐπεσιτίσαντο καὶ ἡτοιμάσαντο[123] καὶ λαβόντες
σάκκους παλαιοὺς ἐπὶ τῶν ὄνων αὐτῶν... ⁵ καὶ τὰ κοῖλα τῶν
ὑποδημάτων[124] αὐτῶν καὶ τὰ σανδάλια αὐτῶν παλαιά

The interpretation of the participle λαβόντες is difficult, because one has problems in identifying a suitable main clause.

Perhaps the clause καὶ ἦλθοσαν πρὸς Ἰησοῦν κτλ in verse 6 may act as a main clause for the participle, but if so, then the syntactic position of verse 5 becomes questionable. In verse 5 a nominal clause might act as a main clause, but then the content of the expression becomes difficult to understand. Should one follow the latter possibility, one has to recognize that the conjunction καί at the

---

[122] In the Pentateuch the books may be arranged according to the use of *part.coni.* to render Hebrew parataxis in the following order: Gen, Dtn, Ex, Num and Lev. Aejmelaeus 1982, 89 gave the statistics.

[123] Margolis made an emendation, omitting ἐπεσιτίσαντο καί against all the manuscripts. He commented on his emendation by saying: "Mas[ius] recognized that we have here a doublet. But he regards επεσιτισαντο as the original. The reverse is probably true." For recent discussion see den Hertog 1996, 88-89 and Moatti-Fine 1996, 142.

[124] The expression κοῖλα τῶν ὑποδημάτων is a *hapax* in the LXX. Here there seems to be a doublet *their boots and sandals*. Margolis 1931, 152 emended the text and omitted the sandals. He commented on the passage as follows: "κοιλα 'soles' amplification. Delete και τα σανδαλια αυτων. σανδαλιον occurs elsewhere only Ju *10 4 16* 9 Is *20 2*." I wonder if we can still follow Margolis. The modern dictionaries indicate a difference between ὑπόδημα and ὑπόδημα κοῖλον and therefore the κοῖλα is not an amplification; see also den Hertog 1996, 89. Margolis's emendation is understandable since the expression τὰ κοῖλα τῶν ὑποδημάτων αὐτῶν is a free rendering even though the Hebrew נעל is generally rendered by ὑπόδημα in the LXX.

beginning of the nominal clause in verse 5 stands between the participial construction and its main clause. Also, the subject of the participle (*the men from Gibea*) differs from the subject of the nominal clause (*boots*).

Josh 10:24

וַיִּקְרָא יְהוֹשֻׁעַ אֶל כָּל אִישׁ יִשְׂרָאֵל וַיֹּאמֶר אֶל קְצִינֵי אַנְשֵׁי
הַמִּלְחָמָה הֶהָלְכוּא אִתּוֹ – καὶ <u>συνεκάλεσεν</u> Ἰησοῦς πάντα Ἰσραὴλ
καὶ τοὺς ἐναρχομένους τοῦ πολέμου τοὺς συμπορευομένους
αὐτῷ <u>λέγων</u> αὐτοῖς

Here the problem lies in the difficulty in linking the translation with the MT. Is it possible that the Hebrew *Vorlage* differed from the MT? If this is the case, was the difference only one of word order? The Greek construction is, on the other hand, straightforward.

Josh 12:4-5

וּגְבוּל עוֹג מֶלֶךְ הַבָּשָׁן מִיֶּתֶר הָרְפָאִים הַיּוֹשֵׁב בְּעַשְׁתָּרוֹת וּבְאֶדְרֶעִי
וּמֹשֵׁל ⁵ בְּהַר חֶרְמוֹן – καὶ Ὢγ βασιλεὺς Βασὰ <u>ὑπελείφθη</u> ἐκ τῶν
γιγάντων, ὁ κατοικῶν ἐν Ἀσταρὼθ καὶ ἐν Ἐδράειν, <u>ἄρχων</u> ἀπὸ
ὄρους Ἀερμών

Verse 5 begins with the participle in Hebrew and in Greek. While the translator uses the participle, he does not use any visible equivalent for the Hebrew co-ordinating conjunction ו. The interpretation of the passage is not quite indispensable, but the most natural way of interpreting the participle ἄρχων is to see it as a part of the *part.coni.* construction, though exceptional.

2.2.15 *Genetivus absolutus*

A parallel construction to the *part.coni.* in Greek is the *genetivus absolutus*. The latter is used in cases where the subject of the participle is not the subject or the object of the main clause.[125] In the LXX, as well as in post-classical Greek in general, there are, however, cases where the *gen.abs* is used instead of the *part.coni.*[126]

---

[125] See footnote no. 108 on p. 56.
[126] See Aejmelaeus 1982, 11-112 and Soisalon-Soininen 1987, 177.

The use of the *gen.abs.* is rarer than the use of the *part.coni.* in
the LXX. According to Soisalon-Soininen, the most common
Hebrew equivalent for the *gen.abs.* is the infinitive construction with
the preposition ב.[127] In many books of the LXX the *gen.abs.* is used
to render co-ordinated clauses, too. In Joshua there is one such case
and in Judges there are five such cases.

Josh 6:5

– יריעו כל העם תרועה גדולה וְנָפְלָה חומת העיר תחתיה
ἀνακραγέτω πᾶς ὁ λαὸς ἅμα. καὶ ἀνακραγόντων αὐτῶν
πεσεῖται αὐτόματα τὰ τείχη τῆς πόλεως
In the LXX the *gen.abs.* is used correctly, but the Hebrew *Vorlage*
was perhaps not quite identical to the MT.

Judg 13:9

וַיָּבֹא – מלאך האלהים עוד אל האשה וְהִיא יוֹשֶׁבֶת בשדה καὶ
παρεγένετο ὁ ἄγγελος τοῦ θεοῦ ἔτι πρὸς τὴν γυναῖκα αὐτῆς
καθημένης ἐν τῷ ἀγρῷ
The Hebrew participle in a clause which is rendered by the *gen.abs.*
is not a rarity.

Judg 18:3

הֵמָה – עם בית מיכה וְהֵמָה הִכִּירוּ את קול הנער הלוי αὐτῶν
ὄντων παρὰ τῷ οἴκῳ Μιχὰ καὶ αὐτοὶ ἐπέγνωσαν τὴν φωνὴν τοῦ
παιδαρίου τοῦ νεωτέρου τοῦ Λευίτου
In this instance the subject of the participle is the same as the subject
of the main clause (*the spies of the Danites*). There is the conjunction καί between the participle and its main clause. Thus, the reader
of the LXX interprets the pronouns αὐτῶν and αὐτοί as referring to
two different groups of people.

Judg 18:22

המה הִרְחִיקוּ מבית מיכה _ והאנשים אשר בבתים אשר עם בית
αὐτῶν δὲ μεμακρυγκότων ἀπὸ –מיכה נזעקו וַיַּדְבִּיקוּ את בני דן

---

[127] Soisalon-Soininen 1987, 176-177. The total number of cases in the LXX is
approximately 200 and there is a considerable difference in the number of
cases between various books of the LXX. E.g. in Job 21 cases exist but in
Judg only 6 cases were reported by Soisalon-Soininen.

τοῦ οἴκου Μιχὰ <u>καὶ</u> ἰδοὺ Μιχὰ καὶ οἱ ἄνδρες οἱ σὺν τῷ οἴκῳ μετὰ Μιχὰ <u>ἔκραζον</u> κατοπίσω υἱῶν Δάν

The LXX contains the phrase καὶ ἰδοὺ Μιχά, a text with no equivalent in the Hebrew. Because it opens the main clause, καί is placed between the participial construction and its main clause.

Judg 19:11

ויאמר הנער אל אדניו הם עם יבוס והיום רד מאד רד – ἔτι αὐτῶν ὄντων κατὰ Ἰεβοὺς καὶ ἡ ἡμέρα κεκλικυῖα σφόδρα· καὶ εἶπεν τὸ παιδάριον πρὸς τὸν κύριον αὐτοῦ

Compare Judg 18:3 above. Interestingly, the translator did not use another *gen.abs.* construction to render the Hebrew מאד רד והיום. Again καί separates the participle and its main clause.

Judg 19:22

המה מיטיבים את לבם והנה אנשי העיר אנשי בני בליעל נסבו את הבית – αὐτῶν δὲ <u>ἀγαθυνθέντων</u> τῇ καρδίᾳ αὐτῶν <u>καὶ ἰδοὺ</u> οἱ ἄνδρες τῆς πόλεως υἱοὶ παρανόμων <u>περιεκύκλωσαν</u> τὴν οἰκίαν

The formula והנה is always rendered as καὶ ἰδού in the LXX of Judges. Here the mechanical translation produced a problematic case of καί separating the participle construction from the rest of the clause. Compare also Judg 18:22 above.

Since in the LXX of Joshua only one case may be found where the translator used the *gen.abs.* to render a parataxis in Hebrew, the *gen. abs.* is a free rendering very rare for him.[128] Almost the same applies to Judges as well. There are five cases and one sees them as free renderings.[129] It might be useful to note that in Judges the *gen.abs.* is one of the most frequent free renderings of the parataxis in Hebrew. It is used when the personal pronoun lies at the beginning

---

[128] There are only two other cases where the *gen.abs* is used in Joshua. In Josh 4:23 the *gen.abs.* is used to render a temporal אשר clause in Hebrew and in Josh 8:29 the *gen.abs* is used as an equivalent for a temporal expression with the preposition כ and the infinitive.

[129] There are two further cases in Judg where the *gen.abs* is used. In Judg 7:19 the Hebrew equivalent is the expression ראש האשמרת התיכונה and in Judg 13:12 the Hebrew equivalent is a עתה clause followed by the question מה יהיה משפט הנער.

of the Hebrew clause transformed into the participial construction. Often the Hebrew clause is also a nominal clause. Since the translator quite often uses the conjunction καί to separate the main clause from the participial construction, and since he occasionally fails to notice that the *gen.abs.* does not suit the context, I believe that the translator of Judges did not bear in mind the context of the passage he was translating.

All the cases listed above include a temporal phrase in Hebrew rendered by the *gen.abs.* According to Soisalon-Soininen, this is the most common way that the *gen.abs.* is used in the LXX. Thus, it often has a temporal function in the LXX.[130] In her study Aejmelaeus pointed out that there are some concessive and conditional cases in the LXX of the Pentateuch,[131] but my material does not include any.

If compared with the Pentateuch, Joshua and Judges do not differ too much from it. The *gen.abs.* is a free, rare and very idiomatic Greek expression. Aejmelaeus concluded that the use of the *gen.abs.* in the Pentateuch shows "the translators' ability to cope with the problems of their work."[132] The same also holds true for the translator of Joshua. The translator of Judges used the *gen.abs.* rather often, but had problems with the construction. One may therefore conclude that he tried to use natural Greek idioms, but was not really successful in doing so.

2.2.16 *An infinitive construction*

There is one more case in the LXX of Joshua to be discussed here. The translation uses an infinitive structure as an equivalent for the Hebrew ‍ו initial main clause.

Josh 4:16

צַוֵּה אֶת הַכֹּהֲנִים נֹשְׂאֵי אֲרוֹן הָעֵדוּת וְיַעֲלוּ מִן הַיַּרְדֵּן – ἔντειλαι τοῖς ἱερεῦσιν τοῖς αἴρουσιν τὴν κιβωτὸν τῆς διαθήκης τοῦ μαρτυρίου Κυρίου ἐκβῆναι ἐκ τοῦ Ἰορδάνου

---

[130] Soisalon-Soininen 1987, 177.
[131] Aejmelaeus 1982, 112. The concessive cases are to be found in Leviticus and the conditional cases in Genesis.
[132] Aejmelaeus 1982, 112.

The case is unique in Joshua,[133] but the use of the infinitive with the verb meaning "to order" is quite common in Greek. There are parallel instances in the other books of the LXX.[134]

The use of an infinitive construction to translate parataxis is a marker of a free rendering. The construction belongs to natural Greek idiom and thus it is straightforward concerning the usage and the style.

2.2.17 No Greek conjunction as an equivalent of the main clause initial Hebrew ו due to rearranging of the text

Often the main clause initial Hebrew ו is rendered by using the Greek co-ordinating conjunction καί. There are, however, cases where another equivalent is used and occasionally the translators have also modified the grammatical structure of the parent text. This is seen in cases where a subordination or an embedded participial or infinitive construction is used. From time to time the translators made such modifications to the structure of the text that the use of the co-ordinating conjunction or any other conjunction became unsuitable. In such cases the translators usually omitted the conjunction appearing in the parent text. There are four such cases in my material. One of the cases exist in Joshua and three in Judges.

Josh 15:5-6

וגבול לפאת צפונה מלשון הים מקצה הירדן ⁶וָעלה הגבול בית חלגה – καὶ τὰ ὅρια αὐτῶν ἀπὸ βορρᾶ καὶ ἀπὸ τῆς λοφιᾶς τῆς θαλάσσης καὶ ἀπὸ τοῦ μέρους τοῦ Ἰορδάνου⁶ ___ ἐπιβαίνει τὰ ὅρια ἐπὶ Βαιθαγλάαμ

The co-ordinating conjunction was moved into a new position in the translation. The expression of place מקצה הירדן is included in the clause in verse 6. Accordingly, the conjunction at the beginning of verse 6 cannot have a visible counterpart in the translation. On the

---

[133] Other instances where ἐντελλόμαι with the infinitive is used in Joshua are 8:35 (= LXX 9:2f) and 17:4.

[134] For similar cases in the LXX see Soisalon-Soininen 1965, 129. Aejmelaeus 1982, 113 discussed the cases in the Pentateuch. She mentioned two close parallels to the case in Joshua, namely Gen 12:20 and 42:25.

other hand, the translator added the conjunction καί before ἀπὸ τοῦ μέρους τοῦ Ἰορδάνου in verse 5.

Judg 3:16

ויעש לו אהוד חרב וַלה שני פיות – καὶ ἐποίησεν ἑαυτῷ Ἀώδ μάχαιραν ___ δίστομον

Here the translator used an adjective instead of a co-ordinated nominal clause in Hebrew and therefore the conjunction was omitted.[135]

Judg 10:10

ויזעקו בני ישראל אל יהוה לאמר חטאנו לך וַכי עזבנו את אלהינו ונעבד את הבעלים – καὶ ἐκέκραξαν οἱ υἱοὶ Ἰσραὴλ πρὸς Κύριον λέγοντες Ἡμάρτομέν σοι, ___ ὅτι ἐγκατελίπομεν τὸν θεὸν ἡμῶν καὶ ἐλατρεύσαμεν ταῖς Βααλίμ.

The translator understood the Hebrew כי clause as subordinated to a preceding clause. Accordingly, he omitted the conjunction. The Hebrew text must be understood in another way if the conjunction ו plays any role here. The conjunction shows that the כי clause explains the following clause (*we have worshipped the Baals*).

Judg 19:7

ויפצר בו חתנו וישב וַילן שם – καὶ ἐβιάσατο αὐτὸν ὁ γαμβρὸς αὐτοῦ, καὶ πάλιν ___ ηὐλίσθη ἐκεῖ

The omission is here due to the excellent free translation. Two clauses have been combined. Two similar cases exist in the Pentateuch (Gen 26:18 and Dtn 30:3).[136]

Summary

The four cases discussed in the present chapter represent omission of the Hebrew ו. It is not possible to offer a waterproof explanation in every instance. Perhaps someone would explain one or two cases differently and speak about the *Vorlage* as deviating from the MT,

---

[135] For similar instances in the LXX of the Pentateuch see Aejmelaeus 1982, 118-119 and especially her example Gen 32:29(28).

[136] Cases in the Pentateuch were discussed by Aejmelaeus 1982, 118.

but I try to explain the cases as results of free modification of the surface structure of the text. The main question here is, why was the Hebrew ו left without a visible counterpart in these cases? Occasionally the question is closely related to the free rendering of the context, thus showing that the "omission" is based on a special interpretation of the context. Clearly the translators of Joshua and Judges introduced some changes - minimal as they are - during the translation process. One may therefore conclude that the overall literal character of the work of these translators left them some room to modify the idiom. Thus, neither the translator of Joshua nor the translator of Judges pursued a word-for-word rendering.

2.2.18 No conjunction at the beginning of the Greek clause (asyndeton)

In many cases the translations lack an equivalent for the Hebrew conjunction ו. The lack of the conjunction often results in an asyndetic linkage between two clauses. Normally classical Greek does not favour the use of asyndeton, but its use is not excluded either.[137] Denniston remarked that the use of asyndeton depends on the stylistic impression the writer desired to give, but often asyndeton is regarded, according to him, as peculiar. He mentioned two examples of writers who used the peculiar asyndeton, namely Xenophon and Andocides.[138] Interestingly, Denniston said that in

---

[137] There are instances where *asyndeton* is preferable, such as an instance where the linkage becomes clear from the preceding context. See further Denniston 1954, xlii-xlv. For a detailed description of the Greek use of *asyndeton* see Kühner-Gerth II:2 § 546.

[138] Denniston 1954, xlv. Indeed, he says that the result in Xenophon and Andocides is "a certain naive awkwardness." Denniston proceeds to mention that already in antiquity the use of *asyndeton* was seen mainly as a stylistic device. This was explicitly mentioned by Aristotle in his *Rhetorics*, where the use of *asyndeton* is mentioned as an example of the feature that formulates the style (*Rh* 1413b3-1414a7). Concerning Andocides Gärtner 1964, 344 says that the style of Andocides was not the best one might hope for. This resulted from the fact that Andocides put more weight on the effect on the listeners than on purity of style. There are an overwhelming number of instances of redundancy, unfinished clauses, and other grammatical

most of the cases of asyndeton, it is linked with the simple co-ordination "and".[139] As Aejmelaeus has pointed out in her study, it is not always clear when asyndeton is based on the Hebrew *Vorlage* of the LXX and when it is a product of the translator's dealing with the Hebrew containing the conjunction ו.[140] There is some degree of difference in the use of the conjunction ו in the Hebrew manuscripts and one may expect that the same holds true for the Hebrew *Vorlage* of the LXX.[141] Also, the asyndetic clauses are not a rarity in the MT either.

In the following discussion the eight cases are grouped according to the degree of certainty that the *Vorlage* contained asyndeton. The main criterion in the grouping has been the possibility of showing an internal Greek reason for the lack of the conjunction. On the other hand, the difficulty in explaining the wording of the Hebrew *Vorlage* has also been taken into account. In cases where the wording of the Hebrew *Vorlage* is felt to be difficult, the reason for asyndeton in Greek has been explained to be the translation process.

a) The Hebrew *Vorlage* was probably close to the MT and the translator left the conjunction without any visible equivalent.

Josh 7:20

– אמנה אנכי חטאתי ליהוה אלהי ישראל וכזאת וכזאת עשיתי
ἀληθῶς ἥμαρτον ἐναντίον Κυρίου θεοῦ Ἰσραήλ. _οὕτως καὶ οὕτως ἐποίησα

At the beginning of verse 20 Achor confesses that he disobeyed the commands of God and then he continues to tell what he has done. The conjunction could be omitted in Greek because the link between

---

incongruencies in his speeches; see also MacDowell 1962, 18-23.

[139] Denniston 1954, xlvi. Other cases mentioned by Denniston are instances where γάρ, γοῦν, 'then' or 'therefore' "has to be supplied."

[140] Aejmelaeus 1982, 83.

[141] See Yevin 1980, 14 (= § 22). The Qumran fragments of Joshua and Judges were published in the DJD I by Barthélemy and in the DJD XII by Ulrich, Tov, and Trebolle Barrera. Preliminary publications appeared in Ulrich 1994 (*4QJosh^a*), Tov 1992 (*4QJosh^b*), Trebolle Barrera 1989 (*4QJudg^a*), and Trebolle Barrera 1992 (*4QJudg^b*). For the text-critical value of the Joshua fragments see Greenspoon 1992.

clauses is clear enough. The adverb οὕτως, because it refers backwards, indicates the connection between clauses.[142]

Josh 7:20-21

וכזאת וכזאת עשיתי 21 וָאראה בשלל אדתר שנער אחת טובה
οὕτως καὶ οὕτως ἐποίησα. 21 _εἶδον ἐν τῇ προνομῇ ψιλὴν ποικίλην καλήν

Verse 21 begins with Achor's explanation as to why he stole some of the spoil. This is preceded by the phrase: *This and this I did.* The co-ordinating conjunction is not needed in Greek, because the preceding context already makes it clear that the following clause is logically linked with the preceding clause.[143]

Josh 8:28

וישרף יהושע את העי ויָשימה תל עולם שממה עד היום הזה
καὶ ἐνεπύρισεν Ἰησοῦς τὴν πόλιν ἐν πυρί. ___χῶμα ἀοίκητον εἰς τὸν αἰῶνα ἔθηκεν αὐτὴν ἕως τῆς ἡμέρας ταύτης

The translator composes an ingenious rendering and by changing the word order he is able to use asyndeton. The linkage between the two clauses is very clear. The explicit marker of the linkage is the pronoun αὐτήν, which refers backwards to the object of the preceding clause.

Josh 22:13-14

וישלחו בני ישראל... את פינחס בן אלעזר הכהן 14 ועשרה נשאים עמו נשיא אחד נשיא אחד לבית אב...[144] וָאיש ראש בית אבותם לאלפי ישראל – המה καὶ ἀπέστειλαν οἱ υἱοὶ Ἰσραήλ ... τόν τε Φεινεὲς υἱὸν Ἐλεαζὰρ υἱοῦ Ἀαρὼν τοῦ ἀρχιερέως 14 καὶ δέκα τῶν ἀρχόντων μετ' αὐτοῦ, ἄρχων εἷς ἀπὸ οἴκου πατριᾶς ἀπὸ πασῶν φυλῶν Ἰσραήλ. ___ἄρχοντες οἴκων πατριῶν εἰσίν χιλί-αρχοι Ἰσραήλ

---

[142] For the use of the adverb οὕτως in asyndetic clause linkages see Smyth 1956 § 2165a. The question is about a specific type of *asyndeton,* called by Kühner-Gerth "apparent *asyndeton*" (*scheinbares Asyndeton*); Kühner-Gerth II:2 § 546.2.

[143] See e.g. Denniston 1954, xliii and Smyth 1956 § 2165.

[144] I have left out the plus in the MT in order to clarify the example.

Probably the translator interpreted the last clause of verse 14 as an explanation concerning the chiefs mentioned in the preceding context. Therefore, the conjunction could be omitted.

b) The Greek text is based on the Hebrew, which differs from the MT

Josh 6:7

וַיֹּאמְרוּ אֶל הָעָם עִבְרוּ וְסֹבּוּ אֶת הָעִיר – ___παραγγείλατε τῷ λαῷ περιελθεῖν καὶ κυκλῶσαι τὴν πόλιν

The whole passage is in direct speech in the LXX, but not in the MT. Also, a major plus in the MT in verse 6 precedes the passage in question. It is difficult to know whether the Hebrew ו appeared in the *Vorlage* of the LXX. καί or any other conjunction may introduce direct speech in Greek and thus it is not self-evident that the translator omitted the conjunction here.

Josh 22:3

לֹא עֲזַבְתֶּם אֶת אֲחֵיכֶם זֶה יָמִים רַבִּים עַד הַיּוֹם הַזֶּה וּשְׁמַרְתֶּם אֵת מִשְׁמֶרֶת מִצְוַת יְהוָה אֱלֹהֵיכֶם – οὐκ ἐγκαταλελοίπατε τοὺς ἀδελφοὺς ὑμῶν ταύτας τὰς ἡμέρας καὶ πλείους ἕως τῆς σήμερον ἡμέρας· ___ἐφυλάξασθε τὴν ἐντολὴν Κυρίου τοῦ θεοῦ ὑμῶν

There is no evident grammatical or stylistic reason why the conjunction should have been omitted here. This is why I conclude that the conjunction ו did not occur in the Hebrew *Vorlage*.

Judg 18:12-13

עַל כֵּן קָרְאוּ לַמָּקוֹם הַהוּא מַחֲנֵה דָן עַד הַיּוֹם הַזֶּה הִנֵּה אַחֲרֵי קִרְיַת יְעָרִים ¹³ וַיַּעַבְרוּ מִשָּׁם הַר אֶפְרָיִם – διὰ τοῦτο ἐκλήθη τῷ τόπῳ ἐκείνῳ Παρεμβολὴ Δὰν ἕως τῆς ἡμέρας ταύτης, ἰδοὺ κατόπισθεν Καριαθιαρὶμ. ¹³ ___παρῆλθαν ἐκεῖθεν καὶ ἦλθαν ἕως τοῦ ὄρους Ἐφράιμ

The difference between the LXX and the MT leads one to ask, what was the wording of the Hebrew *Vorlage*? If the *Vorlage* did contain the Hebrew conjunction ו, then one must conclude, I think, that the omission was due to the beginning of a new section.

Judg 18:22-23

מיכה והאנשים אשר בבתים אשר עם בית מיכה נזעקו וידביקו

‏23 אֶת בני דן וַיִּקְרְאוּ אֶל בני דן ויסבו פניהם ויאמרו למיכה –

Μιχὰ καὶ οἱ ἄνδρες οἱ σὺν τῷ οἴκῳ μετὰ Μιχὰ 23 ___ἔκραζον
κατοπίσω υἱῶν Δάν. καί ἐπέστρεψαν οἱ υἱοὶ Δὰν τὰ πρόσωπα
αὐτῶν καὶ εἶπαν πρὸς Μιχά

The Hebrew Vorlage of the LXX seems to have been shorter than
the MT here. The LXX reflects a text where the final five words of
verse 22 were missing and the beginning of verse 23 belonged to the
same clause as the main part of verse 22.[145]

Summary

The reason for the so-called "omission" in cases where the *Vorlage*
probably did contain the conjunction ו is based on the requirements
of Greek as a language or on the translator's understanding of the
passage. Occasionally there was an opportunity not to use the conjunction in the translation and the translators took that opportunity.
One must say that such cases are not too frequent. The stylistic
impression of the Greek text is merely commanded by the generally
frequent use of the conjunction καί.

2.2.19 *Translation-technical evaluation*

The analysis of the renderings of the main clause initial Hebrew ו is
a fruitful point of departure for study of the translation technique of
a book of the LXX. The different renderings and their uses tell us
about the fundamental elements of the translation technique of a
given book.

---

[145] Perhaps the text of the Vorlage was מיכה והאנשים אשר בבתים אשר עם
בית מיכה קראו אל בני דן. I find it odd that Rahlfs includes the words
ἔκραζον κατόπισω υἱῶν Δάν in verse 22. Also, I wonder why Bodine 1980,
133 seems to follow Rahlfs and even stresses that the given words do not
render the beginning of verse 23 (see his note 75).

This is due to the difference between Hebrew and Greek. The importance lies in the fact that the translator could often vary the rendering employed for the Hebrew conjunction ‏ו‏ if he found it suitable. If, nevertheless, he retained the use of the most common and obvious rendering καί, the result was stylistically special language. Genuine contemporary Greek was, as is well known, colourful when it comes to clause construction. The use of embedding and subordination was frequent, indicating a distance from paratactic Hebrew.

For the analysis discussed with the previous examples the main clauses commencing with ‏ו‏ in the MT were studied. Those main clauses that open with a formula have been excluded from the discussion and will be discussed in a chapter of their own.[146] Also, those main clauses where the LXX differs considerably from the MT have been excluded.[147] The discussion involves 2292 main clauses and the Greek renderings for ‏ו‏ contained in them.

TABLE 4 The renderings of the main clause initial Hebrew ‏ו‏ in the LXX of Joshua and Judges

	Josh	Judg	Josh %	Judg %
καί	716	1451	88.7	97.6
δέ	39	14	4.8	0.9
Part.coni	29	6	3.6	0.4
Other	23	15	2.9	1.0
TOTAL	807	1486	100.0	99.9

The table sets out the number of cases for renderings and the ratio between them. Rare renderings have been included under the title "Other". Such are οὐδέ, μηδέ, εἴτε, οὔτε, οὖν, ἀλλά, ἵνα, ὅτι, γάρ, διὰ τοῦτο, the relative pronoun, the *gen.abs.*, infinitive constructions, and omissions.

The renderings of the main clause initial ‏ו‏ may be summarized by saying that in the LXX of Joshua and Judges one equivalent domi-

---

[146] See chapter 2.3. Formulas in Hebrew on pp. 82-109.
[147] See the introduction on pp. 17-18.

nates the field. In Joshua καί was employed in 88.7% of all cases and in Judges in 97.6%.

This means that the translations are *literal*. The translators used a standard equivalent for the Hebrew conjunction. The literalness of the translations is of a special character, however. Often literalness means the same as word-for-word segmentation and inadequate rendering of the meaning at the same time.[148] The discussion showed that the translators of Joshua and Judges gave a correct idea of the parent text, their *Vorlage*, despite the literalness. They produced renderings of each element in the Vorlage *and* an adequate picture of the whole. Thus, the literalness may be characterized as division into elements (words), high consistency, and accuracy at the same time.[149] By accuracy I mean *a literalness which consists in an accurate rendering of the semantic value of the words of the original*.[150]

One might think that there would be a conflict between the segmentation and accuracy, but here, in renderings of the main clause initial Hebrew ו, conflict does not occur. On the contrary, the accuracy and the segmentation into word-for-word renderings happen to fit together very well. This is due to the similarity in function between καί and ו. Both of them express the simple co-ordination.

The heavy use of καί was not, however, a procedure devoid of problems. Since καί introduces most of the main clauses in the LXX of Joshua and Judges, the style of the LXX differs from genuine Greek. In genuine Greek καί is not used as frequently as in the LXX of Joshua and Judges. καί is simply too common in the LXX, creating a foreign flavour. One must, however, stress that the use of καί in the immediate context of the passages is correct and the problem is a stylistic one.[151]

---

[148] See Barr 1979, 5.

[149] Cf. Barr 1979, 20, who listed different modes of literalism in rendering of the Hebrew text.

[150] Barr 1979, 40. He saw a difference between the logic of segmentation and accuracy, but in my case the difference is not significant. See also Barr, *ibid.* 43.

[151] The detailed analysis of καί appears on pp. 24-35; see esp. pp. 32-35.

The second most frequently used rendering δέ seldom appears in comparison with καί. The ratio of δέ in Joshua is 4.8% and in Judges 0.9%. The rarity of δέ is clearly due to the extensive use of καί. In genuine Greek δέ was far more common than in the LXX. The reason for the rarity of δέ lies basically in the use of καί. The use of δέ required an interpretation that highlighted the dissimilarity between the co-ordinated Hebrew clauses. Should the translators have employed δέ more frequently, the stylistic impression would not have been as foreign as it is.[152]

The difference between Joshua and Judges is not limited to the frequency in use of δέ. The context in which the conjunction is used is also important.[153] The translator of Joshua used δέ more idiomatically than did the translator of Judges, since in the LXX of Joshua δέ is employed in cases where a verb opens the clause in Hebrew. In the LXX of Judges this is not the case.

The rare use of δέ in biblical Greek has received much attention. One of the most interesting theories partly linked with it was developed by *Martin*. He wanted to determine whether a text is versional Greek or genuine language. The method includes seventeen syntactical criteria. Only the ninth criterion is of interest here. According to it the number of times the copulative καί is used to co-ordinate *independent clauses* compared with the postpositive δέ indicates the versional nature of a text if καί is used at least twice as often as δέ.[154] The present analysis supports this claim, but on the other hand the versional status of the LXX of Joshua and Judges is indisputable.

Jobes raised some objections to Martin's use of καί and δέ.[155] She claimed that Martin's premise concerning the word order is not necessarily correct and that the frequent occurrence of καί does not

---

[152] The detailed analysis of δέ appears on pp. 35-43.

[153] Aejmelaeus 1982, 38 and 42-43. For the use of δέ in Joshua and Judges see pp. 40-43.

[154] Martin 1964, 41 and Martin 1974, 16-20. Martin's point of departure is Turner's observation that καί and δέ "as connecting particles between clauses" could be meaningful in discovering the sources used by Luke; see Turner 1955, 107-108. For a discussion about Martin's use of καί – δέ see Aejmelaeus 1982, 46-47.

[155] Jobes 1996, 35-37.

necessarily indicate a Semitic source.[156] These objections seriously question the basis of Martin's methodology.

Oddly enough, these objections did not prevent Jobes from employing Martin's methodology and the καί – δέ relation. Jobes counted *waw-consecutives* (i.e. *wayyiqtol* + *weqatal*) in Esther,[157] but she did not make a distinction between ordinary main clauses and apodoses[158] or count main clauses introduced with another ٦ than *waw-consecutive*. This, I believe, weakens her conclusions. Jobes' way of calculating the minimum occurrences needed for the application of Martin's criteria is also problematic.[159] She took it for granted that there would be a significant average value for the ratio between καί and δέ in versional language and in genuine language and that these are different.[160] So far, the only firm conclusion that can be drawn concerning the use of καί and δέ is that the variation between different authors is fairly wide and that anything that could

---

[156] To support the last objection, Jobes made a reference to Deissmann's study *Licht vom Osten* (Deissmann 1923, 107-108) where four papyri and an inscription were used to illustrate the problem of parataxis in the New Testament. Of these four papyri only P.Paris 51 (= UPZ 1.78) is relevant, since the other documents are much younger, dating to the second and fourth centuries CE. καί is employed seventeen times in P.Paris 51 to introduce a main clause but δέ only twice. Thus, it seems that καί could be used frequently in a genuine Greek text. When evaluating the language of the papyrus the heavy use of *asyndeton* must be taken into account as well. 27 clauses are asyndetic. The style of the papyrus may be illustrated by the following quotation: πάτερ, οὐχ ὁρᾷς τὸ ὅραμα τοῦτο ὃ τεθέαμαι; δι[ηγησά]μην αὐτῷ. ἔδωκέ μοι δύο καλάμους. ἐπιβλέψ[ας τα]χὺ εἶδον τὸν Κνῆφιν. εὐφραίνεσθε οἱ παρ' ἐμοῦ πάν[τες· ἄφ]εσίς μοι γίνεται ταχύ. Thus, I would claim that the use of καί does not influence the style as heavily as *asyndeton*. This makes the papyrus different from the books of the LXX. However, Deissmann's papyri are not really needed here. Had Jobes studied Martin's own statistics for papyri carefully, she would have noted that Martin's statistics do not fully meet his claims, that the genuine language employs καί as often as δέ or that καί is less frequent than δέ; see Martin 1964, 59.

[157] Jobes 1996, 36; her material includes 260 instances of the *waw-consecutive*.

[158] In apodosis the translator did not choose between καί and δέ, but between καί and the total omission of the co-ordinator; see pp. 113-116.

[159] For the way of calculating these see Jobes 1996, 31-33.

[160] According to her, the average for translation language is 95.98 and for genuine language it is 0.298; Jobes 1996, 33.

be described as average value hardly exists. That there is a difference between versional language and genuine Greek is of course clear, but Jobes' idea of the use of Greek is in error.

The *part.coni.* is the third frequently used equivalent. The *part.coni.* introduces very idiomatic Greek style. It appears rather seldom and the translators occasionally had problems when using the *part.coni.* It seems that the problems with the *part.coni.* are linked with the ability to work with wide contexts. The use of the *part.coni.* requires a knowledge of the relationship between the Hebrew clauses planned to be linked together with the *part.coni.* Because the translator of Joshua did not always succeed in producing an idiomatic construction, I conclude that he did not well enough bear the context in mind. The translator of Judges did not stumble when using the *part.coni.*, but one only has to look at his handling of the *gen.abs.* to see that he too encountered problems with memorizing the context.[161]

The best explanation concerning the renderings of the ordinary main clause co-ordinate conjunction in the LXX of Joshua and Judges is grammatical. The function of καί especially comes very close to that of 1 in Hebrew. The **similarity in grammatical function** made it naturally easy and tempting to employ καί to render the main clause initial 1.[162] The similar function of καί and 1 supports the tendency to use the "easy technique," to keep on using the main equivalent.[163] καί, δέ, and *part.coni.* are also very common in genuine Greek and the commonness may also play a role here.

The problems with the context are best explained if we assume that the translators used rather **narrow segmentation**.[164] That is, they did not bear in mind large sections of the parent text.

[161] For the use of the *part.coni.* and *gen.abs.* in renderings of the main clause initial 1 see pp. 56-67.

[162] See pp. 33-34.

[163] For the term "easy technique" see Barr 1979, 26, 50 and Aejmelaeus 1993, 67-68.

[164] For Joshua this is explained by den Hertog 1996, 179-180 but he based his conclusion on the use of the apodotic καί. This will be discussed later in the present study, see pp. 109-129.

Once the suitability of the most common equivalents was established, the translators became accustomed to rendering the main clause initial ו with them, because ו is so common in Hebrew.

The rest of the equivalents for the main clause initial ו in Joshua and Judges are used very rarely by the translators.[165] This is mainly due to the extensive use of the common equivalents, but some additional factors explain why these equivalents are indeed rare.

Often the function of a rare equivalent is different from that of the Hebrew conjunction ו. This is the case with ἀλλά and οὖν, for instance. The conjunctions ἵνα, ὅτι, γάρ and the combination διὰ τοῦτο differ remarkably from ו in respect of their syntactical function.

There are also restrictions in using conjunctions such as μηδέ, οὐδέ, οὔτε, or εἴτε. These conjunctions cannot always act as equivalents for ו, because the context where ו appears in Hebrew is not suitable.

The use of rare equivalents has much to tell regarding the translators' command of Greek. The fact that the normal equivalent for ו is καί does not indicate any problems in the translators' ability to use Greek. The collection of rare equivalents points in the opposite direction. The translators had no major problem with Greek. The use of rare renderings also indicates the wide limits in the translation technique of the translators of Joshua and Judges.

Remarkably, the narrow segmentation did not prevent the translators considering the context. They could find free and suitable ways to render the Hebrew context into Greek. That rare equivalents are indeed rare, on the other hand, shows the power of the segmentation. Free renderings are inventive, but how seldom did the translators detect the possibility of using them! There is a difference between the translator of Joshua and the translator of Judges in their selection of the free renderings used. This kind of variation in the selection of the equivalent is only natural, however, in case of different individuals.

---

[165] The analysis of the use of the free renderings is presented on pp. 45-56 and 67-68.

It is interesting that the translators of Joshua and Judges generally hesitated in changing the co-ordination into subordination.[166] Most of the rare equivalents are co-ordinative conjunctions such as οὐδέ, μηδέ, or ἀλλά. Subordination is used in two ways in rendering the main clause initial ו. In some exceptional cases the co-ordinate clause is rendered with a subordinate clause. In Joshua only two examples occur and in Judges four examples. The more frequently used subordination is the use of embedding, namely the *part.coni.*, the *gen.abs.* and the infinitive construction.

The major **difference** between the LXX of Joshua and Judges concerns the use of καί. For the translator of Judges καί is the equivalent of ו and the rest of the equivalents are only exceptions because he employed καί more frequently than in every nine cases out of ten. One might perhaps think that heavy use would show an attempt to limit the equivalents used, but this need not be the case here. It should be borne in mind that the translator of Judges did not always employ καί, and he could use even a subordinate conjunction to render ו if he chose to do so, and this he did. But then the argument based on the limiting of the equivalents fails if one does not wish to say that the translator failed in his pursuit of limited equivalents. Therefore, the heavy use of καί must be due to its obvious suitability and the very narrow segmentation used by the translator.

When the translations of Joshua and Judges were compared with the translations of the Pentateuch during the analysis, several remarks were made.

Regarding the use of καί, Joshua is close to the translations of Leviticus and Numbers on a statistical level. Judges, on the other hand, was really different from any of the books of the Pentateuch.[167]

When δέ was under discussion, it was found that Joshua resembles the freely translated part of the Pentateuch, but statistically it stands between the freely translated part and the rest of the Pentateuch. The statistics do not alone count here. The ease in using

---

[166] Den Hertog 1996, 179 explained the same concerning the LXX of Joshua, but I doubt if his material really justifies his conclusions. He did not study the renderings of the co-ordinate clauses, but the way the translator used *part.coni* and *gen.abs.* as well as some subordinate clauses.

[167] See p. 35.

δέ in all kinds of contexts characterises the translation technique as much as do the statistics, as has been argued by Aejmelaeus.[168] Judges is close to Leviticus, Numbers and Deuteronomy, yet on the statistical level it stands alone.[169]

If the use of the *part.coni.* is the basis for comparison, Joshua resembles the translations of the Pentateuch. Statistically the closest counterpart to Joshua is Numbers. Judges, again, is clearly separated from the translations of the Pentateuch.[170]

Thus, the position of Joshua and Judges as related to the translations of the Pentateuch depends on the criteria used in the comparison. Nevertheless, Judges is seemingly different as a translation from any of the books of the Pentateuch and from Joshua. Joshua, on the other hand, seems to stand between the different parts of the Pentateuch. It is not as free as Genesis or Exodus, but it is freer than the rest of the books of the Pentateuch.

2.3 Formulas in Hebrew

Hebrew employs special types of idioms to open a main clause. Translation-technically these deserve special treatment since it is not always easy to find Greek idioms to express the same as Hebrew expresses by these idioms. They are the Hebrew formulas והיה,ויהי, והנה and ועתה. In this chapter the formulas are discussed one by one. For modern linguistics the formulas are 'macro-syntactic signs' of narrative.[171] This means that the formula is used to indicate the structuring of the narrative on a wider scale than in the case of clauses.[172] In her study of co-ordination in the Pentateuch Aejme-

---

[168] Aejmelaeus 1982, 38 and 42-43.

[169] See pp. 42-43.

[170] See pp. 62-63.

[171] Niccacci 1986, 32 (= § 28) says concerning the formula ויהי: *"wayᵉhî* è il 'segno macro-sintattico' per eccellenza della narrazione."

[172] For a definition of macro-syntactic signs and their use in Biblical Hebrew see Schneider 1974 § 54.

laeus includes formulas in a larger group of "ordinary" co-ordinate clauses. I feel that the special character of the formulas will be seen more clearly if they are discussed separately. Theoretically, the rendering of the Hebrew conjunction ו in connection with the formula should be bound up with the rendering of the formula as a whole.

The present chapter includes a discussion of renderings of formulas only. Other features, such as the apodotic ו, will be treated later in this study.[173]

2.3.1 *The formula* ויהי

The formula ויהי is normally said to express the beginning of a new narrative or a new paragraph or any turning-point in the narrative.[174] The formula itself is followed by a temporal or circumstantial expression. Greek does not employ any similar structure or sign to indicate a turning-point in the narrative and therefore one might expect the translators to handle ויהי in a special way. The following discussion is arranged according to the Greek equivalents of the formula.

2.3.1.1 καὶ ἐγένετο

It is generally known that ויהי is very often translated in the LXX by the expression καὶ ἐγένετο.[175] Sometimes the verbal form employed in Greek is the passive ἐγενήθη.[176] My material includes 43 cases of καὶ ἐγένετο or καὶ ἐγενήθη. Thirteen of them appear in the LXX of Joshua and the rest are found in the LXX of Judges.

---

[173] For the apodotic ו see pp. 109-129. I have previously discussed the details of the renderings of the formulas ויהי and והיה in their context in Sipilä 1995.

[174] The classical treatment of the formula ויהי (as well as of the formula והיה) is König 1899, 260-278. For a summary of later discussion see Sipilä 1995, 274-275.

[175] For the use of καὶ ἐγένετο in the LXX and in the New Testament see Johannessohn 1925.

[176] Cf. Johannessohn 1925, 163 and Aejmelaeus 1982, 24-25.

Josh 1:1

וַיְהִי אַחֲרֵי מוֹת מֹשֶׁה עֶבֶד יהוה – καὶ ἐγένετο μετὰ τὴν τελευτὴν Μωυσῆ

Josh 10:27

וַיְהִי לְעֵת בּוֹא הַשֶּׁמֶשׁ – καὶ ἐγενήθη πρὸς ἡλίου δυσμάς

Judg 1:14

וַיְהִי בְּבוֹאָהּ – καὶ ἐγένετο ἐν τῷ εἰσπορεύεσθαι αὐτήν

Judg 3:18

וַיְהִי כַּאֲשֶׁר כִּלָּה לְהַקְרִיב אֶת הַמִּנְחָה – καὶ ἐγένετο[177] ὡς συνετέλεσεν Ἀὼδ προσφέρων τὰ δῶρα

Judg 6:25

וַיְהִי בַּלַּיְלָה הַהוּא – καὶ ἐγενήθη[178] τῇ νυκτὶ ἐκείνῃ

The formula is not preserved in the MT in the following instance, but the translation seems to reflect a Hebrew text that includes the formula.

Judg 3:21

וַיִּשְׁלַח אֵהוּד אֶת יַד שְׂמֹאלוֹ – καὶ ἐγένετο ἅμα τοῦ ἀναστῆναι
ἐξέτειλεν Ἀὼδ τὴν χεῖρα τὴν ἀριστερὰν αὐτοῦ
The Hebrew *Vorlage* of the LXX of Judges was probably longer than the present MT here.[179] There seems to be no reason to suppose that the translator would have inserted the plus in the OG.[180] καὶ

---

[177] MS d omits the verb ἐγένετο. The omission of the formula verb is typical of the manuscript. It appears seven times, i.e. in Judg 3:18, 3:27, 6:27, 11:39, 13:20 and 15:17.

[178] MSS glnw omit καὶ ἐγενήθη.

[179] BHK suggests that the Hebrew text was וַיְהִי כְּקוּמוֹ. The infinitive קוּם never appears with the preposition כ, however, and only twice in the MT with the preposition ב (Is 2:19, 21). None of the cases is linked with the formula וַיְהִי.

[180] *Contra* Schreiner 1957, 68. He suggests that the plus was derived from the context. The fact that a plus suits the context well, cannot be used as an argument for its secondary nature, since the original text also suits the context.

ἐγένετο here reflects the Hebrew formula ויהי, as it does in every other instance in Judges.

In most of the cases the Hebrew formula is rendered by the conjunction καί and a complemented verbal form ἐγένετο/ ἐγενήθη. This is in line with our general knowledge concerning the LXX but not concerning the LXX of the Pentateuch.[181] In the LXX of Genesis and Exodus the most frequently employed equivalent of ויהי is ἐγένετο δέ / ἐγενήθη δέ.

It is possible to count from the editions, how often the middle voice is used in contrast with the passive voice. This is, however, misleading, since it is difficult to judge from the manuscripts whether the original translation used the middle voice or the passive voice.[182] One can only say that the middle voice was used more frequently than the passive, but exactly how frequently it was used in the OG is beyond our knowledge.[183]

In comparison with genuine contemporary Greek, one might note that in standard prose the verb γίγνομαι is never used to indicate the beginning of a new paragraph. Instead expressions such as καὶ ἐγένετο (οὕτως) are employed from time to time to mark the opposite, the cessation of an action or the end of a narrative sequence.[184] This being the case, καὶ ἐγένετο only confuses the reader. It does not function in the same manner as the Hebrew

---

[181] See the statistics in Aejmelaeus 1982, 25 and 40.

[182] Sipilä 1995, 277, where the cases in Joshua are listed. In the LXX of Judges the instances are 6:37, 8:33, 9:42, 11:35 and 19:5.

[183] It is possible that the frequent use of the middle voice is due to Greek style. In the Ptolemaic period the passive was used instead of the middle voice. In the classical period the stylistic ideal was the very opposite; see Sipilä 1995, 277 with footnote 24 (ibid., 287-288). The footnote includes an unfortunate misprint. The Greek word παραγίνομαι is printed as paragivnomai.

[184] Johannessohn 1925, 164 and Aejmelaeus 1982, 133-134 discuss the possibility that the verb γίγνομαι carries the narrative forward. This is, however, a very rare occurrence. Besides, in cases where γίγνομαι carries the narrative forward a different construction from καὶ ἐγένετο is used, as Aejmelaeus points out.

formula. Thus it is a slavish rendering of ויהי.[185] The translator
should have avoided employing it when rendering the formula.

It is interesting to note that in the translation of Judges the formula
is *always* rendered by the conjunction καί and the formula verb. The
only choice the translator of Judges had to make was between καί
ἐγένετο and καί ἐγενήθη. In the translation of Joshua, on the other
hand, there are other ways of rendering the formula.

2.3.1.2 καί

The second option for the translator of Joshua when rendering the
Hebrew formula was to omit the verb and use the conjunction καί
only.

Josh 3:14

ויהי בנסע העם מאהליהם לעבר את הירדן – καί ἀπῆρεν ὁ λαὸς
ἐκ τῶν σκηνωμάτων αὐτῶν διαβῆναι τὸν Ἰορδάνην
Here the translator not only omitted the formula verb but also
modified the structure of the passage transforming a ב with infini-
tive-construction into a normal main clause.[186]

Josh 4:1

ויהי כאשר תמו כל הגוי לעבור את הירדן – καί ἐπεὶ συνετέλεσεν πᾶς ὁ λαὸς διαβαίνων τὸν Ἰορδάνην

Josh 6:15

ויהי ביום השביעי – καί τῇ ἡμέρᾳ τῇ ἑβδόμῃ

Josh 8:24

ויהי ככלות ישראל להרג את כל ישבי העי – καί ὡς ἐπαύσαντο
οἱ υἱοὶ Ἰσραὴλ ἀποκτέννοντες πάντας τοὺς ἐν τῇ Γαί

Josh 10:24

ויהי כהוציאם את המלכים האלה אל יהושע – καί ἐπεὶ ἐξήγαγον
αὐτοὺς πρὸς Ἰησοῦν

---

[185] For the definition of "slavish rendering" see the introduction p. 20.
[186] On cases like this see Soisalon-Soininen 1965, 88.

Josh 17:13

וַיְהִי כִּי חָזְקוּ בְּנֵי יִשְׂרָאֵל – [καὶ ἐγενήθη] καὶ ἐπεὶ κατίσχυσαν οἱ υἱοὶ Ἰσραήλ

The Greek text here is very curious.[187] How should one interpret the second καί doubly underlined above? Does it begin a new clause or is it merely an adverb? The opening phrase καὶ ἐγενήθη is not easy to interpret either. Is it possible that here we have a rare case in the LXX where the verb γίγνομαι refers backwards? If the Hebrew *Vorlage* behind the translation was close to the MT, and there is hardly any reason to doubt this, the best explanation for the Greek text is the presence of *a doublet*: both καὶ ἐγενήθη and καί are renderings of the Hebrew formula. The formal expression καὶ ἐγενήθη was probably later added to the passage (cf. Josh 10:24).[188]

In these six cases the complementary verb was omitted. From the point of view of Greek the omission of the verb clearly increases the readability of the translation, since the disturbing element is not present. According to Aejmelaeus' study, there is only one similar case in the Pentateuch (Ex 32:19). In this respect the translation of Joshua reflects some individual and good solutions.[189]

---

[187] See den Hertog 1996, 52.

[188] The manuscript tradition in this instance is complex. There are three major readings:

a) MSS B*(h)r*x (= Rahlfs) read καὶ ἐγενήθη καὶ ἐπεὶ κατίσχυσαν

b) MSS θadeijlpsuvyza₂b₂ A 𝕴 𝕾 (= Margolis) read καὶ ἐγενήθη ἐπεὶ κατίσχυσαν

c) MSS AGNbcfgot read καὶ ἐγενήθη ἐπικατίσχυσαν

I suggest that καὶ ἐγενήθη was later inserted into the passage. The OG is καὶ ἐπεὶ κατίσχυσαν (cf. Josh 4:1 and 10:24). When the formal equivalent of the Hebrew formula, καὶ ἐγενήθη, was added, reading a) was the result. Later the conjunction καί was omitted, resulting in reading b). Further, reading c) is a consequence of misspelling ἐπεί as ἐπι. This is against Margolis 1931, 338 who argues that καί following the formula is a later addition. Due to the misspelt ἐπί for ἐπεί the text was changed from καὶ ἐγενήθη ἐπεὶ κατίσχυσαν (= "OG") to καὶ ἐγενήθη ἐπικατίσχυσαν, and this, he argued, resulted to adding the conjunction καί between ἐγενήθη and ἐπικατίσχυσαν.

[189] Consider the words of Johannessohn 1925, 164: "Da dem Griechischen das einführende εγενετο fremd ist, lassen die LXX-Übersetzer יהי (היה)

2.3.1.3 δέ

In the translation of Joshua the formula ויהי is rendered six times by the conjunction δέ. In these cases the translator did not use any equivalent for the verb היה, but δέ is the only rendering of the formula. Such cases do not exist in Judges, and they are rare in the Pentateuch.[190]

Josh 6:20

ויהי כשמע העם את קול השופר – ὡς δὲ ἤκουσεν ὁ λαὸς τὴν φωνὴν[191] τῶν σαλπίγγων

Josh 9:1

ויהי כשמע כל המלכים – ὡς δ' ἤκουσαν οἱ βασιλεῖς

Josh 10:1

ויהי כשמע אדני צדק – ὡς δὲ ἤκουσεν Ἀδωνίβεζέκ

Josh 10:11

ויהי בנסם מפני ישראל – ἐν τῷ δὲ φεύγειν αὐτοὺς ἀπὸ προσώπου τῶν υἱῶν Ἰσραήλ

Josh 11:1

ויהי כשמע יבין מלך חצור – ὡς δὲ ἤκουσεν Ἰαβεὶν βασιλεὺς Ἀσώρ

Four cases out of the aforementioned five are similar. In these cases the MT employs the introductory formula ויהי כשמע. Only once is this not the case. In that particular case (Josh 10:11) one has

gelegentlich fort. Besonders weit gehen hierin die Übersetzer von Ge, Ex und *Jos* "[italics mine].

[190] Aejmelaeus 1982, 40. Cases where the conjunction δέ is used alone to translate the Hebrew formula ויהי may be found in the following statistics from the Pentateuch: Gen 5 cases, Ex 5, Num 2 and Dtn 1 case. Two examples are listed by Aejmelaeus 1982, 41 (Ex 2:23 and 13:15).

[191] MSS Bq 18 68 122 128 omit τὴν φωνήν. For the evaluation of the omission see den Hertog 1996, 61-62.

difficulties in understanding the formula as introducing a new
paragraph. The Hebrew construction here is close to the text in the
other cases, because the formula is followed by an infinitive
construction.

As Aejmelaeus points out, it is understandable that the translator
chose to use the conjunction δέ in these cases. The formula very
often indicates the transition to a new paragraph, and in Greek δέ is
very suitable in such instances.[192] The fact also explains why in
Joshua δέ is more frequently used as a rendering of the formula than
as a rendering of וּ at the beginning of an ordinary main clause.

It is interesting that the translator of Joshua never added the
complementary verb when using the conjunction δέ as a rendering
of the formula. This is exceptional since even the translators of
Genesis and Exodus frequently used the verb and the conjunction in
Greek.[193] Since the use of δέ and the omission of the verb belong
together in Joshua, one may conclude that the translator considered
the whole formula as a unit when using δέ.

Besides the five cases above there is one instance where δέ is
used, but in this case one cannot be sure how close the Hebrew
Vorlage of the LXX was to the MT. If the *Vorlage* was close to the
MT, the question concerns a free translation. In this case, as well as
the other cases where δέ is used in connection with the formula וַיְהִי,
no equivalent of the verb היה is present.

Josh 5:8

וַיְהִי כַּאֲשֶׁר תַּמּוּ כָל הַגּוֹי לְהִמּוֹל וַיֵּשְׁבוּ תַחְתָּם בַּמַּחֲנֶה עַד חֲיוֹתָם
– περιτμηθέντες δὲ ἡσυχίαν εἶχον, αὐτόθι καθήμενοι ἐν τῇ
παρεμβολῇ ἕως ὑγιάσθησαν

---

[192] Aejmelaeus 1982, 40.
[193] See Aejmelaeus 1982, 40-41. Aejmelaeus concludes that ἐγένετο δέ was the
stereotypical rendering of the formula in Genesis, because it is used almost
constantly.

2.3.1.4 Conclusions

The formula ויהי is employed 27 times in Joshua and 30 times in Judges.[194] The translators of Joshua and Judges frequently used the Greek expression καὶ ἐγένετο to render the formula. This is the normal way of rendering the formula in the LXX.

TABLE 5 The renderings of the Hebrew formula ויהי in the LXX of Joshua and Judges

	Josh	Judg
καὶ ἐγένετο	12	24
καὶ ἐγενήθη	1	6
καί	6	0
δέ	6	0
Minus	1	0

The term *minus* refers to the fact that the Vorlage of the LXX was shorter than the MT. The particular case in question is Josh 8:6.

Only a limited number of alternative equivalents were used by the translators and the complementary verb was often omitted. The cases where καὶ ἐγένετο is employed differ from the cases where the verb is omitted. The omission of the formula verb produces better Greek style than its use. The difference is not only stylistic but translation-technical as well.[195] When the formula verb was omitted, the translator clearly understood the requirements of Greek better than in cases where the verb was used. Aejmelaeus observes that the omission of the verb is often linked with cases where a subordinate

---

[194] I have dealt with the formula ויהי and its treatment in the LXX of Joshua in a IOSCS congress paper (Sipilä 1995). There is an unfortunate error in the paper. I claimed that the formula is employed in Josh 2:5 (ויהי השער לסגור בחשך), but this is not the case.

[195] Aejmelaeus 1982, 41.

clause, and especially a temporal clause, follows the formula. In Joshua the cases where the omission appears each include a temporal expression. The expression in question is mostly an infinitive construction in Hebrew.

Following the example of Sollamo, it is possible to divide the renderings into slavish and literal ones.[196] Cases where the verb is used in Greek are slavish. Cases where the Greek conjunction καί or δέ is used are literal.

When opening the discussion about the formula ויהי, it was expected that the translators would handle the formula in a special way. From the foregoing discussion it is clear that this expectation is not fulfilled. The slavish rendering καί with a formula verb is the main alternative available to the translators. Only the translator of Joshua used the literal renderings καί and δέ. Especially the latter rendering tends to appear in a certain context. Thus, the use of δέ was not as natural as one might perhaps think.

There is a clear difference between the translations of Joshua and Judges. The translator of Joshua used the formula verb in half of the cases. In the other cases he omitted the verb. This fact brings the translation of Joshua close to the translations of Genesis and Exodus. The individual character of the translator is nevertheless seen in the use of καί, which is unique when compared with the Pentateuch.[197] The translation of Judges perhaps resembles the translation of Leviticus.[198]

2.3.2 The formula והיה

As in the case of the Hebrew formula ויהי, the formula והיה is normally said to express a beginning of a new narrative or

---

[196] Sollamo divides the renderings of the Hebrew semiprepositions into slavish, literal and free renderings; see e.g. Sollamo 1979, 30. For the definition of these fairly ambiguous terms see the introduction p. 20.

[197] Aejmelaeus 1982, 25 recognises one passage in Exodus (Ex 32:19) where the formula ויהי is rendered by the conjunction καί only.

[198] According to Aejmelaeus 1982, 25 in the LXX of Leviticus ויהי is rendered by καί ἐγενήθη only, but this is merely a single case in the entire book.

paragraph.[199] As well as ויהי, והיה too can be classified as a macro-syntactic sign. והיה is less common than its counterpart. It may occur in present or future contexts, and the complemented element may be either temporal or conditional. After the discussion of the renderings of the formula ויהי one might expect the translators of Joshua and Judges to have used slavish renderings for the formula והיה. In the following discussion the cases are arranged according to the Greek renderings of the formula, as were the renderings of the formula ויהי in the previous discussion.

2.3.2.1 καὶ ἔσται

The normal rendering of והיה in the LXX is καὶ ἔσται.[200] The use of the formula verb here produces the same problems as the use of the formula verb in the expression καὶ ἐγένετο.

Josh 2:19

והיה כל אשר יצא מדלתי ביתך החוצה דמו בראשו – καὶ ἔσται πᾶς ὃς ἂν ἐξέλθῃ τὴν θύραν τῆς οἰκίας σου ἔξω, ἔνοχος ἑαυτῷ ἔσται

The translation contains two verbs (ἔσται) in the same clause!

Josh 3:13

והיה כנוח כפות רגלי הכהנים נשאי ארון יהוה אדון כל הארץ במי הירדן – καὶ ἔσται ὡς ἂν καταπαύσωσιν οἱ πόδες τῶν

---

[199] The use of והיה as a formula is discussed e.g. by König 1899, 274-278. Niccacci 1990, 182 (= § 156) rejects the assertion that והיה has an initial function. According to him, והיה never begins an independent unit of the narrative or the discourse. On the contrary, according to Nicacci, והיה is used "in placing the circumstance, or rather the paragraph which follows it within the main thrust of the message and of connecting this with the preceding context." From the point of view of the present analysis it is a matter of indifference as to how the function of והיה is actually explained. Greek does not employ any similar construction.

[200] For the use of καὶ ἔσται in the LXX see Johannessohn 1943, and Aejmelaeus 1982, 25-26.

ἱερέων τῶν αἱρόντων τὴν κιβωτὸν τῆς διαθήκης Κυρίου πάσης
τῆς γῆς ἐν τῷ ὕδατι τοῦ Ἰορδάνου

Josh 8:5

והיה כי יצאו לקראתנו – καὶ ἔσται ὡς ἂν ἐξέλθωσιν οἱ κατοικοῦντες Γαὶ εἰς συνάντησιν ἡμῖν

Josh 22:18

והיה אתם תמרדו היום ביהוה – καὶ ἔσται ἐὰν ἀποστῆτε σήμερον
ἀπὸ Κυρίου

Now one asks whether the LXX *Vorlage* of Joshua was different
from the MT. Though there is a formula in the MT, and the LXX
reflects a similar formula, what follows in the LXX may be the
translation of a Hebrew text different from the MT, as BHS suggests.[201] Such a suggestion, however tempting it may be, is nevertheless unnecessary. More probable is the suggestion that the translator
himself was responsible for the "difference". The translation employs the conditional expression ἐὰν ἀποστῆτε κτλ.

Again, as with the formula ויהי, the notion can be entertained that
standard non-translation Greek does not employ the expression καὶ
ἔσται in the same manner as the translations do, namely to introduce
a new paragraph. This may cause problems of interpretation for the
reader of the Greek text. The renderings are seen as slavish, because
the expression καὶ ἔσται is only the result of mechanically
translating the elements ן and the verb היה in the Hebrew formula.

2.3.2.2 καὶ ἐγένετο

In some individual cases the translator of Judges uses the expression
καὶ ἐγένετο or καὶ ἐγενήθη to render the Hebrew formula והיה.

Judg 2:19

והיה במות השופט – καὶ ἐγένετο ὡς ἀπέθνησκεν ὁ κριτής

---

[201] BHS and BHK suppose that the Hebrew *Vorlage* was והיה אם תמרדו
suggesting an error where the letter ת was accidentally omitted. See also
Boling 1982, 506 who argues for the error in the MT.

There seems to be some adversativity in the context of the formula.[202]

Judg 6:3

וַיְהִי אִם זָרַע יִשְׂרָאֵל – <u>καὶ ἐγένετο</u> ὅταν ἔσπειρεν ἀνὴρ Ἰσραήλ

Judg 19:30

וַיְהִי כֹל הָרֹאֶה וְאָמַר – <u>καὶ ἐγένετο</u> πᾶς ὁ ὁρῶν ἔλεγεν
Here the Greek rendering of the formula is clearly erroneous and the reader has difficulties in understanding the Greek text.

Judg 12:5

וַיְהִי כִּי יֹאמְרוּ פְּלִיטֵי אֶפְרַיִם אֶעֱבֹרָה – <u>καὶ ἐγενήθη</u>[203] ὅτι εἶπαν οἱ διεσεσῳσμένοι τοῦ Ἐφραίμ Διαβῶμεν
This is the only case in my material where καὶ ἐγενήθη is used as a rendering of the formula וְהָיָה. One should not, however, exaggerate the significance of the use of the passive.[204]

As the cases show, the translator had a reason for using the aorist form of the verb γίγνομαι in these cases. The exceptional use of the aorist finds its explanation in the context of the formula. The formula וְהָיָה is here used in the narrative. Besides, the action in Hebrew is iterative in these instances[205] and that probably explains the use of the imperfect in the Greek. Instead of the present renderings more natural idiom would probably have been a temporal expression without any counterpart for the Hebrew formula. Thus the renderings must be seen as being slavish.

2.3.2.3 καί

The translator of Joshua occasionally did not use the formula verb when rendering the formula וְהָיָה, but instead used the Greek

---

[202] Compare NEB, NJB and many other modern translations.
[203] MSS glnow read καὶ ἐγένετο and MS d reads καὶ ἐγενήθητε. MSS Beijmqrsuza₂ omit the formula verb and the conjunction ὅτι.
[204] See the discussion about the use of the middle voice *versus* the passive voice on pp. 77-78.
[205] Compare Niccaci 1990, 183 § 158(i).

conjunction καί alone. The translator of Judges never omitted the verb.

Josh 2:14

וַהָיָה בתת יהוה לנו את הארץ ועשׂינו עמך חסד – καὶ αὐτὴ εἶπεν Ὡς ἂν παραδῷ[206] Κύριος ὑμῖν τὴν πόλιν, ποιήσετε εἰς ἐμὲ ἔλεος

In this case one assumes a difference between the MT and the LXX *Vorlage*.[207] Does the LXX conjunction reflect a formula in the *Vorlage* or not? While we do not know the answer, nothing suggests that there could not have been a formula in the *Vorlage* corresponding to the one in the MT.

Josh 7:15

וַהָיָה הנלכד בחרם ישׂרף באשׁ אתו ואת כל אשׁר לו – καὶ ὃς ἂν ἐνδειχθῇ, κατακαυθήσεται ἐν πυρὶ καὶ πάντα ὅσα ἐστὶν αὐτῷ

The use of καί is connected with a free rendering of the Hebrew participle construction as a relative clause.[208]

When discussing the omission of the verb in connection with the renderings of the formula ויהי it was noted that the omission of the verb produces stylistically better Greek. The same notion also applies here. When the formula verb was left without any visible counterpart, the language was more natural Greek.

2.3.2.4 Free rendering

Josh 22:28

ונאמר וַהָיָה כי יאמרו אלינו ואל דרתינו מחר – καὶ εἴπαμεν Ἐὰν γένηταί ποτε καὶ λαλήσωσιν πρὸς ἡμᾶς καὶ ταῖς γενεαῖς ἡμῶν αὔριον

---

[206] MSS Br read παραδοῖ (= Margolis), see den Hertog 1996, 41. For the orthography of the subjunctive of δίδωμι see Mandilaras 1973 § 535.

[207] See e.g. Holmes 1914, 21 and Boling 1982, 142.

[208] Cf. Sipilä 1995, 280.

The introduction of direct speech by the formula והיה is rare in Hebrew, but not impossible. The instance in question is the only case of this type in Joshua. The Greek uses the expression ἐὰν γένηταί ποτε κτλ. The translation is free, and one may only guess at the reasons for the solution adapted. Perhaps the translator interpreted the larger context in such a way that the beginning of the speech means "if that (what is said earlier) happens" etc. This is why he chose to use the conditional clause. The translator's solution is a good one and it produces stylistically correct Greek. The problem is that the translation hardly corresponds to the meaning of the MT.

2.3.2.5 Conclusions

The formula והיה is used 12 times in Joshua and 9 times in Judges. A glance through the renderings in the books of Joshua and Judges reveals that καὶ ἔσται is mostly used as a rendering of the said formula.

TABLE 6 The renderings of the Hebrew formula והיה in the LXX of Joshua and Judges

	Josh	Judg
καὶ ἔσται	7	5
καί	2	0
καὶ ἐγένετο	0	3
καὶ ἐγενήθη	0	1
Free rendering	1	0
Minus	1	0

Minus indicates a case where the LXX does not correspond to the MT. Here the case in question is Josh 8:8.

The translator of Joshua sometimes omitted the formula verb, but the translator of Judges never did so. The translator of Judges, on the other hand, used the verb γίγνομαι to render the formula verb. In Joshua this happens only once and then the question is one of a free rendering. The translator of Judges was found to use only slavish renderings of the formula ויהי, and the same applies to the formula והיה as well. The translator of Joshua, on the other hand, was capable of using literal renderings, and what is more important, even a free rendering (Josh 22:28) on occasion.

Compared with the Pentateuch, the translation of Joshua is close to the translation of Deuteronomy, but the translation of Judges is closer to the translation of Numbers.[209]

2.3.3 *Formula* והנה

The Hebrew formula והנה is used 6 times in Joshua but 21 times in Judges.[210] The use of והנה is more or less closely related to the verb 'to see' or at least to visual perception. It is said to introduce a surprise of some sort.[211] This is, I think, perhaps misleading, since a surprise is not always present. More likely, the formula can be described as marking a turning-point or climax in the text.[212]

2.3.3.1 καὶ ἰδού

In the LXX as a whole the formula והנה is often rendered as καὶ ἰδού.[213] This is the most common rendering of והנה in my material.

---

[209] See Aejmelaeus 1982, 25-26 for the statistics and examples from the Pentateuch. According to her, only the translations of Ex and Dtn omit the formula verb. The translation of Num uses only καὶ ἔσται and καὶ ἐγένετο to render the formula והיה. Thus, my earlier suggestion about the relationship between the LXX of Joshua and the LXX of Numbers (Sipilä 1995, 279) needs to be revised.

[210] הנה without the co-ordinate conjunction appears 9 times in Joshua and 21 times in Judges. In these cases the main equivalent is ἰδού (25 times).

[211] See e.g. Andersen 1974, 94-95..

[212] Schneider 1978, 267. See also Niccacci 1990, 100-101 (= § 70-71).

[213] See Johannessohn 1937, 1939 and 1942. Johannessohn studies the use of the formula והנה and its rendering καὶ ἰδού throughout the Bible. For καὶ ἰδού

In genuine Greek καὶ ἰδού does not mark a surprise or climax or turning-point and therefore it is not a good equivalent of the Hebrew formula.[214]

Josh 7:21

ואחמדם ואקחם והנם טמונים בארץ בתוך האהלי – καὶ ἐνθυμηθεὶς αὐτῶν ἔλαβον. καὶ ἰδοὺ αὐτὰ ἐγκέκρυπται ἐν τῇ γῇ ἐν τῇ σκηνῇ μου

Here the formula is connected by a suffix.

Judg 3:25

ויחילו עד בוש והנה איננו פתח דלתות העליה – καὶ προσέμειναν αἰσχυνόμενοι, καὶ ἰδοὺ οὐκ ἦν ὁ ἀνοίγων τὰς θύρας τοῦ ὑπερῴου

Judg 9:43

וירא והנה העם יצא מן העיר – καὶ εἶδεν καὶ ἰδοὺ λαὸς ἐξῆλθεν ἐκ τῆς πόλεως

Judg 14:8

ויסר לראות את מפלת האריה והנה עדת דבורים בגוית האריה – καὶ ἐξέκλινεν ἰδεῖν τὸ πτῶμα τοῦ λέοντος, καὶ ἰδοὺ συστροφὴ μελισσῶν ἐν τῷ στόματι τοῦ λέοντος

Here a true surprise is present!

Judg 18:9

ראינו את הארץ והנה טובה מאד – εὑρήκαμεν τὴν γῆν καὶ ἰδοὺ ἀγαθὴ σφόδρα

The Greek expression καὶ ἰδού appears 22 times in the LXX of Joshua and Judges as a rendering of והנה. For the translator of Judges καὶ ἰδού was the rendering of והנה. He used it constantly with no variation. The translator of Joshua, on the other hand, used καὶ ἰδού only once. The use of the verb ἰδού in the Greek rendering

_____

as a rendering of והנה in the Pentateuch see Aejmelaeus 1982, 26-28. It appears with especial frequency in Leviticus.

[214] Cf. Johannessohn 1937, 200 who sees the expression καὶ ἰδού as foreign to genuine Greek.

of the formula must be due to the presence of ‎הנה‎ in Hebrew. The rendering καὶ ἰδού does not function in the same way as the formula in Hebrew. Therefore the Greek equivalent is not the best possible choice. It may be characterised as a slavish rendering.

2.3.3.2 καί and δέ

Occasionally the translator of Joshua used only the conjunctions καί[215] or δέ[216] to render the formula ‎והנה‎, but the translator of Judges never did so.

Josh 7:22

‎וירצו האהלה והנה טמונה באהלו‎ – καὶ ἔδραμον εἰς τὴν σκηνήν ... καὶ ταῦτα ἦν ἐγκεκρυμμένα εἰς τὴν σκηνήν

The translator adds the pronoun ταῦτα to increase clarity. Also, he puts the copula into singular as the normal Greek idiom does. These renderings show his abilities as a translator.

Josh 9:13

‎ואלה נאדות היין ... והנה התבקעו‎ – καὶ οὗτοι οἱ ἀσκοὶ τοῦ οἴνου ... καὶ οὗτοι ἐρρώγασιν

When the translator of Joshua used καί alone for a rendering of ‎והנה‎, the Greek also includes a pronoun (ταῦτα / οὗτοι) that has no visible couterpart in Hebrew. One may perhaps think that the translator interpretted the Hebrew ‎הנה‎ as a feminine pronoun, but such an interpretation does not seem probable in the first case (Josh 7:22) where the context refers to masculine entities in Hebrew.

---

[215] For the use of καί as a rendering of ‎והנה‎ in the Pentateuch see Aejmelaeus 1982, 27.

[216] For the use of δέ as a rendering of ‎והנה‎ in Genesis see Aejmelaeus 1982, 42. In the other books of the Pentateuch δέ never renders the Hebrew formula.

Josh 23:14

וְהִנֵּה אָנֹכִי הוֹלֵךְ הַיּוֹם בְּדֶרֶךְ כָּל הָאָרֶץ – ἐγὼ δὲ ἀποτρέχω τὴν ὁδὸν καθὰ καὶ πάντες οἱ ἐπὶ τῆς γῆς

Here the formula is rendered as the conjunction δέ. The logical subject of the speech changes here. It is possible that this change triggered the use of δέ. Otherwise the case does not differ from those where καί alone was used.

The conjunction καί or δέ is a better alternative for the formula than the slavish καὶ ἰδού. Since ἰδού is omitted, it does not disturb the Greek reader. On the other hand, the conjunctions καί and δέ do not mark a climax or any turning point. Therefore, I will classify them as literary renderings. The omission of the visible counterpart for הנה is here probably based on the similar considerations as the omission of the verb with the formulas ויהי and והיה.

2.3.3.3 Omission

Twice the translator of Joshua left the formula והנה without any visible counterpart and used a very free Greek rendering with a construction including the supplementary participle.[217]

Josh 5:13

וַיִּשָּׂא עֵינָיו וַיַּרְא וְהִנֵּה אִישׁ עֹמֵד לְנֶגְדּוֹ – καὶ ἀναβλέψας τοῖς ὀφθαλμοῖς εἶδεν ___ ἄνθρωπον ἑστηκότα ἐναντίον αὐτοῦ

The translator left the Hebrew והנה without any visible equivalent. This happened because the verb ראה immediately precedes the formula. Due to the omission the translator turned the text following the formula into an object in his Greek clause. The result is highly

---

[217] For the use of the supplementary participle see Smyth 1956 § 2110-2112. Kühner-Gerth II:2 § 481.1-2 explains that the participle in such constructions is nothing but a normal attributive participle and that the noun in the accusative related to the participle is the object for a *verbum sentiendi* preceding it. Aejmelaeus 1982, 117 recognizes one instance in the Pentateuch where the supplementary participle is used in rendering of the formula והנה. The instance (Ex 2:6) parallels cases of the supplementary participle in my material.

idiomatic Greek, especially when the supplementary participle acts as the rendering of the Hebrew verb following the formula.

Josh 8:20

וייראו והנה עלה עשן העיר – καὶ ἐθεώρουν ___ καπνὸν ἀναβαί-νοντα ἐκ τῆς πόλεως

2.3.3.4 Conclusions

The Greek renderings of the formula והנה may be classified as slavish, literal or free renderings. καὶ ἰδού is clearly a slavish rendering. The conjunctions καί and δέ are seen as literal renderings and omission with the supplementary participle as a free rendering.

TABLE 7 The renderings of the Hebrew formula והנה in the LXX of Joshua and Judges

	Josh	Judg
καὶ ἰδού	1	21
καί	2	0
δέ	1	0
Free rendering	2	0

The difference between Joshua and Judges is clearly visible when the renderings of the formula והנה are studied. In Judges *every* case of the formula is rendered as καὶ ἰδού. That is, the translator of Judges used only the slavish rendering. In the LXX of Joshua, on the other hand, καὶ ἰδού occurs only once. The translator of Joshua mainly employed καί and δέ. One could therefore argue that the translator of Joshua took Greek idiom better into account, because the rendering καὶ ἰδού is a poor reflection of והנה.

In Joshua, if no subject is explicit in the clause that follows the formula, the translator added the pronoun οὗτος to that clause (see

examples). In the Pentateuch the pronoun ὅδε is occasionally added
as the subject of the clause.[218]

The difference between the translators of Joshua and Judges is
most clearly seen if one examines free renderings. The translator of
Joshua twice used the construction with the supplementary parti-
ciple. The use of the participle shows the abilities of the translator of
Joshua and the difference between the translations of Joshua and
Judges.

In the Pentateuch the use of καί at the beginning of the ordinary
main clause and the use of καί in renderings of the formula do not
significantly differ from one another.[219] In the LXX of Judges this is
the case, but not in the LXX of Joshua. The number of cases is very
limited, however.

2.3.4 *Formula* ועתה

In her study of the rendering of clause initial ו in the Pentateuch,
Aejmelaeus hesitates to classify ועתה as a formula.[220] In this study
the labelling of ועתה as a formula is done only for practical
purposes. After all, ועתה is similar to ויהי, והיה and והנה, because
of the problem how to express the Hebrew idiom in Greek. The
formula introduces an inferential clause and is used in direct
discourse only; it never occurs in narrative.[221] The formula is used 16
times in the MT of Joshua and 15 times in Judges.[222]

---

[218] See Aejmelaeus 1982, 26-27. Her example is are from Num 17:7, but there
is one case in Gen and two additional cases in Lev as well.

[219] Aejmelaeus 1982, 27.

[220] Aejmelaeus 1982, 57.

[221] See eg. Aejmelaeus 1982, 57 and Niccacci 1990, 101 (= § 73). Quite
interestingly Schneider 1978, 264 explains that ועתה is used to indicate that
the speech continues after a break.

[222] עתה without the conjunction ו appears in Joshua only twice. In Judges it is
used 9 times. The main Greek equivalent in these cases is νῦν (7 times).

2.3.4.1 καὶ νῦν

καὶ νῦν is a slavish rendering of the Hebrew formula ועתה. The translators of Joshua and Judges used it frequently to render the formula.

Josh 2:12

ועתה השבעו נא לי ביהוה – καὶ νῦν ὁμόσατέ μοι Κύριον τὸν θεόν

Josh 13:7

ועתה חלק את הארץ הזאת – καὶ νῦν μέρισον τὴν γῆν ταύτην
In this case ועתה does not express inference but consequence.

Judg 11:25

ועתה הטוב טוב אתה מבלק בן צפור מלך מואב – καὶ νῦν μὴ κρείσσων εἶ σὺ τοῦ Βαλὰκ υἱοῦ Σεπφὼρ βασιλέως Μωάβ;

Judg 13:4

ועתה השמרי נא ואל תשתי יין ושכר – καὶ νῦν φύλαξαι καὶ μὴ πίῃς οἶνον καὶ σίκερα

Judg 15:18

אתה נתת ביד עבדך את התשועה הגדלה הזאת ועתה אמות בצמא – σὺ ἔδωκας ἐν χειρὶ τοῦ δούλου σου τὴν σωτηρίαν τὴν μεγάλην ταύτην, καὶ νῦν ἀποθανοῦμαι ἐν δίψει
There is more or less evident adversative function present here.

My material includes an instance to be discussed here, which is interesting from the point of view of textual criticism.

Josh 3:8

ואתה תצוה את הכהנים נשאי ארון הברית לאמר – καὶ νῦν ἔντειλαι τοῖς ἱερεῦσιν τοῖς αἴρουσιν τὴν κιβωτὸν τῆς διαθήκης λέγων
Now the translator perhaps read ועתה and not ואתה as in the MT. We cannot know any longer if the letter ע or א was present in the *Vorlage*. The translation nevertheless supports the letter ע.

The translators of Joshua and Judges very often used the Greek expression καὶ νῦν as a rendering of ועתה. The number of cases is 26. At least in Judges it may be seen as the stereotypical equivalent for ועתה. καὶ νῦν is used in 14 instances out of 15. The translator of Joshua also used it very often (12 instances out of 16). The expression hardly reflects the functions of the Hebrew formula.[223] Consequently, it is not really a suitable equivalent for the formula. The use of καὶ νῦν must be due to the slavish rendering of the elements of the formula: the conjunction ו and the adverb עתה.

2.3.4.2 καί

Once the translator of Judges used only the Greek co-ordinator καί in place of the Hebrew formula.

Judg 7:3

ועתה קרא נא באזני העם לאמר – καὶ εἶπεν Κύριος πρὸς αὐτόν Λάλησον δὴ εἰς τὰ ὦτα τοῦ λαοῦ λέγων
This is the only instance in my material where the LXX has only the conjunction καί to represent the Hebrew ועתה. There is a substantial difference between the MT and the LXX. The LXX starts with a new introduction to the direct speech[224] but the MT has only the formula. This makes it difficult to evaluate the translation. It is, however, possible that the Hebrew *Vorlage* of the LXX did not include the formula at all, but read ויאמר יהוה אליו.[225]

2.3.4.3 νῦν δέ

Twice the translator of Joshua used νῦν δέ to render the Hebrew formula. This expression does not primarily mark the inference in Greek, as καὶ νῦν does not, either.

---

[223] According to LSJ, νῦν is mainly used as either a temporal or an emphatic particle in Greek.

[224] The LXX is supported here by MSS Aabglntw and 𝕾 (sub ※).

[225] Schreiner 1957, 51 explains the LXX reading as the result of the influence of the context, but this seems to me unlikely. On the contrary, the MT could arise from that direction.

Josh 9:12

ועתה הנה יבש והיה נקדים –vῦν δὲ ἐξηράνθησαν καὶ γεγόνασιν
βεβρωμένοι

The Hebrew particle הנה was left without any visible counterpart in
the translation. The last word in the MT, נקדים, is rare and its
meaning is unclear. The translator connected it with eating (cf.
9:5).[226]

Josh 22:4

ועתה הניח יהוה אלהיכם לאחיכם כאשר דבר להם – vῦν δὲ
κατέπαυσεν Κύριος ὁ θεὸς ἡμῶν[227] τοὺς ἀδελφοὺς ἡμῶν[228], ὃν
τρόπον εἶπεν αὐτοῖς

In my material the use of vῦν δέ as a rendering of the formula ועתה
is limited to the book of Joshua. The translator of Genesis used it
once (Gen 20:7), but the expression vῦνὶ δέ is more often found in
the Pentateuch.[229] If the expression καὶ vῦν does not express
inference, the same applies to vῦν δέ as well. It must be seen as a
literal rendering of ועתה.

2.3.4.4 vῦν οὖν

There are several ways of marking inference in Greek. The equivalents discussed so far do not mark it, but the conjunction οὖν does.

---

[226] By basing its conclusion on this particular instance LSJ claims that the verb
βεβρώσκω had a special use. βεβρωμένοι ἄρτοι should mean *mouldy bread*
(similarly Lust-Hauspie 1992, 81). That the root נקד is connected with
mould is probably based on the fact that in later Hebrew נקד means *to sting,
to point*; see Jastrow, 931. The later meaning is valid in Modern Hebrew as
well.

[227] MSS aflstvz and 𝔈 read ὑμῶν (= Margolis). For the evaluation of the
witnesses see den Hertog 1996, 40.

[228] MSS BAbprwy and 𝔖 read ἡμῶν (= Rahlfs) other witnesses ὑμῶν (=
Margolis). For an evaluation of the witnesses see den Hertog 1996, 40.

[229] See Aejmelaeus 1982, 58. Occasionally Rahlfs' edition differs from the
Göttingen edition. Thus, e.g. Gen 32:11 includes vῦν δέ according to Rahlfs.
According to Wevers, the rendering of the formula is vῦνὶ δέ.

Occasionally it is used alone in the Pentateuch to render the Hebrew formula,[230] but in the LXX of Joshua οὖν is always attached to the particle νῦν when used to render the formula ועתה.[231] By using νῦν οὖν the translator showed his ability to use natural Greek expressions.[232] The translator of Judges never used οὖν in renderings of ועתה.

Josh 1:2

משה עבדי מת וְעַתָּה קום עבר את הירדן הזה – Μωυσῆς ὁ θερά-
πων μου τετελεύτηκεν· <u>νῦν οὖν</u> ἀναστὰς διάβηθι τὸν Ἰορδάνην

Josh 22:4

ועתה הניח יהוה אלהיכם לאחיכם כאשר דבר להם וְעַתָּה פנו
ולכו לכם לאהליכם – νῦν δὲ κατέπαυσεν Κύριος ὁ θεὸς ἡμῶν
τοὺς ἀδελφοὺς ὑμῶν, ὃν τρόπον εἶπεν αὐτοῖς· <u>νῦν οὖν</u> ἀποστρα-
φέντες ἀπέλθατε εἰς τοὺς οἴκους ὑμῶν

In both cases where νῦν οὖν is used a participial construction follows the rendering of the formula.

2.3.4.5 Conclusions

Often the formula was rendered very literally in the LXX by καὶ νῦν, but this was not the only possible way to handle the Hebrew formula. The use of καὶ νῦν is not even the best way to render the formula and to open an inferential clause. Greek has more suitable means to do this. One of these is the conjunction οὖν. The translator of Joshua used this when dealing with the formula ועתה. In the cases where οὖν was used, the *part. coni.* was also employed in the immediate context. These features make the instances in question idiomatic Greek.

---

[230] See Aejmelaeus 1982, 58.

[231] For the combination νῦν οὖν in genuine Greek see Kühner-Gerth II:2 § 544.2 (example from Herodotus) and Aejmelaeus 1982, 57-58 (esp. note 1 on p. 58).

[232] Aejmelaeus 1982, 59.

TABLE 8 The renderings of the Hebrew formula ועתה in the LXX of Joshua and Judges

	Josh	Judg
καὶ νῦν	12	14
καί	0	1
νῦν δέ	2	0
νῦν οὖν	2	0

When compared, the translations of Joshua and Judges again diverge in their renderings. The translator of Joshua quite often used καὶ νῦν, but νῦν δέ or νῦν οὖν occur in the translation as well. In the book of Judges one can find only καὶ νῦν (or simple καί). When one uses καὶ νῦν the inference is lost. The best choise among the listed equivalents is, of course, οὖν, since it introduces an inference in Greek and therefore comes close to the use of the formula ועתה.

The translations of Joshua and Judges use καὶ νῦν as the main rendering of the formula. This is mainly true for the books of the Pentateuch also. Aejmelaeus gives the ratio of (νῦν) οὖν in some of the books of the Pentateuch. In Joshua the ratio is 13%. This is less than in Genesis (69%) or Exodus (43%). Of the books of the Pentateuch Numbers is the closest to Joshua, when renderings of the formula are used as the criterion for comparision. For Judges the closest counterpart is perhaps Deuteronomy.[233]

2.3.5 *General remarks concerning the translations of the Hebrew formulas*

Although the formulas include the Hebrew conjunction ו, they do not in fact open an ordinary co-ordinate clause. They are used in Hebrew

---

[233] The statistics for the Pentateuch are given by Aejmelaeus 1982, 58.

in a special way, and therefore they must have often posed difficulties for the translators.

Only occasionally may one find a suitable rendering of them in Greek and the most often used equivalents in the LXX result in stylistically questionable language. The meaning of the Hebrew might even change during the translation process, because the renderings do not necessarily express the idea of the Hebrew.

Only a few literal or free renderings were ranked as being suitable during our discussion. The LXX of Joshua and Judges are different works when it comes to the translations of the formulas. Whereas in Judges the translator very often limited the number of equivalents used to a minimum, in Joshua a wider list of choices was used. Among the equivalents used by the translator of Joshua are free renderings. Their use resulted in appropriate style as well as faithfulness to the content and expression of the parent text.

The use of free renderings thus shows that the translator of Joshua was, on occasion, aware of the difficulties involved in translating the Hebrew formulas. This means that he was also aware of the wider context. The translator of Judges, on the other hand, did not notice the context. I conclude, therefore, that the translator of Joshua used a wider segmentation than did the translator of Judges.

TABLE 9 The ratios of καί and δέ in renderings of the formulas and of ordinary main clauses

%	Joshua		Judges	
	καί	δέ	καί	δέ
Formulas	74	17	100	0
Main clauses	89	5	98	1

Awareness of the problems involved is also seen if one compares the ratios of καί and δέ in renderings of the formulas and of ordinary main clauses. In Joshua δέ is used more often with the formulas than with main clauses. The ratio of δέ for formulas is 12% higher than the ratio for ordinary main clauses.[234] In Judges the difference is unimportant. Thus, the translator of Joshua noticed the special nature of the formulas. This is especially true for the formula וַיְהִי, because most of the cases of δέ appear as renderings of the formula וַיְהִי.

When the translations of Joshua and Judges were compared with the Pentateuch, the closest counterparts for the LXX of Joshua or the LXX of Judges varied depending on the formula under discussion. Statistical comparison is very difficult here because the material is often limited to a handful of cases. Very often the closest counterparts for both of the translators were found among the more literal translators of the Pentateuch. This is only natural, since the translations of Joshua and Judges are literal, the latter being more literal than the former.

2.4 The Hebrew conjunction וֹ at the beginning of an apodosis

2.4.1 Introduction

καί is the principal equivalent for the main clause initial Hebrew וֹ, but the use of καί as a rendering for וֹ is not always suitable. This is especially the case if וֹ introduces an apodosis. καί at the beginning of an apodosis is normally incorrect in Greek prose.

The use of καί to introduce an apodosis has in previous studies been shown to be a criterion that indicates that there are, in fact, clear differences observable between the LXX translators.[235] This makes the phenomenon a very interesting one.

---

[234] A similar observation is made by Aejmelaeus 1982, 25, who notices that the ratio of καί decreases when the renderings of the formula וַיְהִי and the renderings of ordinary main clauses are compared.

[235] See the treatment of the phenomenon in Aejmelaeus 1982, 145-147 and in Aejmelaeus 1993, 57.

An apodosis is a main clause which is preceded by a clause or clauses subordinated to it.[236] The use of the term is explained by the difference between Hebrew and Greek. In Hebrew an apodosis may well begin with the conjunction ו.[237] The use of the conjunction δέ in such instances is correct in Greek.[238] The following quotation from Herodotus illustrates the use of the apodotic δέ:

ἐπεὰν ὁ σκύμνος ἐν τῇ μητρὶ ἐὼν ἄρχηται διακινεόμενος, ὁ δὲ ἔχων ὄνυχας θηρίων πολλὸν πάντων ὀξυτάτους ἀμύσσει τὰς μήτρας. (III.108)[239]

δέ is seldom used in the LXX to open the apodosis, however.[240] The more common way of opening the apodosis is to use the conjunction καί. In Greek καί at the beginning of an apodosis is often seen as either incorrect or otiose by the authors of various studies and grammars.[241] According to the theory, the translators should have avoided καί at the beginning of an apodosis.

---

[236] See e.g. Denniston 1954, 308-309 and Kühner-Gerth II:2 § 570.1. Some grammarians use more general terminology and employ the term apodosis for any main clause with subordinated clauses attached to it. See e.g. Humbert 1960 § 355 or Rijksbaron 1984 § 24.1. Rijksbaron, however, states that a subordinate clause usually precedes an apodosis.

[237] Brockelmann 1956 § 123. See also a detailed description by Joüon-Muraoka § 176. The use of ו to open an apodosis is, according to Joüon-Muraoka, very frequent in conditional and temporal clauses but in causal clauses it is also used frequently. On the other hand, Waltke-O'Connor § 32.2 sees the conditional function of the construction as primary. For the use of the conjunction ו at the beginning of an apodosis in the various Semitic languages see Beyer 1968, 66.

[238] Denniston 1954, 177-185. Denniston points out that the use of apodotic δέ varies among ancient Greek authors and that only Homer and Herodotus use it with any frequency.

[239] For the evaluation of such a claim in Antiquity see Aristotle *Hist.anim.* 579b.

[240] For examples in the LXX of the Pentateuch see my footnote 254 on p. 118.

[241] Aejmelaeus 1993, 57 sees the case of καί introducing an apodosis as "a faulty Greek construction" or "a grammatically unacceptable expression". For the basic grammatical works concerning the phenomenon, see Kühner-Gerth II:2 § 524 Anmerk. 2 and Denniston 1954, 308-309. Most of the cases appear in poetry. E.g. Trenkner, however, sees the use of the apodotic καί as a correct stylistic feature in Greek; Trenkner 1960, 53-54.

Though the conjunction καί is regarded as incorrect, it is used by Greek writers at the beginning of an apodosis. Most of the cases occur in poetry, especially in Homer. Cases in prose are more infrequent.[242] According to the grammar of Kühner and Gerth, the cases in prose may be interpreted as adverbial uses of καί.[243] The following example from Herodotus illustrates this possibility:

ὡς δέ οἱ ταῦτα ἔδοξε, καὶ ἐποίεε κατὰ τάχος (I.79)

This may be understood as: "and as soon as he made this decision, he *also* put it into practice."

Cases of καί at the beginning of an apodosis may also be found in the texts of the Post-Classical period, but these cases are often seen as vulgarisms.[244]

The apodotic καί also appears in the New Testament Luke 2:21 serving as an example:[245]

---

[242] See Kühner-Gerth II:2 § 524.1, Denniston 1954, 308-309 and Trenkner 1960, 53-54. These sources list only 16 cases in prose. They are Herodotus I.79 and VII.128, Plato *Gorgias* 457D, *Kriton* 44D and *Euthyphron* 6E, Thucydides II.21.1, II.93.4, IV.8.9, V.27.1, VII.43.1, VII.75.1, VIII.1.4 and VIII.8.4, Xenophon *Cyr.* IV.2.16, IV.3.14 and V.2.31. The interpretation provided by the literature is not always reliable. E.g. Plato wrote the following in *Gorgias* 457B ἐὰν δὲ οἶμαι ῥητορικὸς γενόμενός τις κᾆθα ταύτῃ τῇ δυνάμει καὶ τῇ τέχνῃ ἀδικῇ, οὐ τὸν διδάξαντα δεῖ μισεῖν (ed. Croiset). According to Denniston, κᾆθα opens an apodosis and the text should be understood as: *If someone becomes clever in rhetoric, he will use his abilities and skills for evil...* Without any difficulty the text could be understood in another way too: *If someone becomes clever in rhetoric and uses his abilities and skills for evil, one should not blame his teacher.* In this interpretation κᾆθα begins, not an apodosis, but a conditional clause.

[243] Kühner-Gerth II:2 § 524.1. Anmerk. 2. Aejmelaeus 1982, 127 follows the interpretation of Kühner-Gerth. Denniston 1954, 309 note 1 remarks that in many cases the grammatical structure of the passage is very similar. There is a temporal protasis followed by an apodosis that begins with καί and the predicate immediately follows it.

[244] See e.g. Beyer 1968, 68.

[245] See Beyer 1968, 69-72. The examples mentioned in the literature are not always well selected. E.g. Turner 1963, 344 mentions three cases in Matthew. Matt 6:4 does not include an apodosis, because the ὅπως clause is subordinated to the preceding clause, not to the following clause. Matt 18:21 and 21:23 do not contain any subordinate clause at all and hence no apodosis exists. This does not, however, mean that the NT does not contain any apodoses introduced by the conjunction καί.

καὶ ὅτε ἐπλήσθησαν ἡμέραι ὀκτὼ τοῦ περιτεμεῖν αὐτὸν <u>καὶ</u>
<u>ἐκλήθη τὸ ὄνομα αὐτοῦ Ἰησοῦς</u>
Often the authors of studies and grammars see here an influence
either of the LXX or of Semitic languages in general.[246]

In the LXX the apodotic καί is no stranger. Aejmelaeus describes
the use of καί in an apodosis in every book of the Pentateuch.[247]
Thus, one would expect to find cases of the apodotic καί in the LXX
of Joshua and Judges, too.

In Joshua 44 relevant cases may be found and in Judges the number is 52. Because the main question is whether the conjunction καί
is used or not, the material in the following discussion is divided into
three groups. First, cases where καί is employed to render the
Hebrew ו at the beginning of an apodosis are discussed, then a case
where δέ is used is discussed. Finally, cases where the translation
does not have any visible equivalent for the Hebrew conjunction are
discussed. In each group the cases are further divided in accordance
with the clause or phrase preceding the main clause with the Hebrew
ו.

2.4.2 καί

In Joshua the conjunction καί is used 23 times to render the Hebrew
conjunction ו at the beginning of an apodosis.[248] In Judges the
number of occurrences is 43.

The cases are divided into subgroups based on the nature of the
expression preceding the apodosis. The majority of the cases consist
of a subordinate clause (1) as the preceding element both in Hebrew

---

[246] Beyer 1968, 68-69. Turner 1963, 334 mentions only the influence of
Aramaic.

[247] Aejmelaeus 1982, 128-138.

[248] Note that Josh 3:8 and 24:33 also contain a case where an apodosis is
introduced by καί but in 3:8 the present-day Hebrew text does not contain
ו at the beginning of the clause in question and in 24:33 the protasis is
missing from the Hebrew. Because of the text critical problems involved
these cases have been excluded from the present analysis.

and in Greek. In some cases the Greek subordinate clause renders a
Hebrew infinitive construction (2). Besides the subordinate clauses,
Greek may also employ infinitive constructions (3) or prepositional
phrases of a temporal nature (4).

Many of the **subordinate clauses** (1) have *temporal force*.

Josh 4:6-7

כי ישאלון בניכם מחר לאמר מה האבנים האלה לכם ⁷ וַאמרתם

להם – ἵνα ὅταν ἐρωτᾷ σε ὁ υἱός σου αὔριον λέγων Τί εἰσιν οἱ
λίθοι οὗτοι ὑμῖν; ⁷ καὶ σὺ δηλώσεις τῷ υἱῷ σου
The Hebrew and Greek contain some differences here, but they do
not affect the present analysis.

Josh 22:7

וברכם וַיברכם אל אהליהם יהושע שלחם כי וגם – καὶ ἡνίκα ἐξαπέστειλεν αὐτοὺς Ἰησοῦς εἰς τοὺς οἴκους αὐτῶν καὶ εὐλόγησεν
αὐτούς

Judg 3:18

ויהי כאשר כלה להקריב את המנחה וישלח את העם נשאי

המנחה – καὶ ἐγένετο ὡς συνετέλεσεν Ἀὼδ προσφέρων τὰ δῶρα,
καὶ ἐξαπέστειλεν [Ἀὼδ]²⁴⁹ τοὺς αἴροντας τὰ δῶρα

Judg 6:3

והיה אם זרע ישראל וַעלה מדין – καὶ ἐνένετο ὅταν ἔσπειρεν
ἀνὴρ Ἰσραήλ, καὶ ἀνέβαινεν Μαδιάμ

Judg 21:21

והנה אם יצאו בנות שילו לחול במחלות וַיצאתם מן הכרמים

וחטפתם לכם איש אשתו – καὶ ἰδοὺ ὡς ἂν ἐξέλθωσιν αἱ θυ-
γατέρες τῶν κατοικούντων Σηλὼ ἐν Σηλὼ χορεῦσαι ἐν χοροῖς,
καὶ ἐξελεύσεσθε ἀπὸ τῶν ἀμπελώνων καὶ ἁρπάσετε ἀνὴρ
ἑαυτῷ γυναῖκα

---

²⁴⁹ MSS bckx read the proper noun. According to Rørdam's emendation 𝔖 uses
an obelus in front of it; Rørdam 1859, 76.

Some *conditional clauses* also occur as the protasis.

Josh 22:18

–וְהָיָה אַתֶּם תִּמְרְדוּ הַיּוֹם בַּיהוָה וּמָחָר אֶל כָּל עֲדַת יִשְׂרָאֵל יִקְצֹף
καὶ ἔσται ἐὰν ἀποστῆτε σήμερον ἀπὸ Κυρίου, καὶ αὔριον ἐπὶ
πάντα Ἰσραὴλ ἔσται ἡ ὀργή

Josh 22:28

וַנֹּאמֶר וְהָיָה כִּי יֹאמְרוּ אֵלֵינוּ וְאֶל דֹּרֹתֵינוּ מָחָר וַאֲמַרְנוּ רְאוּ אֶת
תַבְנִית מִזְבַּח יְהוָה – καὶ εἴπαμεν Ἐὰν γένηταί ποτε καὶ λαλήσωσιν πρὸς ἡμᾶς καὶ ταῖς γενεαῖς ἡμῶν αὔριον, καὶ ἐροῦσιν
Ἴδετε ὁμοίωμα τοῦ θυσιαστηρίου Κυρίου

Judg 6:37

אִם טַל יִהְיֶה עַל הַגִּזָּה לְבַדָּהּ וְעַל כָּל הָאָרֶץ חֹרֶב וְיָדַעְתִּי כִּי
תוֹשִׁיעַ בְּיָדִי אֶת יִשְׂרָאֵל – καὶ ἐὰν δρόσος γένηται ἐπὶ τὸν πόκον
μόνον καὶ ἐπὶ πᾶσαν τὴν γῆν ξηρασία, καὶ γνώσομαι ὅτι
σῴζεις ἐν τῇ χειρί μου τὸν Ἰσραήλ

Judg 14:13

וְאִם לֹא תוּכְלוּ לְהַגִּיד לִי וּנְתַתֶּם אַתֶּם לִי שְׁלֹשִׁים סְדִינִים וּשְׁלֹשִׁים
חֲלִיפוֹת בְּגָדִים – καὶ ἐὰν μὴ δύνασθῆτε ἀπαγγεῖλαί μοι, καὶ
δώσετε ὑμεῖς ἐμοὶ τριάκοντα σινδόνας καὶ τριάκοντα στολὰς
ἱματίων

Three times the subordinate clause has *causal force*. These cases are
to be found in Judges. In Hebrew there is, in these cases, a כי clause
carrying more or less obvious temporal force, but the use of ὅτι in
Greek makes them causal.

Judg 2:18

וְכִי הֵקִים יְהוָה לָהֶם שֹׁפְטִים וְהָיָה יְהוָה עִם הַשֹּׁפֵט וְהוֹשִׁיעָם מִיַּד
אֹיְבֵיהֶם – καὶ ὅτι ἤγειρεν αὐτοῖς Κύριος κριτάς, καὶ ἦν Κύριος
μετὰ τοῦ κριτοῦ καὶ ἔσωσεν αὐτοὺς ἐκ χειρὸς τῶν ἐχθρῶν
αὐτῶν

Judg 6:5-6

כִּי הֵם וּמִקְנֵיהֶם יַעֲלוּ ... [6] וַיִּדַּל יִשְׂרָאֵל מְאֹד מִפְּנֵי מִדְיָן – ὅτι
αὐτοὶ καὶ τὰ κτήνη αὐτῶν ἀνέβαινον ... [6] καὶ ἐπτώχευσεν
Ἰσραὴλ σφόδρα ἀπὸ προσώπου Μαδιάμ

Judg 12:5

והיה כי יאמרו פליטי אפרים אעברה ויאמרו לו אנשי גלעד

האפרתי אתה – καὶ ἐγενήθη ὅτι εἶπαν οἱ διασεσῳσμένοι τοῦ
Ἐφράιμ Διαβῶμεν, καὶ εἶπαν αὐτοῖς οἱ ἄνδρες Γαλαὰδ Μὴ
ὑμεῖς ἐκ τοῦ Ἐφράιμ;

When the Greek **subordinate clause** renders an **infinitive
construction** (2) in Hebrew, the Hebrew formula is often present.
These cases have *temporal force*.

Josh 3:15

וכבוא נשאי הארון עד הירדן וַרגלי הכהנים נשאי הארון נטבלו

בקצה המים והירדן מלא – ὡς δὲ εἰσεπορεύοντο οἱ ἱερεῖς οἱ
αἴροντες τὴν κιβωτὸν τῆς διαθήκης ἐπὶ τὸν Ἰοράνην, καὶ οἱ
πόδες τῶν ἱερέων τῶν αἱρόντων τὴν κιβωτὸν τῆς διαθήκης
Κυρίου ἐβάφησαν εἰς μέρος τοῦ ὕδατος τοῦ Ἰορδάνου ὁ δὲ
Ἰορδάνης ἐπλήρου

Josh 5:13

ויהי בהיות יהושע ביריחו וַישא עיניו וירא והנה איש עמד לנגדו
– καὶ ἐγένετο ὡς ἦν Ἰησοῦς ἐν Ἰερειχώ, καὶ ἀναβλέψας τοῖς
ὀφθαλμοῖς εἶδεν ἄνθρωπων ἑστηκότα ἐναντίον αὐτοῦ

Judg 2:4

ויהי כדבר מלאך יהוה את הדברים האלה אל כל בני ישראל
וַישאו העם את קולם ויבכו – καὶ ἐγένετο ὡς ἐλάλησεν ὁ ἄγγελος Κυρίου τοὺς λόγους τούτους πρὸς πάντα Ἰσραήλ, καὶ
ἐπῆρεν ὁ λαὸς τὴν φωνὴν αὐτῶν καὶ ἔκλαυσαν

Judg 7:15

ויהי כשמע גדעון את מספר החלום ואת שברו וַישתחו – καὶ
ἐγένετο ὡς ἤκουσεν Γεδεὼν τὴν διήγησιν τοῦ ἐνυπνίου καὶ τὴν
σύγκρισιν αὐτοῦ, καὶ προσεκύνησεν Κύριον

Judg 11:35

ויהי כראותו אותה ויקרע את בגדיו ויאמר – καὶ ἐγενήθη ἡνίκα
εἶδεν αὐτήν καὶ διέρρηξεν τὰ ἱμάτια αὐτοῦ καὶ εἶπεν

Infinitive constructions (3) preceding an apodosis are rarer in Greek than subordinate clauses. In my material there are only seven cases and they all have *temporal force*.

Josh 10:11

ויהי בנסם מפני ישראל הם במורד בית חורן ויהוה השליך עליהם אבנים גדלות מן השמים – ἐν τῷ δὲ φεύγειν αὐτοὺς ἀπὸ προσώπου τῶν υἱῶν Ἰσραὴλ ἐπὶ τῆς καταβάσεως Ὡρωνεὶμ, καὶ Κύριος ἐπέρριψεν αὐτοῖς λίθους χαλάζης ἐκ τοῦ οὐρανοῦ

Josh 15:18

ויהי בבואה ותסיתהו לשאול מאת אביה שדה–καὶ ἐγένετο ἐν τῷ εἰσπορεύεσθαι αὐτὴν καὶ συνεβουλεύσατο αὐτῷ λέγουσα Αἰτήσομαι τὸν πατέρα μου ἀγρόν

The Greek apodosis does not fully correspond with the Hebrew but this does not affect the construction.[250]

Judg 1:14

ויהי בבואה ותסיתהו לשאול מאת אביה השדה – καὶ ἐγένετο ἐν τῷ εἰσπορεύεσθαι αὐτὴν καὶ ἐπέσεισεν αὐτὴν [Γοθονιὴλ][251] αἰτῆσαι παρὰ τοῦ πατρὸς αὐτῆς τὸν ἀγρόν

Judg 8:7

ויאמר גדעון לכן בתת יהוה את זבח ואת צלמנע בידי ודשתי את בשרכם את קוצי המדבר – καὶ εἶπεν Γεδεών Οὐκ οὕτως· ἐν τῷ δοῦναι Κύριον τὸν Ζέβεε καὶ Σαλμανά ἐν τῇ χειρί μου καὶ καταξανῶ τὰς σάρκας ὑμῶν ἐν ταῖς ἀκάνθαις τῆς ἐρήμου

Temporal phrases (4) preceding the apodosis are more frequent in Judges than in Joshua. Many of them, indeed almost all, are connected with the formula in Hebrew.

Josh 23:1-2

ויהי מימים רבים אחרי אשר הניח יהוה לישראל מכל איביהם מסביב ויהושע זקן בא בימים²ויקרא יהושע לכל ישראל – καὶ

---

[250] For the various explanations of the differences between the MT and the LXX see Dillmann 1886, 524; Steuernagel 1900, 210; Holmes 1914, 61; Margolis 1931, 290; Noth 1938, 62; Auld 1975, 271 and Butler 1983, 180.

[251] MSS Abcglwx and 𝕮 with 𝕭 omit the proper name (= Rahlfs).

ἐγένετο μεθ' ἡμέρας πλείους μετὰ τὸ καταπαῦσαι Κύριον τὸν
Ἰσραὴλ ἀπὸ πάντων τῶν ἐχθρῶν αὐτῶν κυκλόθεν, <u>καὶ</u> Ἰησοῦς
πρεσβύτερος προβεβηκὼς ταῖς ἡμέραις. ² <u>καὶ</u> συνεκάλεσεν
Ἰησοῦς πάντας τοὺς υἱοὺς Ἰσραήλ

Judg 6:25

ויהי בלילה ההוא ויאמר לו יהוה קח את פר השור אשר לאביך
– <u>καὶ</u> ἐγενήθη τῇ νυκτὶ ἐκείνῃ <u>καὶ</u> εἶπεν αὐτῷ Κύριος Λαβὲ τὸν
μόσχον τὸν σιτευτὸν τοῦ πατρός σου
(Cf. Judg 7:9).

Judg 9:42

ויהי ממחרת ויצא העם השדה – <u>καὶ</u> ἐγενήθη τῇ ἐπαύριον <u>καὶ</u>
ἐξῆλθεν ὁ λαὸς εἰς τὸ πεδίον
(Cf. Judg 21:4).

Judg 11:39

ויהי מקץ שנים חדשים ותשב אל אביה – <u>καὶ</u> ἐγένετο μετὰ τέλος
δύο μηνῶν <u>καὶ</u> ἀνέκαμψεν πρὸς τὸν πατέρα αὐτῆς

The examples in the previous discussion illustrate the various
contexts in which the apodotic καί appear. The element preceding
καί need not be a subordinate clause, but various other constructions
are also possible. Thus, the examples are divided into four main
groups according to the element occurring in front of καί. For the
Pentateuch Aejmelaeus noted the same phenomenon: the element
acting as a protasis may well be a subordinate clause, but often other
constructions appear as well.

Clearly, the use of stylistically problematic καί is triggered by the
presence of the Hebrew conjunction ו. Often the element acting as
a protasis has temporal force or it is preceded by a formula in Hebrew. If the preceding element carries a temporal force, the apodotic
καί appears in 51 cases out of a total of 67 (= 76%). If a formula is
used at the beginning of a protasis, the apodotic καί appears in 50
cases out of a total of 64 (78%). If all the cases are added together,
καί appears in 66 cases out of a total of 95 (=69%).[252] The higher
ratios for καί with temporal apodoses and formulas suggest that the

---

[252] For the complete statistics see p. 126.

temporal constructions or Hebrew formulas and the use of the apodotic καί belong together.[253]

2.4.3 δέ

The cases where the conjunction δέ is used to render the Hebrew ו at the beginning of an apodosis are much rarer than cases where καί is used, though the use of δέ would be correct in Greek.[254] In fact, my material contains only one instance where δέ is used to link a subordinate clause with the apodosis.

Josh 2:7-8

והשער סגרו אחרי כאשר יצאו הרדפים אחריהם ⁸ והמה טרם
ישכבון והיא עלתה עליהם על הגג – καὶ ἡ πόλη ἐκλείσθη. καὶ
ἐγένετο ὡς ἐξῆλθοσαν οἱ διώκοντες ὀπίσω αὐτῶν ⁸ καὶ αὐτοὶ δὲ
πρὶν ἢ κοιμηθῆναι αὐτοὺς αὐτὴ δὲ[255] ἀνέβη ἐπὶ τὸ δῶμα πρὸς
αὐτούς

In the MT no apodosis is present, but because the translator uses a temporal clause at the end of verse 7, the translation contains δέ at the beginning of an apodosis in verse 8.[256] The apodosis is the *anacoluthon* καὶ αὐτοὶ δέ, a very literal rendering of the Hebrew והמה.[257] The next main clause begins with πρὶν ἤ with an *accusa-*

---

[253] For the connection between formulas and the apodotic καί, see Aejmelaeus 1982, 133. For the connection between the apodotic καί and temporal apodoses, see Denniston 1954, 309, note 1.

[254] For the cases in the Pentateuch, see Aejmelaeus 1982, 139. In the Pentateuch only four cases occur. δέ is used three times by the translator of Genesis and once by the translator of Exodus. The case in Exodus is connected with the *part.coni*; Aejmelaeus 1982, 107.

[255] MSS Bcr read αὐτὴ δέ (= Margolis). The majority reading is, however, καὶ αὐτή (= Rahlfs). For the evaluation see den Hertog 1996, 61.

[256] The case is not, however, text-critically obvious. I follow the text of Margolis and Rahlfs here. The conjunction δέ is attested by a number of the best MSS. Yet the Hexaplaric tradition and consequently some other MSS omit it. However, the omission is, as far as I can see, due to a correction towards Hebrew in a literal fashion. Both καί and δέ may be seen as counterparts to the Hebrew ו.

[257] The Greek construction is perhaps due to a misinterpretation of the Hebrew. In Hebrew והמה is not an independent clause, but the pronoun at the head

tivus cum infinitivo (AcI) construction. This is separated from the rest of the clause by another conjunction δέ.[258]

2.4.4 *Omission of the conjunction*

The third group of cases includes instances where the translator did not include any visible equivalent for the Hebrew conjunction ו at the beginning of an apodosis. The omission resulted in a normal Greek idiom. There are 21 cases in Joshua and 17 cases in Judges. Again the block of material may be divided following the expression preceding the apodosis. The cases consist of a subordinate clause (1) as the preceding element. Sometimes the Greek rendering of a Hebrew infinitive construction (2) is a subordinate clause, but cases are limited to Joshua only. Besides the subordinate clauses some infinitive constructions occur in Greek (3) with prepositional phrases of a temporal nature (4) or cases with the Hebrew *casus pendens* (5), but these are rare.

Many of the **subordinate clauses** (1) attached to the apodosis have *temporal force*. This is true for the cases where καί is used as well.

Josh 4:21-22

אֲשֶׁר יִשְׁאָלוּן בְּנֵיכֶם מָחָר אֶת אֲבוֹתָם לֵאמֹר מָה הָאֲבָנִים הָאֵלֶּה
וְהוֹדַעְתֶּם אֶת בְּנֵיכֶם [22] – ὅταν ἐρωτῶσιν ὑμᾶς οἱ υἱοὶ ὑμῶν λέγοντες Τί εἰσιν οἱ λίθοι οὗτοι; [22] __ ἀναγγείλατε τοῖς υἱοῖς ὑμῶν
In the examples illustrating the use of the apodotic καί a similar case is mentioned (Josh 4:6-7).

Judg 13:17

מִי שְׁמֶךָ כִּי יָבֹא דְבָרְךָ וַכִבַּדְנוּךָ – τί ὄνομά σοι, ἵνα, ὅταν ἔλθῃ
τὸ ῥῆμά σου, __ δοξάσωμέν σε;
The temporal clause is embedded in a final clause in Greek.

---

of the clause is in *casus pendens*.

[258] The construction is used only once in Joshua. Normally πρὶν ἤ with AcI is regarded as Ionian, but it is frequently used in Post-Classical language, too; for the Papyri see Mayser II:1, 318-320.

A *conditional clause* may also precede the apodosis with no conjunction at the beginning. In Judges this is the most common type of case with the omission of the Hebrew co-ordinating conjunction. However, if the protasis has conditional force, καί may appear in the translation as well.

Josh 2:20

ואם תגידי את דברנו זה וַהָיִינו נקים משבעתך – ἐὰν δέ τις ἡμᾶς ἀδικήσῃ ἢ καὶ ἀποκαλύψῃ τοὺς λόγους ἡμῶν τούτους, __ ἐσόμεθα ἀθῷοι τῷ ὅρκῳ σου τούτῳ

Josh 14:12

אולי יהוה אותי וַהוֹרשתים כאשר דבר יהוה[259] – ἐὰν οὖν Κύριος μετ' ἐμοῦ ᾖ, __ ἐξολεθρεύσω αὐτοὺς ὃν τρόπον εἶπέν μοι Κύριος
The translation employs a conditional clause to render the Hebrew wish.

Judg 14:12

אם הגד תגידו אותה לי שבעת ימי המשתה ומצאתם וַנתתי לכם שלשים סדינים ושלשים חלפת בגדים – καὶ ἐὰν ἀπαγγείλητέ μοι τὸ πρόβλημα ἐν ταῖς ἑπτὰ ἡμέραις τοῦ πότου, __ δώσω ὑμῖν τριάκοντα σινδόνας καὶ τριάκοντα στολάς

Judg 16:17

אם גלחתי וַסר ממני כחי וחליתי והייתי ככל האדם – καὶ ἐὰν ξυρήσωμαι, __ ἀποστήσεται ἀπ' ἐμοῦ ἡ ἰσχύς μου, καὶ ἀσθενήσω καὶ ἔσομαι κατὰ πάντας τοὺς ἀνθρώπους

Twice the conditional clause is a relative clause. Although the cases appear in different books, the episode described is the same.

Josh 15:16

אשר יכה את קרית ספר ולכדה וַנתתי לו את עכסה בתי לאשה – ὃς ἐὰν λάβῃ καὶ ἐκκόψῃ[260] τὴν Πόλιν τῶν γραμμάτων καὶ

---

[259] There are two אולי clauses in the MT of Joshua. The other instance is Josh 9:7.

[260] MSS B(h)iqra₂ 71 461 with v^mg, z^mg and 𝔈 read καὶ ἐκκόψῃ (= Rahlfs). The rest of the witnesses omit it (= Margolis); see den Hertog 1996, 90 and

κυριεύσῃ αὐτῆς, __δώσω αὐτῷ τὴν Ἀχσὰν θυγατέρα μου εἰς γυναῖκα

Judg 1:12

אשר יכה את קרית ספר ולכדה וַנתתי לו את עכסה בתי לאשה

— ὃς ἂν πατάξῃ τὴν Πόλιν τῶν γραμμάτων καὶ προκαταλάβηται αὐτήν, __δώσω αὐτῷ τὴν Ἀσχὰν θυγατέρα μου εἰς γυναῖκα

Some *causal and comparative clauses* precede the apodosis, too. Similar contexts appear in cases where καί is used.

Josh 15:19

תנה לי ברכה כי ארץ הנגב נתתני וַנתתה לי גלת מים — Δός μοι εὐλογίαν· ὅτι εἰς γῆν Ναγὲβ δέδωκάς με, __δός μοι τὴν Βοθ-θανείς[261]

I interpret this instance differently from the editors of the Greek text and I have changed the punctuation accordingly. By their choice of punctuation the editors suggest that one should read the ὅτι clause as linked with the preceding clause. If this is the case, one should understand the reply as "Give me a present, because you have given me to the land of the Negeb. Give me Bothaneis." Why, then, would the translator omit the co-ordinator at the beginning of the next clause? The omission of the Hebrew co-ordinator becomes understandable if one assumes that the translator considered the last clause to be an apodosis and accordingly left the co-ordinator without any visible equivalent.

Moatti-Fine 1996, 182.

[261] Rahlfs here reads Γολαθμαιν, which seems to be a corrected form for the place-name Γωλαθ μαιμ appearing in many MSS. Margolis gives the name Γωλαθ Μαειν. My text is the reading of MSS B(h*)qr and the Ethiopic. The variants may be based on the corrections towards the MT.

Josh 10:37

ὃν – ככל אשר עשה לעגלון ויחרם אותה ואת כל הנפש אשר בה
τρόπον ἐποίησαν τὴν Ὀδολλάμ[262], __ἐξωλέθρευσαν αὐτὴν καὶ
ὅσα ἦν ἐν αὐτῇ

A Hebrew **infinitive construction** may also be rendered as a subordinate **clause** in Greek (2). Many cases of this type have *temporal
force*.

Josh 3:3

כראותכם את ארון ברית יהוה אלהיכם והכהנים הלוים נשאים
אתו ואתם תסעו ממקומכם – ὅταν ἴδητε τὴν κιβωτὸν τῆς διαθήκης Κυρίου τοῦ θεοῦ ἡμῶν[263] καὶ τοὺς ἱερεῖς ἡμῶν[264] καὶ τοὺς
Λευείτας αἴροντας αὐτήν, __ἀπαρεῖτε ἀπὸ τῶν τόπων ὑμῶν
Not only was the co-ordinator ן omitted, but the explicit subject אתם
was also left without a visible counterpart.

Josh 11:1

ויהי כשמע יבין מלך חצור וישלח אל יובב אל מלך מדון – ὡς δὲ
ἤκουσεν Ἰαβεὶς[265] βασιλεὺς Ἀσώρ, __ἀπέστειλεν πρὸς Ἰωβὰβ
βασιλέα Μαρρών

The Hebrew infinitive construction might be rendered as an
infinitive construction in Greek as well. (3) There are three such
cases in my material.

---

[262] This is the reading of the best MSS as well as of Rahlfs. Margolis makes the
free emendation τῇ Ἐγελάν, which is based on the MT. See also den Hertog
1995, 61. Unfortunately, den Hertog comments on the Greek article only.

[263] Here Margolis reads ὑμῶν against the majority of the MSS. He does not
even recognize the majority reading in his edition. For the evaluation of the
instance in question, see den Hertog 1995, 36. For more general remarks
concerning the use of pronouns in Margolis' edition, see Sipilä 1993, 21.

[264] Here Margolis prefers to read ὑμῶν. See note 261 above.

[265] Rahlfs reads Ιαβιν (an emendation) and Margolis Ιαβειν. The latter is the
majority reading, but MSS ABqru and 𝔉 read Ιαβεις. The situation seems
to resemble that in Josh 15:19; see note 261.

Judg 14:11

‫ויהי כראותם אותו ויקחו שלשים מרעים‬ – καὶ ἐγένετο ἐν τῷ
φοβεῖσθαι αὐτοὺς αὐτὸν __προσκατέστησαν αὐτῷ ἑταίρους
τριάκοντα

The element preceding the apodosis may be a **temporal phrase** (4).
The omission of the co-ordinator between a temporal phrase and the
apodosis is rather rare in Judges.

Judg 11:26

‫בשבת ישראל בחשבון ובבנותיה ובערעור ובבנותיה ובכל הערים‬
‫אשר על ידי ארנון שלש מאות שנה ומדוע לא הצלתם בעת ההיא‬
– ἐν τῷ οἴκῳ Ἰσραὴλ ἐν Ἐσεβὼν καὶ ἐν ταῖς θυγατράσιν αὐτῆς
καὶ ἐν Ἰαζὴρ καὶ ἐν ταῖς θυγατράσιν αὐτῆς καὶ ἐν πάσαις ταῖς
πόλεσιν ταῖς παρὰ τὸν Ἰορδάνην τριακόσια ἔτη __τί ὅτι οὐκ
ἐρρύσαντο αὐτοὺς ἐν τῷ καιρῷ ἐκείνῳ;

In an individual case the apodosis is a *casus pendens* **in Hebrew**
(5). In my material the translator of Judges omitted the co-ordinator
between the *casus pendens* and the apodosis.[266]

Judg 19:30

‫והיה כל הראה ואמר לא נהיתה ולא נראתה כזאת‬ – καὶ ἐγένετο
πᾶς ὁ ὁρῶν __ἔλεγεν Οὔτε ἐγενήθη οὔτε ὤφθη οὕτως
The *casus pendens* is related to a formula in Hebrew (cf. Dtn 21:3).

As was evident in the introductory part of this chapter, an apodosis
in Greek need not be linked in any special way with the subordinate
clauses preceding it. Therefore, when the translators left the Hebrew
ו without a visible counterpart in their Greek text, they followed the
normal Greek procedure in opening an apodosis.

---

[266] In her study Aejmelaeus lists three cases where the co-ordinator separates
the rendering of the *casus pendens* and the apodosis in the LXX of the
Pentateuch; Aejmelaeus 1982, 131-133. She mentions explicitly only Dtn
21:3 but, according to her statistics, there is one case in Leviticus and
another in Numbers as well. In Genesis and Exodus the translators omitted
the co-ordinator in cases including the *casus pendens*.

2.4.5 *Translation-technical evaluation*

The conjunction καί at the beginning of an apodosis is not only unidiomatic, but one may draw conclusions concerning the translation technique of Joshua and Judges based on it. The use of καί to open an apodosis tells us that the translators did not always refine their Greek style. We cannot know if they were aware of the stylistic quality of the translation, but the use of the apodotic καί clearly affects the style of the LXX, especially if its use is extensive. It is quite clear to me that the translators did not intend to produce stylistically questionable language. This may be seen from the fact that they did not always use the apodotic καί. Why then does such a phenomenon occur in their work?

The best single explanation for the phenomenon is the narrow segmentation. The translators probably worked for only short periods of the Hebrew parent text.[267] The personal qualities of the translator then set limits on his ability to take the context into account. If the translator was vigilant, he could bear the context in mind and the most blatant errors could be avoided.

Since the translators of Joshua and Judges use the problematic καί, one may conclude that they only occasionally took the wider context into account.[268] All in all, the length of the subordinate clause or clauses does *not* seem to explain the use of the apodotic καί. One might think that the longer the context the easier it was to forget parts of it and hence use καί. However, in Joshua or in Judges the complexity or the length of the context which the translators needed to bear in mind in order to avoid καί in front of an apodosis does not completely explain the use of καί.

The type of expression preceding the apodosis, on the other hand, does seem to affect the avoidance of καί. If the Hebrew formula, such as ויהי, is present, καί is used more frequently than if the formula is absent.[269] If the expression preceding the apodosis is a subordinate clause, καί is used more frequently than in cases where

---

[267] See e.g. Soisalon-Soininen 1987, 29.
[268] For the translation of Joshua, see den Hertog 1996, 179-180.
[269] Concerning the Pentateuch, see Aejmelaeus 1982, 133-134.

the expression is not a clause.[270] With the Hebrew *casus pendens* καί appears seldom, but one has to bear in mind that such cases are extremely rare.[271]

If the expression preceding the apodosis is temporal in nature, one sees increased ratios of καί. In Judges the omission of the co-ordinator occurs frequently if the preceding clause has conditional force, but in Joshua the use or omission of the co-ordinator seems to depend on the existence of the formula. If the conditional clause is connected with the formula in Joshua, καί is always used. Otherwise, the omission of the co-ordinator occurs.

When Joshua and Judges are compared with the translations of the Pentateuch, some similarities and some differences may be seen. In the Pentateuch only the translation of Genesis uses δέ in front of an apodosis. While in Joshua there is one such case, in Genesis there are three cases.[272] Joshua seems, then, to some extent to resemble Genesis as a translation. More interesting than this is the translator's ability to avoid the use of the apodotic καί. The ratio for Joshua is 48% and for Judges 26%. In the Pentateuch the ratios are: Genesis 55%, Exodus 78%, Leviticus 39%, Numbers 36% and Deuteronomy 30%.[273]

When these percentages are compared with the percentages for Joshua and Judges, two observations may be made. When Joshua was discovered to resemble Genesis in what pertains to the use of δέ in an apodosis, the same cannot be said with respect to the avoidance of the co-ordinator in an apodosis. Joshua lies in between Genesis and the more literal translations of Leviticus, Numbers and Deuteronomy. Judges, on the other hand, is more literal than any of the translations of the Pentateuch. Taking into account the extensive use of καί to render the Hebrew co-ordinator ו in the ordinary main clauses in Judges, this does not perhaps come as a surprise.

---

[270] In the Pentateuch this is not the case — except for Leviticus, where the number of cases with the preceding element not being a clause is very low; see the statistics in Aejmelaeus 1982, 132.

[271] This notion holds true for Genesis and Exodus, too, but again cases are truly rare; see the statistics in Aejmelaeus 1982, 132.

[272] Aejmelaeus 1982, 139. Instances are Gen 6:1-2, 15:3 and 27:37.

[273] Aejmelaeus 1980, 140 provides statistics for the Pentateuch.

TABLE 11 Ratios of the apodotic καί in the various cases

	all cases	cases with formula	other cases
Joshua			
subordinate clause	9/15	6/6	3/9
subordinate clause (MT: infinitive construction)	9/17	7/14	2/3
-----	-----	-----	-----
	(56%)	(65%)	(42%)
-----	-----	-----	-----
infinitive construction	2/3	2/3	0/0
temporal phrase	2/8	2/6	0/1
casus pendens	1/1	0/0	1/1
-----	-----	-----	-----
	(42%)		
-----	-----	-----	-----
TOTAL 52.3%			
Judges			
subordinate clause[274]	21/27	13/13	8/14
subordinate clause (MT: infinitive construction)	5/5	5/5	0/0
-----	-----	-----	-----
	(81%)	(100%)	(57%)
-----	-----	-----	-----
infinitive construction	3/4	2/3	1/1
temporal phrase	13/14	13/13	0/1
casus pendens[275]	1/2	0/1	1/1
-----	-----	-----	-----
	(85%)	(88%)	
-----	-----	-----	-----
TOTAL 82.7%			

The table is composed in accordance with the table provided by Aejmelaeus (1982, 132). In the table the number of instances with the apodotic καί is given in the first column. The first number refers to the number of cases with καί and the second, after a slash, to the total number of cases. The second column gives the number of cases connected with a formula in Hebrew, and the third column gives the number of cases unconnected with a formula.

[274] Judg 16:25 is included in this category, because *kethib* uses the conjunction כי in Hebrew.

[275] In Judg 14:16 the Hebrew *casus pendens* is rendered by a ὅτι clause. The case is included in *casus pendens* cases, however.

2.4.6 The apodotic καί in connection with part.coni. and gen.abs.

As was evident in the previous discussion about the use of the *part.coni.* as a rendering for the normal co-ordinated Hebrew main clause[276] there are some cases where the translation separates the participial construction from its main clause by using the conjunction καί. These cases resemble others where the apodotic καί is employed, since the conjunction is not normally used to separate the participle from its main clause.

Expressions like this are regarded as Hebraisms.[277] Sometimes such unidiomatic expressions may also be found outside the LXX.[278] To take an example of an expression where *part.coni.* is linked by καί to its main clause, consider a section from a letter mentioned by some grammarians:[279]

γράψας, ὅπως εἰδῆις, <u>καὶ</u> σὺ ἀναγωνίατος ἴσθει (*P.Tebt* 1.58.50)

In consequence, Radermacher makes use of the term "clause-initial καί" in his grammar of New Testament Greek. For him the conjunction merely acts as a punctuation mark, not as a conjunction.[280]

In Joshua there are four such cases, but in Judges no such cases exist.[281]

Josh 8:20

‏–ויפנו אנשי העי אחריהם ויראו והנה עלה עשן העיר השמימה
καὶ περιβλέψαντες οἱ κάτοικοι Γαὶ εἰς τὰ ὀπίσω αὐτῶν <u>καὶ</u> ἐθεώρουν καπνὸν ἀναβαίνοντα ἐκ τῆς πόλεως εἰς τὸν οὐρανόν

---

[276] See the chapter *Participium coniunctum* on pp. 51-58.

[277] E.g. Viteau 1893 § 337: "Le participe est au nominatif indépendant, quand il se relie logiquement, mais non grammaticalement, avec le reste de la phrase... Cette construction est hébraïsante."

[278] Mainly basing his claim on this fact, Thumb 1910, 131 points out that the phenomenon cannot be a Hebraism as such. Compare also Mayser II:1 § 51.3 b α. Estimations as to how widespread the phenomenon was, vary and there are studies that consider the phenomenon to be quite common in Attic prose and in *Koiné*; see eg. Trenkner 1960, 52-55.

[279] E.g. Moulton 1906, 223. He lists more examples like this and states that the phenomenon is rare. Nevertheless, he insists that the use of the unidiomatic conjunction does not indicate that the writer had an inferior education.

[280] Radermacher 1911, 177.

[281] Two other cases not listed here are Josh 4:8 and Josh 10:19.

Josh 22:30

וישמע פינחס הכהן ונשיאי העדה... את הדברים... וַיִּיטַב בְּעֵינֵיהֶם

– καὶ ἀκούσας Φεινεὲς ὁ ἱερεὺς καὶ πάντες οἱ ἄρχοντες τῆς συναγωγῆς Ἰσραήλ ... τοὺς λόγους ... καὶ ἤρεσεν αὐτοῖς.

The subject in the main clause (the previous reply) is not the subject of the participle (Phinehas the priest and the elders) here.

When one studies the frequency of καί used to separate the participle from the main clause and compares it with the frequency in using apodotic καί, an interesting observation may be made. In Joshua καί is used in conjunction with *part.coni.* in four cases out of a total of 33 *part.coni.* constructions. The ratio for the omission of the conjunction is therefore 88%. For Judges the ratio is, perhaps surprisingly, 100%. That is, *every* time that the translator of Judges used *part.coni.* to render the Hebrew parataxis he left the co-ordinator without any visible equivalent. Both translators were, then, more cautious when using *part.coni.* than when dealing with the apodoses. The same observation may be made with regard to the Pentateuch, too.[282]

Now, it seems that the translator of Judges was more cautious than the translator of Joshua or the translators of the Pentateuch, since no cases of the *part.coni.* with καί can be detected. This is, however, only half true, since the translator of Judges rather frequently used the *genetivus absolutus* to render the Hebrew parataxis and these cases often contain the use of otiose καί. There are five cases of *gen.abs.* in Judges and in four of these the participle is separated from the main clause by καί. Cases with *gen.abs.* are dealt with in the earlier part of this study, therefore only one example is given here:[283]

Judg 19:11

הם עם יבוס וְהַיּוֹם רַד מְאֹד וַיֹּאמֶר הַנַּעַר אֶל אֲדֹנָיו – ἔτι αὐτῶν ὄντων κατὰ Ἰεβοὺς καὶ ἡ ἡμέρα κεκλικυῖα σφόδρα· καὶ εἶπεν τὸ παιδάριον πρὸς τὸν κύριον αὐτοῦ

---

[282] Aejmelaeus 1982, 104 writes: "The percentages for the cases of the *part. coni.* with καί are comparatively low, certainly lower than the percentages of the apodotic καί generally in the Greek Pentateuch."

[283] See the chapter *Genetivus absolutus* on pp. 64-67.

If the translator of Judges seems to have been cautious when dealing with the *part.coni.*, the *gen.abs.* was more difficult for him, or at least he made more errors when using the latter construction. The ratio for the omission of the co-ordinator with *gen.abs.* is only 20%, a ratio close to the ratio of its omission with an apodosis in Judges.

2.5 The Hebrew conjunction 1 at the beginning of a subordinate clause

2.5.1 *Introduction*

In the previous analysis main clauses beginning with the conjunction 1 were discussed. In the following analysis subordinate clauses will be focussed upon.

In her study Aejmelaeus divided the co-ordinated subordinate clauses into two groups. She discussed in detail clauses where the subordinate clause is opened with both the conjunction 1 and another, i.e. subordinate, conjunction. Cases where the conjunction 1 stands alone at the beginning of a subordinate clause were included in a large collection of cases where an "ordinary" co-ordinate clause appears. The reason for such a division lies, according to her, in the nature of the material itself. Only those cases where the subordinate conjunction is repeated are of special translation-technical value as distinct from other cases. She states that the selection of possible Greek equivalents for the Hebrew 1 decreases in scope in cases where the subordinate conjunction is repeated "unless the repetition ceases."[284]

Now the material is arranged differently than in Aejmelaeus' study.[285] In this chapter co-ordinated subordinate clauses with and

---

[284] Aejmelaeus 1982, 148.

[285] My study also differs from that of Aejmelaeus in another way. In her study Aejmelaeus distinguished subordinate clauses where 1 opens a period con-

without the repetition are discussed. This makes it possible to inves-
tigate whether Aejmelaeus' general remark is valid in the present
material. Thus, my basic question is, does the rendering of the
conjunction ו depend on the repetition of the subordinate conjunction in Hebrew or not. In order to study this, *I shall suppose that the
translators used a wider selection of equivalents in cases where the
repetition did not occur than in cases where it did.*

The material under discussion is small, making the conclusions
reached perhaps less solid. In Joshua only 23 co-ordinated subordinate clauses appear in the MT. In Judges the number of cases is 20.

Theoretically, the difference between co-ordinate main clauses
and co-ordinated subordinate clauses should not be too great.[286] As
we shall see, however, the use of equivalents for the Hebrew conjunction ו between subordinate clauses differs in some respects from
that for the Hebrew conjunction between main clauses. This alone
makes the separation between main clauses and subordinate clauses
relevant.

2.5.2 καί

In Joshua and Judges the most often used equivalent for the Hebrew
conjunction ו is, naturally, καί. Only five times does the translation
of Joshua contain exception to this in my material.

The cases where the conjunction καί is used to link subordinate
clauses together may be divided into two groups. Either the subordi-

---

taining a subordinate clause and a main clause from cases where ו opens an
ordinary main clause. This was significant, because in her material δέ was the
main equivalent for ו in cases with a period; see Aejmelaeus 1982, 155. In
my material this is not the case. Only in three instances was δέ employed as
a rendering of ו if a subordinate clause commences a period. These three
cases contain a conditional clause and an apodosis. Two of them appear in
Joshua (Josh 2:20 and Josh 24:15) and one in Judges (Judg 7:10): וְאִם יָרֵא
אַתָּה לָרֶדֶת רֵד אַתָּה וּפֻרָה נַעַרְךָ אֶל הַמַּחֲנֶה – εἰ δὲ φοβῇ σὺ καταβῆναι,
κατάβηθι σὺ καὶ Φαρὰ τὸ παιδάριόν σου εἰς τὴν παραμβολήν. Since the
number of cases is really low, I did not see any reason to separate the cases
from other cases of main clause initial ו.

[286] See Aejmelaeus 1982, 148.

native conjunction is repeated at the beginning of each clause or the subordinative conjunction is used only at the beginning of the first subordinated clause of the sequence.

In eight instances the Hebrew subordinative *conjunction is repeated* at the beginning of *every co-ordinated subordinate clause*. In these instances the number of co-ordinated subordinate clauses is normally two. Once the first clause and the third clause bear the subordinative conjunction and the second clause in the sequence begins with the Hebrew ו only (Josh 10:1).

Josh 2:10

כי שמענו <u>את אשר</u> הוביש יהוה את מי ים סוף מפניכם בצאתכם

ממצרים <u>ואשר</u> עשיתם לשני מלכי האמרי – ἀκηκόαμεν γὰρ <u>ὅτι</u> κατεξήρανεν Κύριος ὁ θεὸς τὴν ἐρυθρὰν θάλασσαν ἀπὸ προσώπου ὑμῶν ὅτε ἐξεπορεύεσθε ἐκ γῆς Αἰγύπτου <u>καὶ ὅσα</u> ἐποίησεν τοῖς δυσὶ βασιλεῦσιν τῶν Ἀμορραίων

In the Hebrew two relative clauses following a *verbum sentiendi* should be understood as the objects of the verb. Interestingly, the translator used ὅτι for the first relative pronoun, but ὅσα for the second.

Josh 7:15

ישרף באש אתו ואת כל אשר לו <u>כי</u> עבר את ברית יהוה <u>וכי</u>

עשה נבלה בישראל – κατακαυθήσεται ἐν πυρὶ καὶ πάντα ὅσα ἐστὶν αὐτῷ, <u>ὅτι</u> παρέβη τὴν διαθήκην Κυρίου <u>καὶ</u> ἐποίησεν ἀνόμημα ἐν Ἰσραήλ

Here the repetition of the subordinate conjunction כי in Hebrew is not carried over to Greek. On the contrary the second subordinative conjunction was left without a visible counterpart. Obviously καί alone is sufficient in Greek.

Josh 8:21

ויהושע וכל ישראל ראו <u>כי</u> לכד הארב את העיר <u>וכי</u> עלה עשן

העיר – καὶ Ἰησοῦς καὶ πᾶς Ἰσραὴλ εἶδον <u>ὅτι</u> ἔλαβον τὰ ἔνεδρα τὴν πόλιν, <u>καὶ ὅτι</u> ἀνέβη ὁ καπνὸς τῆς πόλεως

Josh 24:31

הזקנים אֲשֶׁר האריכו ימים אחרי יהושע וַאֲשֶׁר ידעו את כל מעשה
יהוה – τῶν πρεσβυτέρων ὅσοι ἐφείλκυσαν τὸν χρόνον[287] μετὰ
Ἰησοῦ καὶ ὅσοι εἴδοσαν πάντα τὰ ἔργα Κυρίου

Judg 2:15

יד יהוה היתה בם לרעה כַּאֲשֶׁר דבר יהוה וְכַאֲשֶׁר נשבע יהוה
להם – καὶ χεὶρ Κυρίου ἦν αὐτοῖς εἰς κακά, καθὼς ἐλάλησεν
Κύριος καὶ καθὼς ὤμοσεν Κύριος

Judg 6:30

וימת כִּי נתץ את מזבח הבעל וְכִי כרת האשרה אשר עליו – καὶ
ἀποθανέτω, ὅτι κατέσκαψεν τὸ θυσιαστήριον τοῦ Βααλ καὶ ὅτι
ἔκοψεν τὸ ἄλσος τὸ ἐπ᾽ αὐτῷ

Josh 10:1

ויהי כשמע אדני צדק ... כִּי לכד יהושע את העי וַיַחרימה ... וְכִי
השלימו ישבי גבעון את ישראל ויהיו בקרבם – ὡς δὲ ἤκουσεν
Ἀδωνιβέζεκ ... ὅτι ἔλαβεν Ἰησοῦς τὴν Γαι καὶ ἐξωλέθρευσεν
αὐτήν ... καὶ ὅτι αὐτομόλησαν οἱ κατοικοῦντες Γαβαὼν πρὸς
Ἰησοῦν καὶ πρὸς Ἰσραήλ

Despite some differences between the LXX and the MT, the grammatical construction in the LXX is close to that in the MT. In both
texts the subordinative conjunction is repeated at the beginning of
the third subordinate clause, but not at the beginning of the second.

The translators usually followed the idiom of the parent text and produced the subordinative conjunction at the beginning of every subordinate clause. There is only one exception to this (Josh 7:15).
Thus, the repetition of the subordinate conjunction in Hebrew is
transferred into Greek as such.

Cases where the Hebrew *does not repeat* the subordinate conjunction form most cases, with 30 instances. A few examples will
illustrate the cases.

---

[287] For ἐφείλκυσαν τὸν χρόνον, see den Hertog 1996, 138 and Moatti-Fine
1996, 238-239.

Josh 1:14-15

¹⁵ וַעֲזַרְתֶּם אוֹתָם <u>עַד אֲשֶׁר</u> יָנִיחַ יְהוָה לַאֲחֵיכֶם כָּכֶם <u>וַ</u>יָרְשׁוּ גַם הֵמָּה
<u>אֶת הָאָרֶץ</u> – καὶ συμμαχήσετε αὐτοῖς ¹⁵<u>ἕως ἂν</u> καταπαύσῃ Κύ-
ριος ὁ θεὸς ὑμῶν τοὺς ἀδελφοὺς ὑμῶν ὥσπερ καὶ ὑμᾶς <u>καὶ</u>
κληρονομήσωσιν καὶ οὗτοι τὴν γῆν

Josh 9:16

וַיִּשְׁמְעוּ <u>כִּי</u> קְרֹבִים הֵם אֵלָיו <u>וַ</u>בְּקִרְבּוֹ הֵם יֹשְׁבִים – ἤκουσαν <u>ὅτι</u>
ἐγγύθεν αὐτῶν εἰσιν, <u>καὶ</u> <u>ὅτι</u> ἐν αὐτοῖς κατοικοῦσιν

Now the translation repeats the subordinative conjunction at the
beginning of both of the subordinate clauses, but the Hebrew uses
כי only at the beginning of the first clause.[288] Because one has
difficulty in finding any reason why the translator should add the
second ὅτι, the translation is probably based on a Hebrew *Vorlage*
different from the present MT.

Josh 23:12-13

כִּי <u>אִם</u> שׁוֹב תָּשׁוּבוּ <u>וַ</u>דְבַקְתֶּם בְּיֶתֶר הַגּוֹיִם הָאֵלֶּה הַנִּשְׁאָרִים הָאֵלֶּה
אִתְּכֶם <u>וַ</u>הִתְחַתַּנְתֶּם בָּהֶם <u>וַ</u>בָאתֶם בָּהֶם <u>וַ</u>הֵם בָּכֶם ¹³ יָדוֹעַ תֵּדְעוּ כִּי ...
– <u>ἐὰν</u> γὰρ ἀποστραφῆτε <u>καὶ</u> προσθῆσθε τοῖς ὑπολειφθεῖσιν
ἔθνεσιν τούτοις τοῖς μεθ᾽ ὑμῶν <u>καὶ</u> ἐπιγαμίας ποιήσητε αὐτούς,
<u>καὶ</u> συγκαταμιγῆτε αὐτοῖς <u>καὶ</u> αὐτοὶ ὑμῖν, ¹³ γινώσκετε ὅτι ...

Judg 4:20

<u>וַ</u>הָיָה <u>אִם</u> אִישׁ יָבוֹא <u>וַ</u>שְׁאֵלֵךְ <u>וַ</u>אָמַר הֲיֵשׁ פֹּה אִישׁ וְאָמַרְתְּ אַיִן – καὶ
ἔσται <u>ἐὰν</u> τις ἔλθῃ πρὸς σὲ <u>καὶ</u> ἐρωτήσῃ σε <u>καὶ</u> εἴπῃ σοι "Εστιν
ἐνταῦθα ἀνήρ; καὶ ἐρεῖς Οὐκ ἔστιν

Note the formula וַהָיָה and the apodosis.

Judg 9:17

<u>אֲשֶׁר</u> נִלְחַם אָבִי עֲלֵיכֶם <u>וַ</u>יַּשְׁלֵךְ אֶת נַפְשׁוֹ מִנֶּגֶד <u>וַ</u>יַּצֵּל אֶתְכֶם מִיַּד
מִדְיָן – <u>ὡς</u> ἐπολέμησεν ὁ πατήρ μου ὑπὲρ ὑμῶν <u>καὶ</u> ἔρριψεν τὴν
ψυχὴν αὐτοῦ ἐξ ἐναντίας <u>καὶ</u> ἐξείλατο ὑμᾶς ἐκ χειρὸς Μαδιάμ
It is difficult to say where is the main clause to which the temporal
clauses relate.

---

[288] Margolis 1931, 161 simply says that the translator added the second ὅτι. If
this is the case, should there perhaps be a particular reason for such an
addition?

Judg 15:6

שמשון חתן התמני כִּי לקח את אשתו וַיִּתְּנָה לְמֵרֵעֵהוּ – Σαμψὼν
ὁ γαμβρὸς τοῦ Θαμναθαίου, ὅτι ἔλαβεν τὴν γυναῖκα αὐτοῦ καὶ
ἔδωκεν αὐτὴν τῷ συνεταίρῳ αὐτοῦ

In cases where the repetition of the subordinate conjunction does not
appear in Hebrew, but the co-ordinator ו opens the subordinate
clause, Greek simply employs the normal equivalent for ו, i.e. καί.
The fact that καί is often used is not surprising. It only shows that
the translators of Joshua and Judges treated the Hebrew ו at the
beginning of a subordinate clause in the same manner as ו at the
beginning of an ordinary main clause.

2.5.3 ἤ

The disjunctive conjunction is a choice to be used if the subordinate
clauses offer alternatives. These cases are rare, because Hebrew
possesses means to indicate the disjunction other than the conjunction ו.[289] The material collected from the LXX of Joshua and Judges
contains only two cases of ἤ. In most of the cases where ἤ is used in
the LXX the Hebrew counterpart is או, the disjunctive conjunction
in Hebrew.

Josh 2:19-20

וְכֹל אֲשֶׁר יִהְיֶה אִתְּךָ בַּבַּיִת דָּמוֹ בְרֹאשֵׁנוּ אִם תִּהְיֶה בּוֹ 20 וְאִם
תַּגִּידִי אֶת דְּבָרֵנוּ זֶה וְהָיִינוּ נְקִיִּם מִשְּׁבֻעָתֵךְ – καὶ ὅσοι ἂν
γένωνται μετὰ σοῦ ἐν τῇ οἰκίᾳ σου, ἡμεῖς ἔνοχοι ἐσόμεθα. ἐὰν

---

[289] GesK § 162 and Joüon-Muraoka § 175. Note that Joüon points out that the
use of ו "often suffices" (*on se contente souvent*), but the translators of the
LXX hardly ever use a disjunctive equivalent for the Hebrew ו.

δέ τις ἡμᾶς ἀδικήσῃ²⁹⁰ 20 ἢ καὶ ἀποκαλύψῃ τοὺς λόγους ἡμῶν τού-τους,²⁹¹ ἐσόμεθα ἀθῷοι τῷ ὅρκῳ σου τούτῳ
Two conditional clauses precede the main clause in Greek, but in the Hebrew the conditional clauses do not belong together.

Josh 22:23
לבנות לנו מזבח לשוב מאחרי יהוה <u>ואם</u> להעלות עליו עולה
– ומנחה <u>ואם</u> לעשות עליו זבחי שלמים יהוה הוא יבקש καὶ εἰ
ᾠκοδομήσαμεν αὐτοῖς βωμὸν <u>ὥστε</u> ἀποστῆναι ἀπὸ Κυρίου τοῦ
θεοῦ ἡμῶν, <u>ὥστε</u> ἀναβιβάσαι ἐπ᾽ αὐτὸν θυσίαν ὁλοκαυτωμάτων
<u>ἢ ὥστε</u> ποιῆσαι ἐπ᾽ αὐτοῦ θυσίαν σωτηρίου, Κύριος ἐκζητήσει
In this instance the translator dealt freely with the Hebrew grammatical construction and produced a conditional clause (καὶ εἰ...) with three embedded ὥστε constructions with an infinitive. Now the Greek conjunction is repeated following the Hebrew wording.

The cases in Joshua share some elements in common. In both cases the Hebrew subordinative conjunction is אם. It is not surprising that the translator chose to use a disjunctive Greek particle in these cases, since the Hebrew construction אם ... ואם may be used to express a disjunctive relation, for example.²⁹² In both cases the translator modified the grammatical structure of the Hebrew. Interestingly the cases are linked with the subordinated clauses only. The

---

²⁹⁰ The first conditional clause ἐὰν δέ τις ἡμᾶς ἀδικήσῃ has received some attention. According to many interpreters, the Greek text is not based on a Hebrew close to the MT. The better candidate for the Hebrew for them is ואם יד תהיה בנו (see Dillmann 1886, 449, Steuernagel 1900, 159, Benjamin 1921, 27, and Margolis 1931, 30). One need not assume a Hebrew *Vorlage* different from the MT. On the contrary, I find it at least possible that the "difference" was produced by the translator (cf. Butler 1982, 27).

²⁹¹ Note the translation by Moatti-Fine 1996, 104: "et si *tu révèles* ces paroles qui sont les nôtres" [italics mine]. She explains that this is due to a correspondence to the MT, but in cases like this should one take the MT into account at all?

²⁹² Constructions such as אם ... ו, אם ... או or או ... או may be characterized as disjunctive together with אם ... (ו)אם. See e.g. Clines 1993, 305.

disjunction between the main clauses does not occur in the LXX of Joshua.[293]

In the cases where ἤ appears as a rendering of the conjunction ו the subordinative conjunction is repeated in the Hebrew. The rare counterpart ἤ was used contrary to expectation.

2.5.4 *Free renderings*

Three times in my material the Hebrew conjunction ו at the beginning of a co-ordinated subordinate clause has been left without any visible counterpart in the translation. Every time the translator rearranged the grammatical structure of the passage so that the use of any conjunction became unnecessary. The cases are found in the LXX of Joshua.

Josh 2:9

– ידעתי כִּי נתן יהוה לכם את הארץ וְכִי נפלה אימתכם עלינו

ἐπίσταμαι ὅτι δέδωκεν ὑμῖν Κύριος τὴν γῆν, ἐπιπέπτωκεν γὰρ ὁ φόβος ὑμῖν ἐφ' ἡμᾶς

The Hebrew has two co-ordinate כי clauses that express what the citizens of Jericho knew about God's acts. The translator makes the second כי clause an explanation for the main clause (*I know that ... for the fear of you has fallen upon us.*) This has been made by using the Greek conjunction γάρ. The Hebrew ו was then naturally left without any visible equivalent.

Josh 17:16

ורכב ברזל בכל הכנעני הישב בארץ העמק לַאֲשֶׁר בבית שאן

ובנותיה וְלַאֲשֶׁר בעמק יזרעאל – καὶ ἵππος ἐπίλεκτος καὶ σίδη-

---

[293] In the LXX of the Pentateuch some cases of ἤ between main clauses do occur, see Aejmelaeus 1982, 67. Her listing of cases where ו is rendered by ἤ is incomplete. See Num 5:20 as a case that should be mentioned in her Chapter 3. Her conclusions, however, are valid despite the missing cases.

ρος τῷ Χαναναίῳ τῷ κατοικοῦντι ἐν Ἐμὰκ __ τῷ²⁹⁴ ἐν Βαιθσὰν
καὶ ἐν ταῖς κώμαις αὐτῆς __ἐν κοιλάδι Ἰεζραήλ
The co-ordinate Hebrew relative clauses have been transformed into
prepositional phrases. The location of the city Beth-Shean in the
Valley of Jezreel is made clear by omitting the conjunction.²⁹⁵ This
suggests that the translator was well-informed about the geographi-
cal details of Palestine.

Josh 22:22
‎יהוה הוא ידע וישראל הוא ידע אם במרד ואם במעל ביהוה‎ –
θεὸς αὐτὸς οἶδεν, καὶ Ἰσραὴλ αὐτὸς γνώσεται. εἰ ἐν ἀποστασίᾳ
__ἐπλημμελήσαμεν ἔναντι τοῦ Κυρίου
By modifying the clause structure the translator could omit the conjunction. He transformed the first subordinate clause into a prepositional phrase.

In the three cases listed the translator used a free rendering for the
conjunction ‎ו‎ and the subordinate Hebrew conjunction attached to it.
This is once again contrary to the supposition made in the introduction to the present chapter. I supposed that other renderings than
καί should be used in cases where the repetition of the Hebrew
subordinate conjunction does not occur.

2.5.5 Translation-technical evaluation

The Greek conjunction καί is the main equivalent for ‎ו‎ at the beginning of a co-ordinated subordinate clause. Here the use of καί is
unproblematic and corresponds to the Greek idiom.²⁹⁶

---

²⁹⁴ ἐν Ἐμὰκ τῷ is Margolis' emendation. The instance is complicated due to
many variants; e.g. MSS Bhqr with 𝔊 read ἐν αὐτῷ and MSS Gbckx with
𝔖 ἐν τῇ γῇ ἐν ἐμοι. For the evaluation of the variants see den Hertog 1996,
77.

²⁹⁵ The location indicated by the translator is in fact quite correct. The biblical
city Beth-Shean (the Hellenistic Σκυθόπολις) lies in the middle of the Valley
of Jezreel in between Mt. Gilboa and the River Jordan.

²⁹⁶ Aejmelaeus 1982, 155.

The translator of Joshua occasionally varied the rendering of ו. He did not always use καί as did the translator of Judges. The difference only confirms the general notion of the more literal character of Judges.

If one compares the translations of Joshua and Judges with those of the Pentateuch, one may note that Joshua is closest to the translations of Exodus and Numbers. The translation of Judges does not really correspond to any of the translations of the Pentateuch.[297] The similarities or differences are of very little significance here due to the limited material, however. Thus no valid conclusions can be drawn.

The material was intended to test Aejmelaeus' conclusion that instances where ו is attached to another conjunction in Hebrew would be more interesting from the translation-technical point of view. The repetition could perhaps trigger a free rendering of the co-ordinator.

TABLE 11 The renderings of the Hebrew conjunction ו at the beginning of a subordinate clause in the LXX of Joshua and Judges

	Joshua	Judges
Subordinator repeated		
καί	5	2
ἤ	2	0
Free	3	0
Subordinator not repeated		
καί	13	18

The clauses are divided into two groups; clauses where the subordinate conjunction is repeated at the beginning of every subordinate clause and clauses where the sub-ordinator appears only with the first subordinate clause in the chain.

---

[297] For the statistics concerning the Pentateuch see Aejmelaeus 1982, 155.

To test the conclusion an opposite theory was formed. I supposed that the translators would use a wide selection of equivalents in cases where the subordinate conjunction in Hebrew is not repeated. To verify my theory, I needed to collect all instances where 1 links two subordinate clauses. The advantage of my approach is that we can compare the renderings of the subordinate clauses where the subordinator is repeated with those where it is not repeated.

In my material the repetition is hardly ever avoided and the co-ordinator καί very often appears as the equivalent of 1. In cases where the Hebrew subordinator is not repeated the translators of Joshua and Judges employed καί alone as the rendering for 1.

Other renderings alongside καί were used if the repetition appears, but only in Joshua. Thus my theory was proved wrong. The "wider" collection of equivalents appears in renderings of 1 when the repetition is present. This, of course, verifies the statement by Aej-melaeus. On the other hand, one must remember that cases where an optional equivalent for the Hebrew co-ordinator appears are exceptional, since the selection of the Greek rendering is connected with the free rendering of the context. They also appear in Joshua alone.

3 The renderings of the Hebrew conjunction כי

3.1 The use of כי in Hebrew

The Hebrew conjunction כי is a multipurpose connective. This means that כי may be used to express various types of logical relationship between clauses.[1] In traditional grammars many different usages have been proposed but no agreed understanding about the functions of כי has been reached. It is, nevertheless, clear that כי is used at least to express nominalization[2] and to introduce various types of adverbial clauses.[3]

Aejmelaeus proposed a different way of understanding the use and function of כי in Hebrew. According to her, the use of כי may be divided into different groups depending on the *position* of the כי clause relative to the main clause. If the clause expressing the main event follows the כי clause, the כי clause is a circumstantial clause. If, on the other hand, the main event precedes the כי clause, the כי

---

[1]   Joüon-Muraoka's Hebrew grammar mentions the following instances as uses of כי: object clause and nominalization (§157), oaths (§165), and conditional clauses (§167, both protasis and apodosis!). Alongside these כי may function as an emphatic (§164), temporal (§166), consecutive (§169), causal (§170), concessive (§171), or adversative (§172) particle. Recently Kaddari compared the syntactical status of כי in Ben Sirach and in the OT by using a very similar approach to the use of כי; Kaddari 1997, 87-91. See also Clines 1998, 383-390.

[2]   Schoors 1981, 253-264. The use of כי to indicate nominalization is, according to Schoors, the most common way of using כי in the OT. He compared the nominalizing כי to the Greek conjunction ὅτι. The term 'nominalizing כי' is taken from Williams 1976 § 451.

[3]   Schoors 1981, 264-271.

clause is in the majority of cases a causal clause.[4] The כִּי clause following the main clause may also be an object clause or it may express a positive alternative after a negative clause, but in such cases the context clearly guides the reader. In this study Aejmelaeus' proposal has been followed, since it helps the modern reader to understand the possibilities the translators had at hand.

Independently of Aejmelaeus and prior to her study Bandstra suggested an almost identical way of understanding the Hebrew conjunction כִּי. Bandstra's main point was the question of the existence of the emphatic כִּי, which he wished to deny, but he enlarged the study to govern the whole syntax of כִּי in Classical Hebrew. The relative order of a כִּי clause and the clause with which it is linked is important in order to understand the function of the כִּי clause in Hebrew. A כִּי clause that precedes another clause is, according to Bandstra, either a circumstantial, conditional, or concessive clause. If the כִּי clause follows the other clause it is a causal, consequential, or adversative clause. By the term 'consequential clause' Bandstra refers to a clause that gives either a reason or a motivation for another clause. An 'adversative clause' means in his terminology the same as a clause expressing a positive alternative in Aejmelaeus' terminology.[5]

The multipurpose conjunction posed difficulties for the translators. Hebrew כִּי was a difficult conjunction to interpret and translate. There is no suitable standard equivalent to it in Greek. The translators, therefore, had to analyse the context of the כִּי clause in order to be able to render it correctly.[6] How did the translators of Joshua and Judges cope with כִּי?

Approximately 4000 Hebrew clauses commence with the conjunction כִּי in the Old Testament.[7] In the MT of Joshua it occurs 103

---

[4] Aejmelaeus 1986, 198-199.
[5] Bandstra 1982, 90-91. For the definitions of 'consequential' and 'adversative' see *ibid*, 136 and 149.
[6] Cf. Aejmelaeus 1993, 59: "before translating the translator had to check which kind of כִּי clause he was dealing with."
[7] Schoors 1981, 240. The figure is almost 4500 according to Clines 1998, 383.

times and in the MT of Judges 113 times.[8] In the following chapters the analysis of the material is divided into four categories. The first category includes cases where כי introduces a causal clause. The second category is made up of circumstantial clauses, the third category includes object clauses, and finally the fourth category includes clauses that express a positive alternative after a negative clause. This categorization of clauses is based on Hebrew, not on Greek. Also, it should be understood that the categorization here is based primarily on the logical relationship between the כי clause and its main clause. The position of the כי clause plays only a subsidiary role in the categorization.

3.2 Causal כי

Many instances where a כי clause in Hebrew follows the main clause have causal force. Causality here is to be understood in the wide sense of the word, since it may include such functions as reason, motivation, explanation, and cause.[9] Many Indo-European languages make a division between strong and weak causality by using different morphemes and different syntactical constructions,[10] but in other languages, including Hebrew, the same morpho-syntax marks various types of causality.[11]

Greek has several ways of expressing causality. It makes the distinction known from other Indo-European languages, and uses ὅτι

---

[8]   The following eight instances have been excluded from the analysis due to the differences between the MT and the OG: Josh 2:9, 2:15, 5:5, 5:7, 6:17, 14:3, 20:5 (x2).

[9]   Aejmelaeus 1993, 177. See also Bandstra 1982, 159-170.

[10]   See e.g. Hentschel 1989, 68. Hentschel discusses German, French, Serbo-Croatian, and English in its older form. The conjunctions *denn, car, jer*, and *for* in these languages express weaker causality, and they also commence — as traditional grammars state — co-ordinated clauses. The conjunctions *weil, parce que, zato što*, and *because*, on the other hand, commence a subordinated clause and express strong causality.

[11]   See Givón 1990, 834-835. According to Givón, the majority of languages do not distinguish between various aspects of causality. He called a clause expressing strong causality a *cause clause* and a clause expressing weaker causality a *reason clause*.

to express strong causality and γάρ to express weaker causality.[12] Thus, the Greek translator had to judge by assessing the content of the passage which Greek conjunction should be used to express the Hebrew parent text properly. Did the translators of Joshua and Judges take this kind of consideration into account?

In the MT of Joshua 62 causal clauses begin with the conjunction כִּי. In the MT of Judges the number of כִּי initial causal clauses is 75. The following discussion is divided according to the Greek equivalents used by the translators.

3.2.1 ὅτι

The most common rendering of the causal כִּי in the LXX is ὅτι. Yet ὅτι is not the most common causal conjunction in genuine Greek.[13] When Aejmelaeus searched for causal ὅτι clauses in genuine Greek, she found that ὅτι is extremely rare as a causal conjunction. Only a "handful" of cases occur in the text used by her.[14] She argues that ὅτι is not always the best possible equivalent for the causal כִּי in Hebrew. ὅτι expresses causality in a very precise way, but כִּי in Hebrew also expresses causality in the broader sense of the word. In cases where the causal clause provides only motivation or explanation on a rather general level, genuine Greek makes use of the conjunction γάρ.[15] It is therefore best to try to distinguish the idiomatic causal ὅτι from the unidiomatic motivational ὅτι.

---

[12] In addition to ὅτι one may use διότι, ἐπεί or ἐπείδη to express strong causality and ἐπεί or ὡς together with γάρ to express weaker causality; see Aejmelaeus 1993, 18. Aejmelaeus calls strong causality *direct* and weak causality *indirect*.

[13] For ὅτι as a causal conjunction in Greek see Kühner-Gerth II:2 § 569.2.

[14] Aejmelaeus 1993, 23-24. The texts used by Aejmelaeus are: the First Book of Polybius' *History*, Theophrastus' *Characters*, Epicurus' *Three Epistles*, Philodemus' ΠΕΡΙ ΟΙΚΟΝΟΜΙΑΣ, a selection of Ptolemaic papyri and inscriptions, the Letter of Aristeas and 2 Maccabees. For the editions she used see *ibid.*, 23 note 12.

[15] Aejmelaeus 1993, 20: "the Septuagint translators...used ὅτι even to introduce a motivation or an explanation in loose connection with the preceding context, although such expressions should really be governed by γάρ."

In the translation of Joshua ὅτι is used 30 times to render the Hebrew כי at the beginning of a causal clause.[16] In Judges the number
of cases is 71. Aejmelaeus divides the causal ὅτι clauses in the LXX
of the Pentateuch into idiomatic cases and unidiomatic cases. She
also describes the rest of the books of the LXX in the same manner,
but unfortunately she does not provide in her study a clear medium
for others to make a distinction in similar fashion to her.[17] Making a
complete distinction between idiomatic and unidiomatic cases is
difficult. The distinction may only be based on an interpretation of
the Greek text and the interpreter's ability to distinguish between a
motivational use and a causal use of ὅτι. As far as I can see, in the
LXX of Joshua 18 clauses represent the idiomatic use and 12 the
unidiomatic use. In Judges 51 cases represent the unidiomatic use of
ὅτι and only 19 cases represent the idiomatic use.[18]

The following examples illustrating the use of causal ὅτι are
divided into two groups. There are cases where the causal ὅτι has
been used correctly and cases where the ὅτι clause expresses merely
motivation and the use of the conjunction is therefore questionable.

Examples where ὅτι is used according to *normal Greek idiom*:

Josh 2:12

ועתה השבעו נא לי ביהוה כי עשיתי עמכם חסד ועשיתם גם אתם
עם בית אבי חסד – καὶ νῦν ὀμόσατέ μοι Κύριον τὸν θεόν, ὅτι
ποιῶ ὑμῖν ἔλεος, καὶ ποιήσατε καὶ ὑμεῖς ἔλεος ἐν τῷ οἴκῳ τοῦ
πατρός μου

---

[16] According to Aejmelaeus 1993, 27 sixty-nine cases are to be found in
Judges. This means that she interprets only one case differently than I, but
I am unable to tell which is the case in question.

[17] Aejmelaeus' expressions "in loose connection" (1993, 20), "little causal
force" (1993, 22) or "which would necessitate the rendering 'for'"(1993, 24)
are rather subjective in nature.

[18] Cf. Aejmelaeus 1993, 27: Two-thirds of the causal כי clauses represent the
type of usage where γάρ should have been preferred. The way I have divided
the material fits in with Aejmelaeus' description.

This instance is interpreted in such a way that כי or ὅτι introduces
a causal clause preceding the main clause.[19] It should be noted that
cases where the causal כי clause precedes the main clause are rather
rare and this example therefore represents an exception in my
material.

Josh 9:18

ולא הכום בני ישראל כי נשבעו להם נשיאי העדה ביהוה אלהי
ישראל – καὶ οὐκ ἐμαχέσαντο αὐτοῖς οἱ υἱοὶ Ἰσραήλ, ὅτι
ὤμοσαν αὐτοῖς πάντες οἱ ἄρχοντες Κύριον τὸν θεὸν Ἰσραήλ

Josh 14:12

ועתה תנה לי את ההר הזה אשר דבר יהוה ביום ההוא כי אתה
שמעת ביום ההוא – καὶ νῦν αἰτοῦμαί σε τὸ ὄρος τοῦτο, καθὰ
εἶπεν Κύριος τῇ ἡμέρᾳ ἐκείνῃ, ὅτι σὺ ἀκήκοας τὸ ῥῆμα τοῦτο
τῇ ἡμέρᾳ ἐκείνῃ

Judg 8:20

ולא שלף הנער חרבו כי ירא כי עודנו נער – καὶ οὐκ ἔσπασεν
τὸ παιδάριον αὐτοῦ τὴν μάχαιραν αὐτοῦ, ὅτι ἐφοβήθη, ὅτι ἦν
νεώτερος
This instance contains two causal ὅτι clauses. We may, therefore,
conclude that the translator did not always care to avoid repetition.

Judg 9:5

ויותר יותם בן ירבעל הקטן כי נחבא – καὶ ἀπελείφθη Ἰωαθὰμ
υἱὸς Ἰεροβάαλ ὁ νεώτερος, ὅτι ἐκρύβη

Judg 10:10

חטאנו לך וכי עזבנו את אלהינו ונעבד את הבעלים – ἡμάρτομέν
σοι, ὅτι ἐγκατελίπομεν τὸν θεὸν ἡμῶν καὶ ἐλατρεύσαμεν ταῖς
Βααλιμ
The use of the co-ordinating conjunction ו makes this case difficult
to interpret. The causal interpretation adopted by the translator is

---

[19] Compare the translation of Moatti-Fine (1996, 102): "*parce que* je pratique
la pitié envers vous, alors vous aussi vous pratiquerez la pitié envers la
maison de mon père" [Italics mine].

correct,[20] but it might also be possible to interpret the case as temporal.

Examples where ὅτι is used *contrary* to the normal Greek idiom are quite easy to find. These cases may be grouped into various subgroups. The largest of the subgroups includes cases where the ὅτι clause provides *a motivation for a command or prohibition.*[21]

Josh 1:11

הכינו לכם צידה כִּי בעוד שלשת ימים אתם עברים את הירדן הזה – ἑτοιμάζεσθε ἐπισιτισμόν, <u>ὅτι</u> ἔτι τρεῖς ἡμέραι καὶ ὑμεῖς διαβαίνετε τὸν Ἰορδάνην τοῦτον

Josh 3:5

התקדשו כִּי מחר יעשה יהוה בקרבכם נפלאות – ἁγνίσασθε εἰς αὔριον, <u>ὅτι</u> αὔριον ποιήσει ἐν ὑμῖν Κύριος θαυμαστά
The LXX plus εἰς αὔριον strengthens the linkage between the command and its explanation.

Josh 10:6

ועזרנו כִּי נקבצו אלינו כל מלכי האמרי – καὶ βοήθησον ἡμῖν <u>ὅτι</u> συνηγμένοι εἰσὶν ἐφ᾽ ἡμᾶς πάντες οἱ βασιλεῖς τῶν Ἀμορραίων

Judg 4:14

קום כִּי זה היום אשר נתן יהוה את סיסרא בידך – ἀνάστηθι, <u>ὅτι</u> αὕτη ἡ ἡμέρα, ἐν ᾗ παρέδωκεν Κύριος τὸν Σισαρὰ ἐν χειρί σου
Compare Judg 7:9, Judg 7:15, and Judg 8:21 for similar commands.

Judg 4:19

השקיני נא מעט מים כִּי צמאתי – πότισόν με δὴ μικρὸν ὕδωρ, <u>ὅτι</u> ἐδίψησα

---

[20] A similar interpretation is adopted in many modern translations too; see e.g. NRSV, NJB, Einheitsübersetzung, and TOB.

[21] For examples where a command or prohibition in the Pentateuch is motivated by a ὅτι clause see Aejmelaeus 1993, 21.

Judg 5:23

ארו ארור ישביה כי לא באו לעזרת יהוה – καταράσει καταρά
σασθε τοὺς ἐνοίκους αὐτῆς, ὅτι οὐκ ἤλθοσαν εἰς τὴν βοήθειαν
Κυρίου

This example is the only causal ὅτι clause in the poetic sections in
my material.

Josh 14:9

לך תהיה לנחלה ולבניך עד עולם כי מלאת אחרי יהוה אלהי –
σοὶ ἔσται ἐν κλήρῳ καὶ τοῖς τέκνοις σου εἰς τὸν αἰῶνα, ὅτι
προσετέθης ἐπακολουθῆσαι ὀπίσω Κυρίου τοῦ θεοῦ ἡμῶν

In fact the case is not a command but a *declaration*.

Josh 7:15

ישרף באש אתו ואת כל אשר לו כי עבר את ברית יהוה –
κατακαυθήσεται ἐν πυρὶ καὶ πάντα, ὅσα ἐστὶν αὐτῷ, ὅτι
παρέβη τὴν διαθήκην Κυρίου

Perhaps one should speak here of an *exhortation* or an *instruction*
rather than a command.

Judg 6:31

אם אלהים הוא ירב לו כי נתץ את מזבחו – εἰ ἔστιν θεός, αὐτὸς
ἐκδικήσει αὐτόν, ὅτι κατέσκαψεν τὸ θυσιαστήριον αὐτοῦ

Here the question in Hebrew is not one of a command but one of an
exhortation. In Greek the use of the future turns the Hebrew exhortation into an expression of belief or even conviction (*If he is God,
he will punish him*).

Josh 11:6

אל תירא מפניהם כי מחר כעת הזאת אנכי נתן את כלם חללים
לפני ישראל – μὴ φοβηθῇς ἀπὸ προσώπου αὐτῶν, ὅτι αὔριον
ταύτην τὴν ὥραν ἐγὼ παραδίδωμι τετροπωμένους αὐτοὺς ἐναν
τίον τοῦ Ἰσραήλ

Using a ὅτι clause to give a reason for fear is possible in genuine Greek.[22] Now, however, the explanation is so loose that one should not use ὅτι.

Occasionally (five times in the LXX of Judges) the ὅτι clause *explains a question*. In these cases there is the possibility of using a final clause as an equivalent of the Hebrew כי clause, but the translator did not use any final conjunction to render the Hebrew כי.

Judg 8:15

μὴ – הכף זבח וצלמנע עתה בידך כִּי נתן לאנשיך היעפים לחם
χεὶρ Ζέβεε καὶ Σαλμανὰ νῦν ἐν τῇ χειρί σου, ὅτι δώσομεν τοῖς ἀνδράσιν σου τοῖς ἐκλελυμένοις ἄρτους;
In this case, one wonders whether the translator intended to use a final clause despite the presence of the causal conjunction ὅτι, because he rendered the Hebrew *yiqtol* in the כי clause by the future tense. See also Judg 8:6 and Judg 14:3.

Judg 9:28

τί ἐστιν 'Αβιμέλεχ, καὶ τίς – מי אבימלך ומי שכם כִּי נעבדנו
ἐστιν ὁ υἱὸς Συχέμ, ὅτι δουλεύσομεν αὐτῷ;
Here too, the future tense gives a final colour in the Greek causal clause. Cf. Judg 9:38 and Judg 18:23.

Judg 11:12

τί ἐμοὶ καὶ σοί, ὅτι – מה לי ולך כִּי באת אלי להלחם בארצי
ἥκεις πρός με σὺ πολεμῆσαί με ἐν τῇ γῇ μου;
The Hebrew in this instance is commented on in KBL reference and described as a peculiar phrase.[23]

---

[22] Kühner-Gerth II:2 § 553.b.9.e. Consider e.g. an example from Xenophon (*Hist.* III.5.10): ὅτι δὲ πολλῶν ἄρχουσι, μὴ φοβηθῆτε, ἀλλὰ πολὺ μᾶλλον διὰ τοῦτο θαρρεῖτε "and do not be afraid *because* they rule over many, but much rather be of good courage on that account" (transl. Brownson).
[23] See also Aejmelaeus 1993, 176-177.

Judg 14:3

האין בבנות אחיך ... אשה כִּי אתה הולך לקחת אשה מפלשתים
– μὴ οὐκ ἔστιν ἀπὸ τῶν θυγατέρων τῶν ἀδελφῶν σου ... γυνή,
ὅτι σὺ πορεύῃ λαβεῖν γυναῖκα ἐκ τῶν ἀλλοφύλων;

Sometimes the ὅτι clause *motivates a question.*

Judg 21:5

מי אשר לא עלה בקהל מכל שבטי ישראל אל יהוה כִּי השבועה
הגדולה היתה לאשר לא עלה אל יהוה המצפה – τίς ὁ μὴ
ἀναβὰς ἐν τῇ ἐκκλησίᾳ ἐκ πασῶν φυλῶν Ἰσραὴλ πρὸς Κύριον;
ὅτι ὅρκος μέγας ἦν τῷ μὴ ἀναβάντι πρὸς Κύριον εἰς Μασσηφά

Judg 21:16

מה נעשה לנותרים לנשים כִּי נשמדה מבנימן אשה – τί ποιήσωμεν
τοῖς ἐπιλοίποις εἰς γυναῖκας; ὅτι ἠφάνισται ἐκ τοῦ Βενιαμὶν
γυνή

A negation may also be motivated by using a ὅτι clause.

Judg 2:17

וגם אל שפטיהם לא שמעו כִּי זנו אחרי אלהים אחרים וישתחוו
להם – καί γε τῶν κριτῶν αὐτῶν οὐκ ἐπήκουσαν, ὅτι ἐξεπόρνευ-
σαν ὀπίσω θεῶν ἑτέρων καὶ προσεκύνησαν αὐτοῖς

Often the linkage between the ὅτι clause and its main clause is very
opaque or the ὅτι clause provides an odd explanation for the main
incident.

Josh 17:1

ויהי הגורל למטה מנשה כִּי הוא בכור יוסף – καὶ ἐγένετο τὰ
ὅρια φυλῆς υἱῶν Μανασσή, ὅτι οὗτος πρωτότοκος τῷ Ἰωσήφ
Why is the status of Manasseh as Joseph's oldest son used to
explain the division of the land?

Judg 1:34

וילחצו האמרי את בני דן ההרה כי לא נתנו לרדת לעמק – καὶ
ἐξέθλιψεν ὁ Ἀμορραῖος τοὺς υἱοὺς Δὰν εἰς τὸ ὄρος, ὅτι οὐκ
ἀφῆκεν αὐτὸν καταβῆναι εἰς τὴν κοιλάδα

The explanation states the same thing as the main clause, but in other
words.

Judg 12:4

וילחם את אפרים ויכו אנשי גלעד את אפרים כי אמרו פליטי
מנשה אפרים אתם גלעד בתוך אפרים בתוך מנשה – καὶ ἐπολέμει τὸν
Ἐφραίμ, καὶ ἐπάταξαν ἄνδρες Γαλαὰδ τὸν Ἐφραίμ, [ὅτι εἶπαν
Οἱ διασεσωσμένοι τοῦ Ἐφραὶμ ὑμεῖς, Γαλαὰδ ἐν μέσῳ Ἐφραὶμ
καὶ ἐν μέσῳ Μανασσή][24]

Could the words of the Ephraimites be the reason for their defeat?[25]

Judg 13:16

ויאמר מלאך יהוה אל מנוח אם תעצרני לא אכל בלחמך ואם
תעשה עלה ליהוה תעלנה כי לא ידע מנוח כי מלאך יהוה הוא
– καὶ εἶπεν ὁ ἄγγελος Κυρίου πρὸς Μανῶε Ἐὰν βιάσῃ με, οὐ
φάγομαι τῶν ἄρτων σου, καὶ ἐὰν ποιήσῃς ὁλοκαύτωμα, Κυρίῳ
ἀνοίσεις αὐτό· ὅτι οὐκ ἔγνω Μανῶε ὅτι ἄγγελος Κυρίου ἐστίν

The fact that Manoah did not know that the man was an angel does
not explain anything here.

Judg 20:39

ובנימן החל להכות חללים באיש ישראל כשלשים איש כי אמרו
אך נגוף נגף הוא לפנינו – καὶ Βενιαμὶν ἦρκται τοῦ τύπτειν
τραυματίας ἐν τῷ ἀνδρὶ Ἰσραὴλ ὡσεὶ τριάκοντα ἄνδρας, ὅτι[26]
εἶπαν Πλὴν τροπούμενος τροποῦται ἐναντίον ἡμῶν

---

[24] MSS gloptv(w) and 𝔏 omit the ὅτι clause. It is difficult to decide whether
the omission is based on an attempt to increase the clarity of the text or
whether the MSS and 𝔏 represent the OG here.

[25] Interestingly NRSV adds a footnote referring to this verse: "Meaning of Heb
uncertain: Gk omits *because...Manasseh*." The MT does not contain any
strange words or expressions difficult to understand as such, but maybe the
logic of the passage is not quite clear. The assertion that the LXX omits the
Hebrew כי clause is based on the assumption that MSS gloptv (w) and 𝔏
represent the OG here.

[26] MSS Zglnoptvw have καί here.

Is the reply of the Benjaminites perhaps an indicator of their great courage?

Conclusions

ὅτι is the most frequently used equivalent of the Hebrew causal כִּי in my material. This is perhaps surprising, since ὅτι is not the most common causal conjunction in Greek. It seems therefore that the LXX translators used ὅτι more often as a causal conjunction than genuine Greek authors. One may conclude that the extensive use of ὅτι as a causal conjunction is a special feature of the LXX and perhaps a Hebraism.

TABLE 12 The use of unidiomatic causal ὅτι in the Pentateuch[27], Joshua and, Judges

N	Causal ὅτι	Unidiomatic ὅτι	%
Gen	68	23	34
Ex	12	1	8
Lev	40	26	65
Num	55	30	56
Dtn	102	74	73
Josh	30	12	40
Judg	71	52	73

Why, then, did the translators adopt ὅτι so often? To be able to understand the procedure followed by the translators one should

---

[27] The figures for the Pentateuch are based on Aejmelaeus 1993, 26. She does not provide the exact figures for the unidiomatic use of ὅτι in the various books of the Pentateuch, but it is possible to compute them from the figures she gives.

broaden one's view of the Hebrew causal כי clauses. If one widens one's perspective and takes into account all instances where the Hebrew has כי, it is easier to understand why the translators selected the conjunction ὅτι as a primary equivalent for the Hebrew causal כי. Besides the causal use of כי there are also many cases where כי introduces an object clause and ὅτι is a very suitable rendering for such occurrences of כי. This makes the use of ὅτι natural. Because the majority of כי clauses may be seen as either causal clauses or object clauses, ὅτι may be used in the majority of cases. Perhaps it is not the best possible choice every time that the translators employed it, but at least one may tolerate it.

Besides general considerations, there are special reasons for favouring ὅτι as a causal conjunction. ὅτι has advantages as a causal conjunction when compared with other Greek causal conjunctions, such as ἐπεί, ἐπείδη or ὡς. It expresses normal straightforward causality.[28] When discussing the use of καί and δέ as renderings of the ordinary main clause-initial Hebrew ו it was proposed that the translators might favour καί because of the word order. Perhaps the same holds true here too. ὅτι was probably favoured rather than γάρ because of the word order. One may consider one further possible explanation concerning the extensive use of ὅτι in the translations of Joshua and Judges – the usage in the Pentateuch. Once the use of ὅτι as a primary causal conjunction was established in the LXX of the Pentateuch, it must have been easier for other translators to adopt the same usage.

As the above examples show, ὅτι is used both in instances where it fits well and in instances where it is not the best available choice for the translators. A similar twofold usage is common in the LXX as a whole.

If the statistical data are used to arrange the books of the Pentateuch and Joshua and Judges in descending order the following list may be composed: Exodus, Genesis, Joshua, Numbers, Leviticus, Deuteronomy, Judges.

Joshua, in this respect, lies between Genesis and Numbers. This seems to fit in quite well with other available statistical data concerning these translations. *Judges*, on the other hand, resembles

---

[28] See Aejmelaeus 1993, 45.

Deuteronomy, because the translations contain an approximately
equal frequency of unidiomatic ὅτι clauses.

3.2.2 γάρ

Greek frequently uses γάρ to introduce a causal clause. The causal
force introduced by γάρ is weaker than causality introduced by ὅτι.[29]
From the point of view of the present study this is perhaps the most
important thing about γάρ. The use of γάρ is also syntactically different from the use of ὅτι. The former is often explained as introducing a co-ordinate clause, the latter a subordinate clause. Besides,
γάρ is never used as the first word in a clause.

In the LXX γάρ occurs more seldom than ὅτι. Nevertheless, in
cases where γάρ is employed its use is idiomatic. In the translation
of Joshua γάρ is used in 22 cases as a rendering of the Hebrew
causal כִּי. In Judges γάρ is really rare. It is used only *once* to render
causal כִּי.[30]

The examples in the following discussion are arranged in the same
way as the examples in the discussion concerning ὅτι as a rendering
of causal כִּי in the previous chapter.

The Greek γάρ clause explains *a command, an exhortation or a
prohibition*.

Josh 1:6

חֲזַק וֶאֱמָץ כִּי אַתָּה תַּנְחִיל אֶת הָעָם הַזֶּה אֶת הָאָרֶץ – ἴσχυε καὶ
ἀνδρίζου, σὺ γὰρ ἀποδιαστελεῖς[31] τῷ λαῷ τούτῳ τὴν γῆν

---

[29] See Kühner-Gerth II:2 § 545 and Denniston 1954, 56-98. For the use in
Papyri see Mayser II:3 § 164.4. Rijksbaron 1976, 158 sees the difference
between γάρ and ὅτι in a different way. According to Rijksbaron, γάρ introduces information that the reader does not know beforehand. In the LXX his
assertion, however, finds no support, since some γάρ clauses make reference
to known information. See e.g. Josh 10:4, where reference is made to the
beginning of chap. 10.

[30] There are only two γάρ clauses in Rahlfs' A text of Judges (19:14 and
21:22).

[31] MSS B*cmr with θ' read διελεῖς (= Margolis) the most widely attested
reading being ἀποδιαστελεῖς (= MSS AFMNθ multi = Rahlfs). Greenspoon

Josh 5:15

של נעלך מעל רגלך כִּי המקום אשר אתה עמד עליו קדש הוא
– λῦσαι τὸ ὑπόδημα ἐκ τῶν ποδῶν σου· ὁ γὰρ τόπος, ἐφ᾿ ᾧ νῦν[32]
ἕστηκας ἅγιός ἐστιν

Josh 10:8

אל תירא מהם כִּי בידך נתתים – μὴ φοβηθῇς αὐτούς, εἰς γὰρ
τὰς χεῖράς[33] σου παραδέδωκα αὐτούς
In Josh 11:6, an aforementioned example, the Greek ὅτι clause was
used to explain an exhortation not to fear.[34]

Josh 24:18

גם אנחנו נעבד את יהוה כִּי הוא אלהינו – ἀλλὰ καὶ ἡμεῖς λατρεύσομεν Κυρίῳ, οὗτος γὰρ θεὸς ἡμῶν ἐστίν
Note the interesting rendering ἀλλὰ καί.

Judg 21:22

חנונו אותם כי לא לקחנו איש אשתו במלחמה כִּי לא אתם נתתם
להם – ἐλεήσατε αὐτούς, ὅτι οὐκ ἔλαβον ἀνὴρ γυναῖκα αὐτοῦ
ἐν τῷ πολέμῳ· οὐ γὰρ ὑμεῖς δεδώκατε αὐτοῖς
This is the only case in Judges where γάρ is used to render the causal כי. It is quite possible that the translator wished to avoid repeat-
ing the same conjunction and therefore rendered the second כי by
γάρ. This is not, however, always the case with the translator of
Judges. E.g. in Judg 8:20, an example discussed earlier, he twice
used the conjunction ὅτι, even in very close proximity.[35]

In Joshua γάρ is quite common with commands, exhortations or
prohibitions. ὅτι occurs only seven times but γάρ is employed eleven
times. As one may conclude from the examples given, this is due to
the fact that the causality between the explanation and the command,

---

1983, 38 supports Margolis, but den Hertog 1996, 33 and Moatti-Fine 1996,
35 support Rahlfs.

[32] MSS Befjrsuz read νῦν (= Margolis). The majority of witnesses read σύ (=
Rahlfs). For the evaluation of the variants see den Hertog 1996, 88.

[33] The LXX seems to follow the *Kethib* here; see Margolis 1931, 175.

[34] The example is discussed on p. 147.

[35] The discussion appears on p. 145.

exhortation or prohibition is often weak. γάρ is simply a better alternative for expressing such causality.[36]

In Joshua γάρ is used in commencing a causal clause in other kinds of instances as well. There are eight cases in this category.

Josh 2:9-10

וכי נפלה אימתכם עלינו[37]... [10] כי שמענו את אשר הוביש יהוה את מי ים סוף – ἐπιπέπτωκεν γὰρ ὁ φόβος ὑμῶν ἐφ' ἡμᾶς· [10] ἀκηκόαμεν γὰρ ὅτι κατεξήρανεν Κύριος ὁ θεὸς τὴν ἐρυθρὰν θάλασσαν

Now the explanation is connected with the fear of the Israelities. Interestingly, the object clause (את אשר) commences with ὅτι.

Josh 10:2

וייראו מאד כי עיר גדולה גבעון – καὶ ἐφοβήθησαν ἐν αὐτοῖς[38] σφόδρα. ᾔδει γὰρ[39] ὅτι μεγάλη πόλις Γαβαών

The LXX includes a plus here, and it is quite possible that the translator had a Hebrew *Vorlage* different from the MT.

Josh 18:6-7

ויריתי לכם גורל פה לפני יהוה אלהינו [7] כי אין חלק ללוים בקרבכם כי כהנת יהוה נחלתו – καὶ ἐξοίσω ὑμῖν κλῆρον ἔναντι Κυρίου τοῦ θεοῦ ἡμῶν. [7] οὐ γὰρ ἔστιν μερὶς τοῖς υἱοῖς Λευεὶ ἐν ὑμῖν, ἱερατεια γὰρ[40] Κυρίου μερὶς αὐτοῦ

This instance includes two occurrences of γάρ.

---

[36] See also Aejmelaeus 1985, 118.
[37] The MT here includes a plus וכי נמגו כל ישבי הארץ מפניכם.
[38] MSS Bchqru and the margins of MSS v and z read ἀπ' αὐτῶν (= Margolis). For the evaluation of the variant, see den Hertog 1996, 36-37.
[39] MS G and 𝔖 preserve the obelus in front of ᾔδει.
[40] The conjunction ὅτι is supported by MSS Aθadgiklmnptuya₂b₂ 18 64 68 71 74 76 84 118 122 127 128 134 461 and 610. MS c does not include any conjunction. Margolis gives a different list for the evidence for ὅτι, but this is due to his misreading of the apparatus of BrM.

There are also three *special cases*.

Josh 2:9

ידעתי כי נתן יהוה לכם את הארץ וכי נפלה אימתכם עלינו –
ἐπίσταμαι ὅτι δέδωκεν ὑμῖν Κύριος τὴν γῆν, ἐπιπέπτωκεν γὰρ
ὁ φόβος ὑμῶν ἐφ' ἡμᾶς

The translation includes a causal clause, but the use of the co-ordinating conjunction ו shows that כי is, in fact, employed to mark nominalization.

Josh 17:1

למכיר בכור מנשה אבי הגלעד כי הוא היה איש מלחמה – τῷ
Μαχεὶρ πρωτοτόκῳ Μανασσὴ πατρὶ Γαλαάδ, ἀνὴρ γὰρ[41]
πολεμιστὴς ἦν

This instance is quite problematic, because the Hebrew text is un-clear. It states that the reason why Machir received a plot of land by lottery is connected with his warlike character.

Josh 23:11-13

ונשמרתם מאד לנפשתיכם לאהבה את יהוה אלהיכם כי אם 12
שוב תשובו ... 13 ידוע תדעו כי לא יוסיף יהוה אלהיכם להוריש
את הגוים האלה – καὶ φυλάξασθε σφόδρα τοῦ ἀγαπᾶν Κύριον
τὸν θεὸν ὑμῶν. 12 ἐὰν γὰρ ἀποστραφῆτε ... 13 γινώσκετε ὅτι οὐ
μὴ προσθῇ Κύριος τοῦ ἐξολεθρεῦσαι τὰ ἔθνη ταῦτα

Conclusions

The examples given indicate that the translators employed γάρ in an idiomatic way. The basic question regarding the use of γάρ does not, therefore, lie in the grammatical correctness of the translation. Instead, the question is one of the frequency of γάρ. It is well known that γάρ is a very common conjunction in Greek.[42] In the LXX, and especially in the translations of Joshua and Judges, the situation is

---

[41] MSS gn 127 read the conjunction ὅτι and MSS elq do not include any conjunction at all. The conjunction γάρ is supported by MSS Gab*b*ckx 18 64 and 128. 𝔖 also seems to support γάρ.

[42] Aejmelaeus 1993, 24 writes: "γάρ was found to be extremely common in all texts, except in the official papyrus texts and inscriptions."

quite the opposite of the genuine use of the conjunction: γάρ is rare.[43]

The immediate reason for the rarity of γάρ in the LXX seems to be the heavy use of ὅτι as the causal conjunction. The translators regarded ὅτι as the primary equivalent of the Hebrew כִּי, despite the differing function of כִּי. Because the Hebrew causal כִּי was very often rendered by ὅτι, the use of other causal conjunctions as equivalents was naturally less frequent. The extensive use of γάρ in renderings of the Hebrew causal כִּי would have been an easy procedure to adopt. If the translators had used γάρ, many problematic cases would have disappeared. γάρ bearing only weak causal force fits in very well as the counterpart of the Hebrew causal כִּי.

But if the translator wished to express strong causality, γάρ was unsuitable, since the causal force carried by γάρ is weak. Perhaps the syntactical position of γάρ also played some part here. γάρ is a postpositive conjunction. Here there seems to be an analogy to the use of the co-ordinating conjunction δέ, which is also a postpositive conjunction and rather seldom used in the LXX. Perhaps the word order made it difficult to use a postpositive conjunction.

The translators seem to be aware that ὅτι is not always the best choice for the Hebrew causal כִּי; they did not always use it. One may conclude that the translators' linguistic abilities matched the task of translation, but their products, the translations, do not fully reflect their abilities. This must be due to the translation techniques applied.

When γάρ is compared with the use of ὅτι in the translations of Joshua and Judges the following figures may be computed. The ratio of γάρ to all renderings of the Hebrew causal כִּי in Joshua is 34% and in Judges 1%.

Aejmelaeus compares the use of γάρ with the total number of occurrences of γάρ and of unidiomatic ὅτι cases and describes this total as cases where γάρ "could have appeared".[44] If such figures are

---

[43] For a general description of the use of γάρ in the LXX see Aejmelaeus 1993, 26-29.

[44] One has to bear in mind that Aejmelaeus claims that the most suitable way to use γάρ would have been to employ it in every case where the unidiomatic ὅτι appears but not in cases where ὅτι is used idiomatically. Here I see a problem, because γάρ is used to mark weak causality and one may

computed for Joshua and Judges, the following percentages are
revealed: for Joshua the ratio of γάρ to all potential cases is 65% and
for Judges it is 2%.

TABLE 13 The use of γάρ in the LXX of the Pentateuch[45], Joshua
and Judges

	Number of γάρ clauses	% of all causal יכ clauses	% of potential clauses
Gen	87	55	78
Ex	79	85	96
Lev	23	35	45
Num	20	27	40
Dtn	35	26	32
Josh	**22**	**34**	**65**
Judg	1	1	2

In the Pentateuch the freer translators, those of Exodus and Genesis, used the conjunction γάρ more often than did the literal translators. The translator of Joshua almost matches the free translators
of the Pentateuch, but the translator of Judges seemingly worked in
quite a different way from any of the translators of the Pentateuch.
He used γάρ only once, and the only instance may be explained as
a result of attempting to avoid using ὅτι twice within a limited context. Thus, the result of using the conjuction γάρ resembles the result
of using the causal ὅτι discussed earlier.[46]

---

use it idiomatically in *every possible* causal clause. It is only the use of ὅτι
that imposes certain limitations.

[45] The statistics for the Pentateuch are based on Aejmelaeus 1993, 26.

[46] See pp. 151-153.

3.2.3 διότι

διότι is the third causal conjunction used in renderings of the Hebrew causal כי in the LXX of Joshua and Judges. διότι is closely related to the conjunction ὅτι and may be used, like ὅτι, to introduce both causal clauses and object clauses. According to the reference works, the first author to employ διότι was Herodotus.[47] διότι appears infrequently in the LXX. In my material it is used twice to render the causal כי.[48]

Josh 6:25

– וַתֵּשֶׁב בְּקֶרֶב יִשְׂרָאֵל עַד הַיּוֹם הַזֶּה כִּי הֶחְבִּיאָה אֶת הַמַּלְאָכִים
καὶ κατῴκησεν ἐν τῷ Ἰσραὴλ ἕως τῆς σήμερον ἡμέρας, <u>διότι</u> ἔκρυψεν τοὺς κατασκοπεύσαντας

Judg 11:13

וַיֹּאמֶר מֶלֶךְ בְּנֵי עַמּוֹן אֶל מַלְאֲכֵי יִפְתָּח כִּי לָקַח יִשְׂרָאֵל אֶת אַרְצִי
בַּעֲלוֹתוֹ מִמִּצְרַיִם – καὶ εἶπεν βασιλεὺς υἱῶν Ἀμμὼν πρὸς τοὺς ἀγγέλους Ἰεφθάε <u>Διότι</u> ἔλαβεν Ἰσραὴλ τὴν γῆν μου ἐν τῇ ἀναβάσει αὐτοῦ ἐξ Αἰγύπτου
Whether one should interpret this as a causal clause or as an object clause, depends on the interpretation of the wider context. Since the question concerns an answer given by the king of Ammon, it is natural to interpret the instance as a causal clause.[49]

3.2.4 διὰ τό with an infinitive

As is well known, using an infinitive construction instead of a subordinate clause is quite possible in Greek. The construction διὰ

---

[47] See Kühner-Gerth II:2 § 550, Smyth 1956 § 2578 and Aejmelaeus 1993, 18.

[48] In the Pentateuch similar cases are Gen 26:22, 29:32, Lev 22:20, 25:23, 25:42, and Dtn 31:17 (עַל כִּי).

[49] Cf. Aejmelaeus 1993, 27 note 15. On p. 184 Aejmelaeus writes: "Further-more, when direct speech is introduced by כי, this need not be understood as an emphatic particle. We are often dealing with an answer to a why question, or כי may otherwise be understood as causal."

τό with an infinitive bears causal force in Greek[50] and it is from time to time used to render a Hebrew causal clause in the LXX.[51] There are two cases in the translations of Joshua and Judges.

Josh 5:7

ואת בניהם הקים תחתם אתם מל יהושע כִּי ערלים היו כי לא

בדרך אותם מלו – ἀντὶ δὲ τούτων ἀντικατέστησεν τοὺς υἱοὺς αὐτῶν οὓς Ἰησοῦς περιέτεμεν <u>διὰ τὸ</u> αὐτοὺς <u>γεγενῆσθαι</u> κατὰ τὴν ὁδὸν ἀπεριτμήτους

The whole paragraph is quite freely rendered here.

Judg 3:12

ויחזק יהוה את עגלון מלך מואב על ישראל <u>עַל כִּי</u> עשו את הרע

בעיני יהוה – καὶ ἐνίσχυσεν Κύριος τὸν Ἐγλὼμ βασιλέα Μωὰβ ἐπὶ τὸν Ἰσραὴλ <u>διὰ τὸ πεποιηκέναι</u> αὐτοὺς τὸ πονηρὸν ἔναντι Κυρίου

In this instance the Hebrew conjunction כי is linked with the preposition על.[52]

3.2.5 ὅτε

Once the Greek text employs a temporal ὅτε clause[53] to render a weak causal כי clause.[54] The instance is, of course, a special case.

---

[50] See Kühner-Gerth II:2 § 478.3-4 and Blass-Debrunner-Rehkopf § 402.1.

[51] Soisalon-Soininen 1965, 133. See also p. 130, where Soisalon-Soininen mentions Ex 33:3 as an example of a Hebrew כי clause rendered by the construction διὰ τό with an infinitive.

[52] The case is mentioned by Soisalon-Soininen 1965, 133 and 152. The combination על כי is found only five times in the MT (Dtn 31:17, Judg 3:12, Ps 139:14, Jer 4:28, and Mal 2:14)

[53] Nilson 1907, 51 notes that the temporal function (in his terminology *Bedeutung*) of ὅτε may easily be changed to a causal one.

[54] In the Pentateuch no such cases exist. Instead ὅτε is used to render a construction ב with the *inf.c.* There are only three instances where this is not the case (Gen 11:10, a co-ordinated clause in Hebrew; Gen 24:30, a construction ב + *inf.c.*; and Lev 26:45, an אשר clause). In Joshua ὅτε is used in the same way as in the Pentateuch. Note, however, Josh 14:11, where ביום שלח אותי משה is rendered as ὅτε ἀπέστειλέν με Μωυσῆς. In Judges the major-

Judg 8:1

מה הדבר הזה עשית לנו לבלתי קראות לנו כי הלכת להלחם
במדין – τί τὸ ῥῆμα τοῦτο ἐποίησας ἡμῖν τοῦ μὴ καλέσαι ἡμᾶς,
ὅτε ἐξεπορεύου πολεμῆσαι ἐν τῇ Μαδιάμ;

Here the Hebrew כי clause expresses the reason for the question.[55]
Similar כי clauses are rendered by ὅτι instead.[56] Now, the translator
probably saw the כי clause as related to the verb קרא in Hebrew
and thus thought it possible to use a temporal equivalent for the
causal כי.

3.2.6 εἰ

Sometimes the כי clause may be interpreted as expressing the conditions under which the main action takes place. Thus it is understandable that the translators could use conditional clauses to render
the causal כי clauses. In my material only the translator of Joshua
employed conditional clauses to render causal כי clauses.

Josh 2:5

רדפו מהר אחריהם כי תשיגום – καταδιώξατε ὀπίσω αὐτῶν, εἰ
καταλήμψεσθε αὐτούς

Josh 17:15

עלה לך היערה ובראת לך שם בארץ הפרזי והרפאים כי אץ
לך הר אפרים – ἀνάβηθι εἰς τὸν δρυμὸν καὶ ἐκκάθαρον σεαυτῷ,
εἰ στενοχωρεῖ σε τὸ ὄρος τὸ Ἐφράιμ

Here the MT provides a longer text than the LXX, but the grammatical structure is similar.[57]

---

ity of cases include in Hebrew the combination ויהי כי. In Judg 2:2 מה
עשיתם זאת is rendered as ὅτε ταῦτα ἐποιήσατε.

[55] Many modern translations employ a temporal clause to render the particular
כי clause; see e.g. NRSV, Einheitsübersetzung, or TOB.
[56] See pp. 148-149..
[57] Cf. Moatti-Fine 1996, 195.

The aforementioned two cases constitute the conditional renderings of the causal כי clauses in my material. In both cases the question is one of indefinite conditions in Greek.

3.2.7 *Free renderings*

The cases where the translators used either καί or δέ to translate the causal כי are results of free rendering. The translator modified the Hebrew grammatical construction by using the co-ordinating conjunction. There are four cases in my material.

Josh 8:6

ויצאו אחרינו עד התיקנו אותם מן העיר כי יאמרו נסים לפנינו
– καὶ ὡς ἂν ἐξέλθωσιν ὀπίσω ἡμῶν, ἀποσπάσομεν αὐτοὺς ἀπὸ τῆς πόλεως. καὶ ἐροῦσιν Φεύγουσιν οὗτοι ἀπὸ προσώπου ἡμῶν
The translator recast the grammatical structure of his parent text.[58] The main clause was turned into a temporal clause and the infinitive construction into a main clause. Thereafter it was probably natural to employ a co-ordinated main clause instead of a causal clause.

Judg 16:24

ויראו אתו העם ויהללו את אלהיהם כי אמרו נתן אלהינו בידינו
את אויבנו – καὶ εἶδεν αὐτὸν ὁ λαὸς καὶ ἤνεσαν τοὺς θεοὺς αὐ-τῶν καὶ εἶπαν Παρέδωκεν ὁ θεὸς ἡμῶν τὸν ἐχθρὸν ἡμῶν ἐν χειρὶ ἡμῶν
In this instance the translator transformed the Hebrew כי clause into a co-ordinated main clause. It is possible that the verb אמר followed by direct speech affected the translator's rendering.

Judg 20:41

ויבהל איש בנימן כי ראה כי נגעה עליו הרעה – καὶ ἔσπευσεν ἀνὴρ Βενιαμὶν καὶ εἶδεν ὅτι ἧπται αὐτοῦ ἡ κακία

---

[58] See Soisalon-Soininen 1965, 114, who saw the Greek as either the result of free rendering or as a rendering based on a Hebrew *Vorlage* different from the MT.

Here the Hebrew text includes two כִּי conjunctions following one another in a very narrow context. Probably the following context (כִּי רָאָה) affected the translator's choice of words.

Josh 11:10

וַיִּלְכֹּד אֶת חָצוֹר וְאֶת מַלְכָּה הִכָּה בֶחָרֶב כִּי חָצוֹר לְפָנִים הִיא רֹאשׁ כָּל הַמַּמְלָכוֹת הָאֵלֶּה – καὶ κατελάβετο Ἀσὼρ καὶ τὸν βασιλέα αὐτῆς. ἦν δὲ Ἀσὼρ τὸ πρότερον ἄρχουσα πασῶν τῶν βασιλειῶν τούτων

Now the translator of Joshua employed δέ as a rendering of the Hebrew כִּי. The relationship between the Hebrew כִּי clause and its immediate context is a very loose one. Clearly the כִּי clause does not explain or provide circumstances for the military operation against Hazor.

3.2.8 *Omissions*

Occasionally the visible Greek counterpart for כִּי does not appear in the LXX. The difficulty with these cases lies in the question of the Hebrew *Vorlage* of the LXX. How do we know if and when the *Vorlage* deviated from the present Massoretic text? Despite the problem I shall try to explain the cases as resulting from the translator's interpretation of the Hebrew. The cases appear in the LXX of Joshua alone.

Josh 1:8

תִּשְׁמֹר לַעֲשׂוֹת כְּכָל הַכָּתוּב בּוֹ כִּי אָז תַּצְלִיחַ אֶת דְּרָכֶךָ – συνῇς[59]

---

[59] Margolis reads εἰδῇς as MS B and the margins of MSS M and z. The majority reading is συνῇς. It is difficult to know which is more likely to have been the OG. The translator very often used φυλάσσω to render שמר. Only here and in verse 22:2 (שמר = ἀκούω) did he alter the rendering. Besides, συνίημι (*to understand*) does not differ too much in meaning from ὁράω (*to see*) in this context. Den Hertog 1996, 33-34 recognizes the difficulty involved here, but follows the majority reading, arguing that εἰδῇς is a stylistic correction.

ποιεῖν πάντα τὰ γεγραμμένα. ___ τότε εὐοδωθήσῃ καὶ εὐοδώσεις[60] τὰς ὁδούς σου

Possibly the translator considered the equivalent for כי as unnecessary because of the presense of τότε.

Josh 5:14

ויאמר לא כי אני שר צבא יהוה – ὁ δὲ εἶπεν αὐτῷ _ Ἐγὼ ἀρχιστράτηγος δυνάμεως Κυρίου

The translator seems to have read לו instead of לא. Consequently, the translator probably simply left כי at the beginning of the direct speech without any visible counterpart.

Josh 7:13

התקדשו למחר כי כה אמר יהוה אלהי ישראל חרם בקרבך – ἁγιασθῆναι εἰς αὔριον· _ τάδε λέγει Κύριος ὁ θεὸς Ἰσραήλ Τὸ ἀνάθεμα ἐν ὑμῖν ἐστιν

Here כי following a command expresses rather loose causality. The omission does not affect the content and it is even possible that the translator thought it better not to use any equivalent for כי.

Josh 7:15

ישרף באש אתו ואת כל אשר לו כי עבר את ברית יהוה וכי עשה נבלה בישראל – κατακαυθήσεται ἐν πυρὶ καὶ πάντα, ὅσα ἐστιν αὐτῷ, ὅτι παρέβη τὴν διαθήκην Κυρίου καὶ _ ἐποίησεν ἀνόμημα ἐν Ἰσραήλ

The omission is understandable because the instance includes two co-ordinated causal כי clauses in Hebrew.

Josh 9:22, 24

וידבר אליהם לאמר למה רמיתם אתנו ... 24 ויענו את יהושע ויאמרו כי הגד הגד לעבדיך את אשר צוה יהוה אלהיך את משה את הארץ לכם לתת עבדו – καὶ εἶπεν αὐτοῖς Διά τί παρελογίσασθέ με ...; 24 καὶ ἀπεκρίθησαν τῷ Ἰησοῖ λέγοντες _ Ἀνηγγέλη ἡμῖν ὅσα συνέταξεν Κύριος ὁ θεός σου Μωυσῇ τῷ παιδὶ αὐτοῦ δοῦναι ὑμῖν τὴν γῆν ταύτην

---

[60] εὐοδωθήσῃ καὶ εὐοδώσεις is a double reading. Margolis tries to solve the problem by following the reading of MSS Bcz, but omits the first part (εὐοδωθήσῃ καί). See den Hertog 1996, 83-84.

The causal כִּי introduces an answer to the question 'why' posed by Joshua. The omission is probably the consequence of rendering וַיֹּאמְרוּ as the participle λέγοντες. The case has, therefore, similarities to Josh 5:14, discussed earlier.

Josh 24:16-17

חֲלִילָה לָּנוּ מֵעֲזֹב אֶת יְהוָה לַעֲבֹד אֱלֹהִים אֲחֵרִים¹⁷כִּי יְהוָה אֱלֹהֵינוּ הוּא הַמַּעֲלֶה אֹתָנוּ – μὴ γένοιτο ἡμῖν καταλιπεῖν Κύριον ὥστε λατρεύειν θεοῖς ἑτέροις. ¹⁷__ Κύριος ὁ θεὸς ἡμῶν αὐτὸς θεός ἐστιν, αὐτὸς ἀνήγαγεν ἡμᾶς

Since the LXX differs slightly from the MT at the beginning of verse 17, it has been proposed that the *Vorlage* deviated from the MT.⁶¹ This explanation is, however, unnecessary. Probably the translator wished to emphasize monotheistic belief and thus turned the causal clause into a main clause.

3.2.9 *Translation-technical evaluation*

ὅτι is the most frequently used rendering of the causal כִּי in the LXX of Joshua and Judges. It appears 101 times in my material. 30 instances occur in Joshua and 71 in Judges. The frequency of ὅτι in relation to all causal כִּי clauses in Joshua is 48% and in Judges 95%. The frequent use of causal ὅτι is foreign to genuine Greek; thus the LXX bears a foreign flavour.

Not only is the relative frequency of causal ὅτι very high, but occasionally it is not even the best possible choice of rendering. ὅτι marks strong causality, but not all of the causal כִּי clauses carry strong causality. Even so, perhaps the use of ὅτι is tolerable at least.⁶²

---

⁶¹ Margolis 1992, 464 supposes that the Hebrew text might have been יהוה אלהינו הוא האלהים המעלה but he followed here a minority Greek reading and restored the LXX as Κύριος ὁ θεὸς ἡμῶν αὐτὸς θεός ἐστιν ὅς ἀνήγαγεν κτλ. His comment was: "ὅς is restored from Or_g; comp. the doublet in S; ὅς was corrupted into αυτος (ουτος)." I am relying on Rahlfs and the best MSS here. Cf. den Hertog 1996, 91.

⁶² See pp. 151-152 and examples on pp. 146-151.

Four reasons for the frequent use of ὅτι may be posited. ὅτι is suitable and idiomatic *in other cases* of כי than the causal. If כי marks nominalization, ὅτι is almost the only possible way to translate it. Also, the grammatical function of ὅτι resembles in some respects that of כי. Both conjunctions mark *normal straightforward causality* despite the fact that כי is often merely motivational. Perhaps the *word order* plays some role here, too. When using ὅτι, the translator did not need to change the word order of the parent text. Had he employed γάρ, another main equivalent for causal כי, he would have needed to change the word order. A close analogy to the use of καί instead of δέ in renderings of the main clause initial ו is clear. There is, to my mind, the possibility that the translators of Joshua and Judges adopted the frequent use of causal ὅτι from *a model*, viz. the older translations of the Pentateuch.[63]

TABLE 14 The renderings of the causal כי in the LXX of Joshua and Judges

N	Josh	Judg	Josh %	Judg %
Causal ὅτι	18	19	28	25
Motivational ὅτι	12	52	19	68
γάρ	22	1	34	1
διότι	1	1	2	1
διὰ τό + inf	1	1	2	1
ὅτε		1	0	1
εἰ	2		3	0
Free renderings	2	2	4	3
Omissions	6		9	0
Total .	**64**	**77**	**101**	**100**

---

[63] For the discussion of the reasons for using causal ὅτι, see pp. 151-152.

The use of ὅτι is important as concerns translation technique. It shows that the translators picked up the equivalent without thorough consideration. Otherwise, they would surely have employed ὅτι far more seldom than they actually did. At least the cases where ὅτι is used unidiomatically to mark a loose causality would not appear in the LXX. The manner of translating the causal כי thus fits very well the description of narrow segmentation and "easy" technique.

The second most frequent equivalent of the causal כי in the LXX of Joshua and Judges is γάρ. The difference between γάρ and ὅτι is of interest for the translation-technical analysis. Whereas ὅτι has a limited function as a causal conjunction, the function of γάρ is broader. γάρ may be used to introduce practically any causal clause. This being the case, it is perhaps surprising that γάρ is not the basic equivalent for the causal כי while ὅτι is.

My material contains 23 cases of γάρ as the equivalent of the causal כי. The difference between Joshua and Judges is remarkable. While the translator of Joshua employed γάρ 22 times to render the causal כי the translator of Judges used it only once.[64] This fact shows that the translators did not employ the same translation technique. Since the translator of Judges really seldom perceived the need for another causal conjunction than ὅτι, one may safely conclude that he was not always aware of the context.

The translators of Joshua and Judges used other conjunctions besides ὅτι and γάρ to render the causal כי. Usually the use of another rendering than the conjunctions ὅτι and γάρ seems to fit the context in question. The use of rare equivalents therefore indicates that the translators considered the Hebrew parent text and tried to express the meaning, as they saw it, within the limits of their working habits, their translation technique.

These rare cases indicate that the translators could employ a free rendering if they chose to do so. In order to understand the translation technique of Judges this is, naturally, an important notion. Only taking ὅτι and γάρ into consideration one might perhaps think that the translator of Judges actively attempted to limit the number

---

[64] The translator of Judges employed γάρ twice. The cases appear in Judg 19:14 and 21:22. See p. 54 and 154.

of equivalents and thus tried to mark the conjunction in the parent text. Since he sometimes even used a temporal clause to render a causal כי clause, this cannot be the case. The explanation for the monotonous character of the translation should be sought in another direction, that is, the narrow segmentation as the strong basis of the translation technique.

If we compare the translators of Joshua and Judges with the translators of the Pentateuch, the translator of Joshua evidently comes closer to the translators of Genesis and Exodus. The translator of Judges is different from all the translators of the Pentateuch. The difference culminates in the use of the conjunction γάρ. The very low ratio of γάρ clauses in relation to all renderings of the causal כי clauses is exceptional and shows how great was the influence of the narrow segmentation.

3.3 Circumstantial כי

According to Aejmelaeus, when a כי clause precedes the main clause, it expresses the circumstance(s) pertaining to the following main clause.[65] These כי clauses may be interpreted as causal, conditional or temporal, depending on the relationship between the circumstance and the main event.

If the narrow segmentation sets limits to the process of translation, and I do not see any reason to argue against this, we may suppose that the translators had difficulty in recognising the context and its implications outside the segment being translated. If the translation of כי demanded that the translator check the nature of the כי clause, there might occur several cases where the translators made a *faux pas* in choosing the Greek counterpart for כי. Also, we may suppose that they knew the context that was already translated better than the context following the segment on which they were concen-

---

[65] Aejmelaeus 1993, 170-171. See also Bandstra 1982, 90 and 121, who recognizes three different types of circumstantial כי: temporal, conditional and concessive.

trating.[66] The latter supposition is really relevant when studying the renderings of the circumstantial כי. We must, therefore, ask how far the translators of Joshua and Judges could consider the context and especially the following main clause.

The best way to answer the question is to look at the actual cases where the circumstantial כי appears in Joshua and Judges. These books include 16 circumstantial clauses. Again, the following discussion is arranged according to the Greek equivalents used by the LXX translators of Joshua and Judges.

3.3.1 ὅτε

The Greek conjunction ὅτε is the equivalent most often employed in the LXX of Joshua and Judges. ὅτε occurs in cases where the action in the main clause takes place at the time indicated in the temporal clause.[67] The cases appear in the translation of Judges only[68] and they all resemble each other.[69]

Judg 1:28

ויהי כי חזק ישראל וישם את הכנעני למס – καὶ ἐγένετο ὅτε ἐνίσχυσεν Ἰσραήλ, καὶ ἔθετο τὸν Χαναναῖον εἰς φόρον

The כי clause is preceded by the formula ויהי. The translator employed the apodotic καί to link the temporal clause and the main clause. This often happens if the subordinate clause bears temporal force.

Judg 16:16

ויהי כי הציקה לו בדבריה כל הימים ותאלצהו ותקצר נפשו למות – καὶ ἐγένετο ὅτε κατειργάσατο αὐτὸν τοῖς λόγοις αὐτῆς

---

[66] Soisalon-Soininen 1987, 28-39 and Aejmelaeus 1993, 11.

[67] Kühner-Gerth II:2 § 566.1 and § 569.1. See also Brandt 1908, 28.

[68] ὅτε is never employed as the equivalent for כי in the Pentateuch or in Joshua. The most common Hebrew equivalent for a ὅτε clause in these books is the construction ב + inf.c. See note 55 on pp. 160-161.

[69] There are 5 ὅτε clauses in the LXX of Judges. One of these is discussed earlier in this study on page 161 (Judg 8:1) and the fifth case is in Judg 2:2, where the ὅτε clause is employed to render a מה clause in the Hebrew.

ὅλην τὴν νύκτα καὶ παρηνώχλησεν αὐτόν, καὶ ὠλιγοψύχησεν
ἕως εἰς θάνατον

Judg 16:25

וַיְהִי כִּי טוֹב [70] לִבָּם וַיֹּאמְרוּ – καὶ ἐγένετο ὅτε[71] ἠγαθύνθη ἡ καρδία αὐτῶν, καὶ εἶπαν
Here the *kethib* is followed.

In cases where ὅτε is used the Hebrew clauses have things in
common. Every time the conjunction כִּי is preceded by the formula
וַיְהִי marking the temporal nature of the clause. The action in the
main clause is a consequence of the action in the כִּי clause.[72] Thus,
the equivalent ὅτε is suitable in these cases. The cases appear in the
narrative only.

3.3.2 *ὅταν*

The Greek conjunction ὅταν is a combination of ὅτε and ἄν. Like
ὅτε, it introduces a temporal clause. The difference between ὅτε and
ὅταν is not notable. The use of ὅταν introduces a hypothetical
colouring.[73] The action of the main clause takes place when and if
the temporal clause is fulfilled.

Josh 4:6

כִּי יִשְׁאָלוּן בְּנֵיכֶם מָחָר לֵאמֹר מָה הָאֲבָנִים הָאֵלֶּה לָכֶם [7] וַאֲמַרְתֶּם
לָהֶם – ἵνα ὅταν ἐρωτᾷ σε ὁ υἱός σου αὔριον λέγων Τί εἰσιν οἱ
λίθοι οὗτοι ὑμῖν; [7] καὶ σὺ δηλώσεις τῷ υἱῷ σου

---

[70] The *Qere* is וַיְהִי כְּטוֹב.

[71] MSS dp read ὅταν.

[72] The logical relationship between the כִּי clause and the main clause comes
close to causality. Cf. Aejmelaeus 1993, 173, who refers to the ambiguity
between temporal and causal clauses on a general level.

[73] Brandt 1908, 16. See also LSJ. The special colouring is here due to the pro-
spective subjunctive; see Kühner-Gerth II:1 § 394. The use of the pro-
spective subjunctive in renderings of כִּי clauses with *yiqtol* in the Pentateuch
is discussed by Voitila 1995, 207-209. His material includes two temporal
ὅταν clauses (Ex 3:21 and Num 11:29).

The temporal construction in Hebrew looks towards the future. This makes the use of ὅταν appropriate. Why the translator employed both ἵνα and ὅταν to render the Hebrew כִּי, is difficult to say. The use of ἵνα links the passage with the preceding context and with the command to pick up stones from the River Jordan. The use of ὅταν, on the other hand, ties the clause and the embedded question to the following answer.

Josh 17:18

והיה לך תצאתיו כִּי תוריש את הכנעני כי רכב ברזל לו – καὶ
ἔσται σοι, καὶ[74] ὅταν ἐξολεθρεύσῃς τὸν Χαναναῖον, ὅτι ἵππος
ἐπίλεκτός ἐστιν αὐτῷ

The interpretation of the present case depends on the solution of the text-critical problem in the LXX: did the translator employ καί before the conjunction ὅταν or not? If so, and I think it very plausible, then the temporal clause begins a new sentence.[75] However, no suitable main clause exists!

Judg 13:17

וכבדנוך[76] כִּי יבא דבריך כִּי שמך מי – Tί ὄνομά σοι, ἵνα ὅταν[77]
ἔλθῃ τὸ ῥῆμά σου, δοξάσωμέν σε;

The translator employed the Greek conjunction ὅταν for the Hebrew כִּי, and the Greek ἵνα expresses the same as the Hebrew co-ordinator ו before כבדנוך.[78]

---

[74] MSS Gab*b*cdefgjlnptvxz 18 64 74 76 84 127 128 134 343 610 omit καί together with 𝔄 𝔈 𝔖 and Aldina.

[75] Cf. den Hertog 1996, 48, 178. Den Hertog concludes that the omission of καί is probably secondary, since the MT does not include any counterpart for καί and the conjunction καί does not fit syntactically in the context. Thus καί is hardly a corruption. But he also claims that the conjunction separates the temporal clause from its main clause *before it* (it is yours *and* when you shall drive out the Canaanites). This is hardly the case. A more plausible explanation is to say that the conjunction indicates that the temporal clause is not subordinated to the main clause before it.

[76] The *Qere* reads the singular.

[77] Against ἵνα ὅταν MSS Bu and the margin of z read ὅτι and MSS oa₂ read ὅταν.

[78] Accordingly many modern translations use a temporal clause here. See e.g. GNB, NEB, Einheitsübersetzung, or TOB.

Judg 21:22

καὶ –והיה כִּי יבאו אבותם או אחיהם לרוב אלינו ואמרנו אליהם
ἔσται ὅταν[79] ἔλθωσιν οἱ πατέρες αὐτῶν ἢ οἱ ἀδελφοὶ αὐτῶν
κρίνεσθαι πρὸς ὑμᾶς, καὶ ἐροῦμεν πρὸς αὐτούς

The content of the passage carries iterative force. This is why one
might also use a conditional clause to render the כי clause.[80]

The Hebrew clauses behind the ὅταν clauses have something in
common. The temporal construction in Hebrew looks towards the
future. This makes the use of ὅταν suitable. Once the כי clause is
preceded by the formula והיה (Judg 21:22), which made it easier for
the translator of Judges to note the temporal character of the כי
clause.

3.3.3 ἐπεί

The Greek conjunction ἐπεί may introduce a temporal clause, but
not always. Often the ἐπεί clause had causal force in the Hellenistic
period.[81] The borderline between the causal and the temporal functions of the ἐπεί clause is unclear, however. Nevertheless, if the ἐπεί
clause has temporal force, the action of the main clause follows the
action of the ἐπεί clause.[82]

Josh 17:13

[καὶ ἐγενήθη] –ויהי כִּי חזקו בני ישראל ויתנו את הכנעני למס
καὶ ἐπεί κατίσχυσαν οἱ υἱοὶ Ἰσραὴλ καὶ ἐποίησαν τοὺς
Χαναναίους ὑπηκόους

The translation contains, quite correctly, a temporal rendering of the
Hebrew ויהי כי. The problems of this case have been dealt with
earlier in this study.[83] Probably the formal equivalent καὶ ἐγενήθη
for the formula ויהי is a later addition.

---

[79] MS a₂ reads ἐάν.
[80] MS a₂ reads the conjunction ἐάν.
[81] Radermacher 1925, 201.
[82] Kühner-Gerth II:2 § 566.1.
[83] See p. 87.

Judg 6:7-8

ויהי כִּי זעקו בני ישראל אל יהוה על אדות מדין ⁸ וישלח יהוה
אִישׁ נביא אל בני ישראל – καὶ ἐγένετο ἐπεὶ ἐκέκραξαν οἱ υἱοὶ
Ἰσραὴλ πρὸς Κύριον διὰ Μαδιάμ, ⁸ καὶ ἐξαπέστειλεν Κύριος
ἄνδρα προφήτην πρὸς τοὺς υἱοὺς Ἰσραήλ

The two cases in my material have many things in common. The
formula ויהי precedes the כי clause and the predicate of the כי
clause is in *qatal*. Moreover, the cases appear in narrative only. The
predicate of the temporal clause in Greek is in the aorist indicative
as well as the predicate of the main clause. Because of the content
of the passages, one could speculate whether the ἐπεί clauses have
a causal function, which only shows how vague is the borderline
between causality and temporality here.

3.3.4 ἡνίκα (ἄν)

The use of the temporal conjunction ἡνίκα denotes that the action
of the main clause happens at the same time as the action of the
ἡνίκα clause. Thus the function of ἡνίκα resembles that of ὅτε. The
action in the ἡνίκα clause is somehow definite.[84] The use of ἄν with
the subjunctive introduces a hypothetical colouring into the temporal
clause.[85]

Josh 22:7-8

ו ⁸ ... – וגם כִּי שלחם יהושע אל אהליהם ויברכם – καὶ ἡνίκα ἐξαπέστειλεν αὐτοὺς Ἰησοῦς εἰς τοὺς οἴκους αὐτῶν καὶ εὐλόγησεν αὐτοὺς ⁸ καὶ ...
The Hebrew in this passage should be understood as having a
temporal force.[86] The main event takes place at the time indicated by
the כי clause.

---

[84] Kühner-Gerth II:2 § 566.1.
[85] Voitila 1995, 208 mentions Ex 1:10 as an example in the Pentateuch of a כי
clause rendered by ἡνίκα ἄν with the subjunctive.
[86] See Schoors 1981, 268.

Josh 24:20

ἡνίκα – כִּי תעזבו את יהוה ועבדתם אלהי נכר ושב והרע לכם
ἐὰν[87] ἐγκαταλίπητε Κύριον καὶ λατρεύσητε θεοῖς ἑτέροις, καὶ
ἐπελθὼν κακώσει ὑμᾶς

The כי clause in Hebrew could be understood as either conditional
or temporal (cf. the preceding context). Consequently, the use of
ἡνίκα ἄν with the subjunctive is appropriate.

3.3.5 ὡς ἄν

ὡς is one of the multipurpose conjunctions in Greek.[88] It may introduce a temporal, causal or comparative clause, among other things.[89]
If the ὡς clause precedes the main clause, the ὡς clause has temporal force.[90] The temporal construction ὡς ἄν with the subjunctive
is rare in the classical period but it is more common in the post-
classical period.[91]

Josh 8:5

καὶ – והיה כִּי יצאו לקראתנו כאשר בראשנה ונסנו לפניהם
ἔσται ὡς ἄν ἐξέλθωσιν οἱ κατοικοῦντες Γαὶ εἰς συνάντησιν
ἡμῖν καθάπερ καὶ πρῴην καὶ φευξόμεθα ἀπὸ προσώπου αὐτῶν

---

[87] MSS Babcorz read ἐάν, other MSS read ἄν. The apparatus of Margolis'
edition does not indicate the variation. Even though Bauer's Greek
Dictionary of the New Testament sees a difference between ἡνίκα ἄν and
ἡνίκα ἐάν, these two combinations are only orthographical variants of the
same expression. See e.g. Thackeray 1909, 65.

[88] Muraoka 1964, 51-72 deals extensively with the use of ὡς in the LXX and
NT.

[89] See e.g. LSJ. According to Muraoka 1985, 160 note 156, "[t]he Greek
particle hōs [ως] is the closest possible parallel to ki in its etymology and
variety of uses." However, the translators of Joshua and Judges mainly
employed ὅτι as the rendering for כי.

[90] Rijksbaron 1976, 107.

[91] See Mayser II:1 § 47 II (esp. p 275). On ὡς ἄν + subj. in the NT see Blass-
Debrunner-Rehkopf § 455.2 and Muraoka 1964, 65-66. According to
Mandilaras 1973 § 598.20, the temporal ὡς ἄν with the subjunctive is not
used at all in post-Ptolemaic papyri. Voitila 1995, 208 mentions Gen 12:12
as an example in the Pentateuch of כי clause rendered by the temporal ὡς
ἄν with the subjunctive.

The Hebrew formula והיה precedes the כי clause. The temporal construction looks towards the future: it is expected that the men of Ai come to fight against the Israelites. In the translation of Joshua ὡς clauses frequently occur in the renderings of the Hebrew ב with an infinitive construction.[92] The present case is an exception, though by no means a failure.

3.3.6 ὅτι

In some circumstantial cases the translators employed a causal equivalent for the Hebrew כי. This should not surprise anyone, since quite possibly a causal clause may be used to express a circumstance.[93]

Judg 2:18

וכי הקים יהוה להם שפטים והיה יהוה עם השפט – καὶ ὅτι[94] ἤγειρεν αὐτοῖς Κύριος κριτάς, καὶ ἦν Κύριος μετὰ τοῦ κριτοῦ Here the כי clause may be understood either as causal or as temporal.[95] Therefore the interpretation adopted by the translator is at least possible.

Judg 12:5

והיה כי יאמרו פליטי אפרים אעברה ויאמרו לו אנשי גלעד האפרתי אתה – καὶ ἐγενήθη ὅτι εἶπαν οἱ διασεσῳσμένοι τοῦ Ἐφραίμ Διαβῶμεν, καὶ εἶπαν αὐτοῖς οἱ ἄνδρες Γαλαάδ Μὴ ὑμεῖς ἐκ τοῦ Ἐφραίμ; The combination והיה כי often introduces an iterative temporal clause. However, the translator did not make use of a temporal rendering. It would, perhaps, be possible to use a conditional clause here, but a causal equivalent for the Hebrew כי seems unsuitable.

---

92 Sipilä 1995, 282.
93 See Aejmelaeus 1993, 172.
94 MSS defghijklnprstvwz and 𝔄 𝔈 𝔏 read ὅτε. Cf. modern translations such as NJB, GNB, or Einheitsübersetzung.
95 See Aejmelaeus 1993, 172. She uses this instance as an example of a case where the formal distinction is difficult to make.

The translator missed the iterative force of the context and employed the aorist indicative for the Hebrew *yiqtol*, because the passage appears in the narrative. There is the possibility of interpreting the Greek as an object clause, but as such it would be an exception, since in the LXX of Judges object clauses introduced by ὅτι are always connected with a *verbum dicendi* or *sentiendi*.[96]

3.3.7 ἐάν

Occasionally the circumstance may be expressed by using a conditional clause.[97] Such a case occurs once in the translation of Joshua, but clearly here the question is that of a special free rendering.

Josh 22:28

והיה כִּי יאמרו אלינו ואל דרתינו מחר ואמרנו – ἐὰν γένηται ποτε καὶ λαλήσωσιν πρὸς ἡμᾶς καὶ ταῖς γενεαῖς ἡμῶν αὔριον, καὶ ἐροῦσιν[98]

Now the Hebrew is best understood as expressing an iterative condition: *Every time they say to us and our descendants, we*[99] *reply.* The free rendering of the formula and the כי clause did not prevent the translator from using the apodotic καί.

3.3.8 *Free rendering*

Josh 8:6

ויצאו אחרינו עד התיקנו אותם מן העיר כִּי יאמרו נסים – καὶ ὡς ἂν ἐξέλθωσιν ὀπίσω ἡμῶν, ἀποσπάσομεν αὐτοὺς ἀπὸ τῆς πόλεως· καὶ ἐροῦσιν Φεύγουσιν οὗτοι

---

[96] See the discussion concerning the nominalizing כי on pp. 180-189.

[97] Aejmelaeus 1993, 171. She also states that the borderline between conditional and temporal interpretations of the Hebrew circumstantial כי is extremely vague.

[98] MSS abcoqx 18 64 128 and the margin of MS v with 𝕮 and 𝕾 read the first person plural (ἐροῦμεν = Margolis). For the evaluation of the variant see Greenspoon 1983, 152-153 and den Hertog 1996, 32.

[99] The translator employed the third person plural (ἐροῦσιν) and perhaps had the descendants in mind.

The use of an exceptional counterpart for the Hebrew כִּי, the conjunction καί, is due to the free rendering of the context.[100]

3.3.9 Translation-technical evaluation

The circumstantial כִּי clauses are a minority when compared with other כִּי clauses. The MT of Joshua and Judges include only 16 cases. The most frequent Greek conjunction is ὅτε but it is not a standard equivalent for the circumstantial כִּי. If compared with other כִּי clauses, the clauses where the circumstantial כִּי appears are rendered in a special way in the LXX of Joshua and Judges. We may conclude that the translators recognised the special character of these Hebrew clauses. Thus the circumstantial כִּי clauses posed no problems for the translators.[101]

Often the circumstantial כִּי clause is rendered in the present material by using a temporal clause in Greek (twelve cases). The temporal clauses in the LXX of Joshua have recently been studied by den Hertog.[102] Unfortunately from the point of view of the present analysis, he is not interested in the temporal clauses themselves. His main concern is the use of the apodotic καί with temporal clauses.[103] This is why he only lists the cases and discusses the appearance of the apodotic καί. The apodotic καί has been dealt with earlier in this study. There it became evident that it is used especially in cases where the protasis is a temporal clause or in cases where a formula precedes the protasis in Hebrew.[104]

But why did the translators employ the temporal clause in any case? This question is not formulated by den Hertog. The temporal

---

[100] See Margolis 1931, 126. Soisalon-Soininen 1965, 114 leaves open the possibility of a Hebrew *Vorlage* deviating from the MT.

[101] Cf. Aejmelaeus 1993, 171: "the choice ... in most cases is not at all difficult."

[102] Den Hertog 1996, 177-180.

[103] This is only natural if his method is taken into account. He starts with the Greek text and collects the temporal and conditional clauses, commencing with ἐπεί, ἡνίκα, ὅταν, and ὡς. This makes it difficult to study the choice of equivalents, since a clear picture of the parent Hebrew text is then unattainable.

[104] See p. 117-118 and Aejmelaeus 1982, 133.

clause was, after all, not the only available possibility for rendering a circumstantial כי clause. A closer look at the temporal cases shows that there are some clear reasons for the temporal inter-pretation of certain passages. Often the כי clause is preceded by the formula ויהי or והיה. Only once does a formula not appear (Judg 13:17). In Joshua the formula is used twice, and once the כי clause includes the temporal adverb מחר (Josh 4:6). These temporal mark-ers in the immediate context of כי made the temporal interpretation a natural and easy choice for the translators.

TABLE 15 Temporal conjunctions used as equivalents for the circumstantial כי in the LXX of Joshua and Judges

Conjunction	Josh	Judg
ὅτε	0	3
ὅταν	2	2
ἐπεί	1	1
ἡνίκα	2	0
ὡς	1	0

A clear temporal marker is not always present to trigger the tem-poral interpretation (see e.g. Josh 22:7). Thus the translators surely considered the wider context when rendering circumstantial כי clauses. This is seen from the fact that the interpretations adopted by the translators fit the contexts.

The choice of equivalent for the temporal כי differed from the choice of equivalent for ו or the causal כי, since there is no major equivalent. Instead various temporal conjunctions were used: ὅτε, ὅταν, ἐπεί, ἡνίκα, and ὡς. The use of the equivalent turns out to be natural. The translators clearly used normal Greek temporal expres-sions.

There is a difference between the LXX of Joshua and the LXX of Judges in respect of the temporal clauses, as one might expect. How-ever, the nature of the difference is not like the difference in respect of causal clauses. The difference lies in the corpus of the equivalents used by the translators. The conjunctions employed by both of the translators are ὅταν and ἐπεί. The translator of Joshua also employed ἡνίκα and ὡς, but the translator of Judges did not. The latter, on the other hand, employed ὅτε, which is not used by the translator of Joshua. That the translator favoured a particular conjunction is only natural. Personal style and liking probably mattered here. Therefore, the difference in the selection of rare conjunctions used by the translators is not significant. Interestingly, the use of equivalents is not limited in the same way as the use of equivalents for the causal כִּי. One should, however, bear in mind that the total number of cases under discussion here is very low.

TABLE 16 The non-temporal renderings for the circumstantial כִּי in the LXX of Joshua and Judges

Rendering	Josh	Judg
ὅτι	0	2
ἐάν	1	0
Free	1	0

Beside the temporal clauses the translator of Joshua employed other ways of rendering the circumstantial כִּי clause. Once he used a conditional clause as part of a free rendering (Josh 22:28). Once he used the co-ordinator καί to render כִּי (Josh 8:6), and the use of the co-ordinator is motivated by a free rendering.

The translator of Judges twice employed ὅτι to render a circumstantial כִּי. Sometimes ὅτι is a possible rendering but not always. Especially in Judg 12:5 a temporal clause would have been better. The use of ὅτι here indicates, I think, that the translator was not informed of the context. The use of the conjunction ὅτι, although it did not fit the context, is best explained as due to a mechanical rendering.

The conjunction alone does not mark the nature of the subordinate clause in Greek. The verbal form of the predicate is related to the function of the clause as well. Thus it is of interest to study what kind of verbal form the translators used for the predicate.

In the present material, the renderings of the circumstantial כי clauses, the translations adopted for the Hebrew verbal forms seem to follow a pattern. The Hebrew *yiqtol* is always rendered by the subjunctive and *qatal* mainly by the indicative. But the subjunctive is used for *qatal*, if the clause is part of direct discourse. In narrative the predicate is mainly in the aorist indicative. Only once is the imperfect indicative used. This is why I think that the overall context affects the use of the verbal form in the predicate of the circumstantial clause more than the Hebrew verbal form it contains.[105]

It is, then, plausible to conclude that the translators analysed the context of the circumstantial cases when rendering them. The appearance of a Hebrew temporal marker surely guided the translator in temporal cases. Since it does not always occur, the logical relationship of the circumstantial clause and the following main clause played an important role in the process of translation. Consequently, the narrow segmentation that is assumed to have affected the translation profoundly, did not exclude the possibility of taking the context of a כי clause into account when translating. The generally literal character of the translators' work did not, then, affect their ability to translate properly.[106]

3.4 Nominalizing כי

Many כי clauses may be understood as object clauses. The particle introducing such clauses is said to be a nominalizing particle and

---

[105] Kühner-Gerth II:2 § 567 explains that the subjunctive is used in temporal clauses if a future event is in question.

[106] Barr 1979, 297 (= 23) expresses the same idea perhaps even more clearly when he says that "it is therefore not necessarily true that the literal translator was stupid or unintelligent, as has often been implied."

accordingly Hebrew כִּי may be called in these cases 'nominalizing כִּי'.[107]

My material, the כִּי clauses in Joshua and Judges, includes cases of nominalizing כִּי after verbs of perception (*verba sentiendi*) and verbs of saying (*verba dicendi*). Since the use of object clauses after *verba sentiendi* differs from the use of object clauses after *verba dicendi* both in Hebrew and in Greek, these two groups are here separated from each other.

3.4.1 Cases with *verba sentiendi*

A *verbum sentiendi* expresses perception, and often it requires grammatical object to describe the object of perception. In Hebrew such an object may be a כִּי clause.[108] The books of Joshua and Judges include 33 כִּי-initial object clauses following a *verbum sentiendi*. The Hebrew verbs are יָדַע, זָכַר, רָאָה, and שָׁמַע. The discussion of cases in the following is organized according to the Greek equivalent for כִּי in the Hebrew.

3.4.1.1 ὅτι

There are 27 cases of ὅτι in my material. It is the most common equivalent of the Hebrew כִּי before an object clause following a *verbum sentiendi*. The examples listed in the following will reflect various contexts where the object clause appears.

a) The object clause belongs to direct speech

Josh 2:9

יָדַעְתִּי כִּי נָתַן יְהוָה לָכֶם אֶת הָאָרֶץ – ἐπίσταμαι ὅτι δέδωκεν ὑμῖν Κύριος τὴν γῆν

---

[107] The terminology is taken from Williams 1976 § 451. Bandstra 1982, 97 prefers the term complementizing כִּי, because the content of the כִּי clause completes the structure of the main clause.

[108] See e.g. Aejmelaeus 1993, 174, who describes instances where a כִּי clause follows a *verbum sentiendi* as "the most unambiguous cases".

Josh 4:24

ὅπως – לְמַעַן דַּעַת כָּל עַמֵּי הָאָרֶץ אֶת יַד יהוה כִּי חֲזָקָה הִיא
γνῶσιν πάντα τὰ ἔθνη τῆς γῆς ὅτι ἡ δύναμις τοῦ Κυρίου
ἰσχυρά ἐστιν

Judg 4:9

הָלֹךְ אֵלֵךְ עִמָּךְ אֶפֶס כִּי לֹא תִהְיֶה תִפְאַרְתְּךָ עַל הַדֶּרֶךְ אֲשֶׁר אַתָּה
הוֹלֵךְ –πορευομένη πορεύσομαι μετὰ σοῦ· πλὴν γίνωσκε ὅτι οὐκ
ἔσται τὸ προτέρημά σου εἰς τὴν ὁδόν, ἣν σὺ πορεύῃ
The plus πλὴν γίνωσκε turns the ὅτι clause into an object clause.
In Hebrew אֶפֶס כִּי restricts the preceding statement.[109]

Judg 9:2

וּזְכַרְתֶּם כִּי עַצְמְכֶם וּבְשַׂרְכֶם אָנִי – καὶ μνήσθητε ὅτι σάρξ ὑμῶν
καὶ ὀστοῦν ὑμῶν ἐγώ εἰμι

Judg 15:11

הֲלֹא יָדַעְתָּ כִּי מֹשְׁלִים בָּנוּ פְלִשְׁתִּים – οὐκ οἶδας ὅτι ἄρχουσιν
ἡμῶν οἱ ἀλλόφυλοι;
A similar case is to be found in Judg 18:14.

b) The object clause is in the narrative.

Josh 8:21

וִיהוֹשֻׁעַ וְכָל יִשְׂרָאֵל רָאוּ כִּי לָכַד הָאֹרֵב אֶת הָעִיר – καὶ Ἰησοῦς
καὶ πᾶς Ἰσραὴλ εἶδον ὅτι ἔλαβον τὰ ἔνεδρα τὴν πόλιν

Josh 10:1

וַיְהִי כִּשְׁמֹעַ אֲדֹנִי צֶדֶק מֶלֶךְ יְרוּשָׁלַ͏ִם כִּי לָכַד יְהוֹשֻׁעַ אֶת הָעַי – ὡς
δὲ ἤκουσεν Ἀδωνιβέζεκ βασιλεὺς Ἰερουσαλὴμ ὅτι ἔλαβεν
Ἰησοῦς τὴν Γαί

Judg 16:20

וְהוּא לֹא יָדַע כִּי יהוה סָר מֵעָלָיו – καὶ αὐτὸς οὐκ ἔγνω ὅτι
Κύριος ἀπέστη ἀπ' αὐτοῦ

---

[109] See Clines 1993, 359, who provides the meaning 'except that' for אֶפֶס כִּי.
The combination is found in Dtn 15:4, Judg 4:9, 2 Sam 12:14, and Am 9:8
as well as in 1QH 2.33.

Josh 8:14

והוא לא ידע כי ארב לו מאחרי העיר – καὶ αὐτὸς οὐκ ᾔδει ὅτι
ἔνεδρα αὐτῷ ἐστιν ὀπίσω τῆς πόλεως
The translator added a copula to the nominal clause. The use of the
present tense ἐστιν is noteworthy.

Josh 9:16

וישמעו כי קרבים הם אליו ובקרבו הם ישבים – ἤκουσαν ὅτι ἐγγύθεν αὐτῶν εἰσιν, καὶ ὅτι ἐν αὐτοῖς κατοικοῦσιν
Here too the translator employed the present tense. Now the verb
εἰσιν corresponds to the Hebrew personal pronoun הם.[110] Similar
cases are to be found in Judg 6:22, 13:16, 13:21, 14:4 and, 18:26.

Judg 20:34

והם לא ידעו כי נגעת עליהם הרעה – καὶ αὐτοὶ οὐκ ἔγνωσαν
ὅτι ἀφῆπται αὐτῶν ἡ κακία
The Hebrew participle is rendered by the perfect indicative. The
same Greek verbal form is used in the following two examples, too.
The use of the perfect tense indicates that the translator wished to
highlight the point of view of the perceptor in these cases.[111]

Judg 20:36

ויראו בני בנימן כי נגפו – καὶ εἶδεν Βενιαμὶν ὅτι τετρόπωται

Judg 20:41

ראה כי נגעה עליו הרעה – καὶ εἶδεν ὅτι ἧπται αὐτοῦ ἡ κακία

ὅτι is a very suitable counterpart for Hebrew כי before an object
clause after a *verbum sentiendi*. The translations follow the Greek
idiom in this respect. It might be noted that the Greek way of

---

[110] Cf. Soisalon-Soininen 1987, 75: "Die üblichste Übersetzungsweise des in
einem Nominalsazt als Subjekt stehenden Personalpronomens ist seine Wiedergabe mit dem Verb εἶναι" and *ibid*, 76: "Es beruht auf dem Charakter
des hebräischen Nominalsatzes, daß in den meisten Fällen das in Frage
kommende Tempus das Präsens ist, aber auch Imperfekt und Futur kommen
vor, z.B. in Gen Imperfekt 8mal, Futur 5mal. Beispiele: Gen 3:7 וידעו כי
עירמם הם – καὶ ἔγνωσαν ὅτι γυμνοὶ ἦσαν".

[111] See e.g. Aejmelaeus 1993, 70-71.

introducing an object clause resembles that of Hebrew. Most object clauses are introduced in Hebrew by using כי and in Greek by ὅτι. Therefore, the translators naturally employed ὅτι to introduce an object clause.

3.4.1.2 διότι

διότι is similar to ὅτι as to its usage in Greek. Therefore one may expect to find cases where διότι introduces an object clause following a *verbum sentiendi*. In my material this happens once.

Josh 23:14

וידעתם בכל לבבכם ובכל נפשכם <u>כי</u> לא נפל דבר אחד מכל הדברים – καὶ γνώσεσθε τῇ καρδίᾳ ὑμῶν καὶ τῇ ψυχῇ ὑμῶν <u>διότι</u> οὐ διέπεσεν[112] εἰς λόγος ἀπὸ πάντων τῶν λόγων

3.4.1.3 Special case

My material includes a special case where the Greek conjunction δέ is used to render the Hebrew כי and it may be interpreted as opening an object clause.

Josh 14:12

ועתה תנה לי את ההר הזה אשר דבר יהוה ביום ההוא כי אתה שמעת ביום ההוא <u>כי</u> ענקים שם – καὶ νῦν αἰτοῦμαί σε τὸ ὄρος τοῦτο, καθὰ εἶπεν Κύριος τῇ ἡμέρᾳ ἐκείνῃ· ὅτι σὺ ἀκήκοας τὸ ῥῆμα τοῦτο[113] τῇ ἡμέρᾳ ἐκείνῃ. νῦνι <u>δὲ</u> οἱ Ἐνακεὶμ ἐκεῖ εἰσιν

The Hebrew is not easy to understand. The best possibility is to see the כי clause as the object of שמע (*you heard that there are the Anakim*),[114] but this interpretation is not obvious.[115] It is possible that

---

[112] MSS BA^{a7} read οὐκ ἔπεσεν (= Margolis); see den Hertog 1996, 67.

[113] For the plus in the LXX see e.g. Holmes 1914, 59.

[114] Cf. e.g. NRSV.

[115] When the last כי clause in this instance is understood as an object, the first כי clause, obviously causal in nature, seems to provide an odd explanation for the request.

the Greek expression νῦνι δέ reflects the problems the translator encountered in finding a suitable rendering. It is also possible that the Hebrew *Vorlage* of the LXX read וְעַתָּה.

3.4.1.4 Omission

In one instance the translation does not contain any visible counterpart for the Hebrew conjunction initiating an object clause after a *verbum sentiendi*.

Josh 3:7

אָחֵל גַּדֶּלְךָ בְּעֵינֵי כָל יִשְׂרָאֵל אֲשֶׁר יֵדְעוּן כִּי כַּאֲשֶׁר הָיִיתִי עִם

מֹשֶׁה אֶהְיֶה עִמָּךְ – ἄρχομαι ὑψῶσαί σε κατενώπιον πάντων υἱῶν Ἰσραὴλ ἵνα γνῶσιν __[116] καθότι ἤμην μετὰ Μωυσῆ οὕτως ἔσομαι καὶ μετὰ σοῦ

The translator omitted any equivalent for the Hebrew כִּי commencing an object clause. This is perhaps due to the first Greek word in the object clause, καθότι.

3.4.1.5 Translation-technical evaluation

In terms of translation technique the object clauses after *verba sentiendi* were not difficult for the translators. This may be seen from the fact that they almost always used an appropriate Greek counterpart for the object clause initial Hebrew כִּי. The nominalizing use of כִּי is easy to recognize after the reader of the Hebrew text notes the verb denoting perception. Only once, regarding my material, may one ask whether the translator did not note that the Hebrew conjunction כִּי introduces an object clause, but in that particular case (Josh 14:12) the context of the Hebrew clause is difficult to understand.

---

[116] MSS adghknptwd₂ 71 72 76 84 118 127 add ὅτι (cf. 𝔄 ℭ 𝔏). For the evaluation of the addition, see den Hertog 1996, 95.

In classical Greek the author may employ the verbal forms of direct speech in object clauses following a *verbum sentiendi* (the point of view of the perceptor) if he or she prefers to do so.[117] The narrative verbal forms may also be used (the point of view of the narrator). It seems that the system is no longer used in the post-classical period and that the authors used the verbal forms of direct speech only.[118] Accordingly, the translators of Joshua and Judges employed the verb forms of direct speech.

3.4.2 Cases with *verba dicendi*

When the Hebrew conjunction כי is preceded by a *verbum dicendi*, such as אמר, the Greek equivalent ὅτι is often very suitable. It may act as ὅτι *recitativum*. This is due to the fact that often a *verbum dicendi* is followed by direct speech in Hebrew. Yet כי in Hebrew perhaps does not act as כי *recitativum*[119] causing some problems of interpretation.[120]

---

[117] See e.g. Rijksbaron 1984, 51-52 with some examples.

[118] See Mayser II:3 § 155.1.c, Blass-Debrunner-Rehkopf § 324 and especially Voitila 1995, 53.

[119] Schoors 1981, 258 denies the existence of כי *recit.* and interprets such cases as examples of emphatic כי. Bandstra 1982, 165-166 also denies the existence of כי *recit.* Muraoka 1985, 163 note 164 refers to an article by Esh where the possibility of using כי *recit.* in Hebrew is also rejected. Muraoka himself explains that such a use of כי is quite natural, since according to him כי bears demonstrative force. Aejmelaeus 1993, 38-42 sees כי *recit.* as a part of the substantival function of כי.

[120] Often the Hebrew grammarians explain that there exists an emphatic use of כי (see e.g. Muraoka 1985, 158-164 and Waltke-O'Connor 1990, 657; Van Wolde 1995, 635-636 discusses כי before *verba sentiendi* as emphatic) that might explain cases where direct speech is introduced by כי. The majority of potential cases come from oaths and conditional apodoses; otherwise there seems to be little room for the emphatic use of כי; see Aejmelaeus 1993, 184. Because of this the emphatic use of כי need not be the only way of explaining the use of כי after a *verbum dicendi*. At least in some cases כי may be explained as causal. This is particularly true in cases where what is in question is an answer to a 'why' question; Aejmelaeus 1993, 184.

3.4.2.1 ὅτι

If the Hebrew כִּי is preceded by a *verbum dicendi*, the translators of Joshua and Judges used ὅτι to render the Hebrew conjunction. Only one exception to this habit is to be found (Judg 6:16). I am following the suggestion made by Aejmelaeus that ὅτι should be seen as ὅτι *recitativum* in cases where such an interpretation produces more fluent Greek than seeing ὅτι as a causal conjunction.[121] Therefore, in the present discussion ὅτι is always seen as ὅτι *recitativum*. The cases where ὅτι is seen as causal are dealt with along with other cases of causal כִּי in chapter 3.1.[122]

Two cases with the verb אמר:

Josh 2:24

וַיֹּאמְרוּ אֶל יְהוֹשֻׁעַ כִּי נָתַן יְהוָה בְּיָדֵנוּ אֶת כָּל הָאָרֶץ – καὶ εἶπαν πρὸς Ἰησοῦν <u>ὅτι</u> Παρέδωκεν Κύριος πᾶσαν τὴν γῆν ἐν χειρὶ ἡμῶν

This is a clear case for ὅτι *recitativum* in Greek. The particular case is, however, difficult to interpret in Hebrew.[123]

Jugd 15:2

וַיֹּאמֶר אָבִיהָ אָמֹר אָמַרְתִּי כִּי שָׂנֹא שְׂנֵאתָהּ וָאֶתְּנֶנָּה לְמֵרֵעֶךָ – καὶ εἶπεν ὁ πατὴρ αὐτῆς Εἴπας εἶπα <u>ὅτι</u> μισῶν ἐμίσησας αὐτήν, καὶ ἔδωκα αὐτὴν τῷ συνεταίρῳ σου

Should one interpret this case as ὅτι *recitativum*?[124] The conjunction is preceded by several אמר verbs. What follows is direct speech. Rahlfs uses a small letter o to indicate ὅτι *recitativum*.

---

[121] Aejmelaeus 1993, 43.

[122] See pp. 143-153.

[123] Schoors 1981, 258 explains that Josh 2:24 is an example of the emphatic use of כִּי. Aejmelaeus 1993, 43, on the other hand, discusses the possibility of explaining Josh 2:24 as follows: "the spies told what happened to them and said that..."

[124] The present case is not mentioned by Aejmelaeus 1993, 45 note 20 among cases of ὅτι *recitativum* in the LXX of Judges.

Three cases with the verb נגד:

Judg 4:12

כי עלה ברק בן אבינעם – ויגדו לסיסרא – καὶ ἀνήγγειλαν τῷ Σισαρὰ ὅτι ἀνέβη Βαρὰκ υἱὸς Ἀβινέεμ

Judg 9:47

כי התקבצו כל בעלי מגדל שכם – ויגד לאבימלך – καὶ ἀπηγγέλη τῷ Ἀβιμέλεχ ὅτι συνήχθησαν πάντες οἱ ἄνδρες τοῦ πύργου Σικίμων

Judg 14:9

כי מגוית האריה רדה הדבש – ולא הגיד להם – καὶ οὐκ ἀπήγ-γειλεν αὐτοῖς ὅτι ἐκ τῆς ἕξεως τοῦ λέοντος ἐξεῖλεν τὸ μέλι

A case with the verb קרא:

Josh 22:34

כי עד הוא בינתינו – ויקראו בני ראובן ובני גד למזבח – καὶ ἐπωνόμασεν Ἰησοῦς τὸν βωμὸν τῶν Ῥουβὴν καὶ τῶν Γὰδ καὶ τοῦ ἡμίσους φυλῆς Μανασσή, καὶ εἶπεν ὅτι Μαρτύριόν ἐστιν ἀνὰ μέσον αὐτῶν

Now it is not absolutely clear whether the Greek conjunction ὅτι is ὅτι *recitativum*, because the following words need not be direct speech. Yet I count this case as being among the cases of ὅτι *recitativum*.[125]

3.4.2.2 Omission

Judg 6:16

כי אהיה עמך והכית את מדין כאיש אחד – ויאמר אליו יהוה – καὶ εἶπεν πρὸς αὐτὸν ὁ ἄγγελος Κυρίου ___ Κύριος ἔσται μετὰ σοῦ, καὶ πατάξεις τὴν Μαδιὰμ ὡσεὶ ἄνδρα ἕνα

---

[125] See Aejmelaeus 1993, 45 note 20.

Now the translator omitted the equivalent for כִּי.[126] The Hebrew should be interpreted as a reply to the question in 6:15: "How can I deliver Israel?" The translator probably saw no need to use any Greek conjunction here. The Greek constantly describes the heavenly being as an angel in verses 6:11-18, but in the MT the angel appears only in verses 11 and 12. After that יהוה himself speaks with Gideon.

3.4.2.3 Translation-technical evaluation

The object clause following a *verbum dicendi* most naturally commences with the conjunction ὅτι in Greek and thus the translator could easily employ ὅτι as an equivalent for the Hebrew כִּי preceded by a *verbum dicendi*. The result is idiomatic Greek in spite of the interpretative problems that one may encounter in Hebrew.

If a *verbum dicendi* is followed by indirect speech in Greek, the author should use the verbal forms of direct speech for indirect speech.[127] In my material this does happen, indicating the translators' good command of Greek.

3.5 כִּי marks a positive alternative

As pointed out earlier, the Hebrew conjunction כִּי may express a positive alternative after a negative clause.[128] In Greek there is no obvious way of expressing the same. Instead in my material the translators came to employ an adversative conjunction as an equivalent for the Hebrew conjunction.

---

[126] MSS abglnptvwx 𝔏 𝕾, add ὅτι which is ὅτι *recitativum*.
[127] See e.g. Rijksbaron 1984, 53-55 with examples.
[128] Bandstra 1982, 149-150 calls this type of a כִּי clause as adversative.

3.5.1 ἀλλά

The Greek conjunction ἀλλά expresses strong adversativity. In cases where the Hebrew כי is used after a negative statement to mark a positive alternative, ἀλλά fits the context very well.[129] In the following all cases are listed.

Josh 11:20

ἵνα – למען החרימם לבלתי היות להם תחנה כִּי למען השמידם
ἐξολεθρευθῶσιν, ὅπως μὴ δοθῇ αὐτοῖς ἔλεος ἀλλ' ἵνα ἐξολεθρευθῶσιν

The negation preceding the כי clause is לבלתי.

Josh 22:28

אשר עשו אבותינו לא לעולה ולא לזבח כִּי עד הוא בינינו
ὃ ἐποίησαν οἱ πατέρες ἡμῶν οὐχ ἕνεκεν καρπωμάτων – וביניכם
οὐδὲ ἕνεκεν θυσιῶν, ἀλλὰ μαρτύριόν ἐστιν ἀνὰ μέσον ὑμῶν καὶ
ἀνὰ μέσον ἡμῶν

The negation preceding the כי clause is לא – ולא.

Josh 24:21

οὐχί, ἀλλὰ Κυρίῳ λατρεύσομεν – לא כִּי את יהוה נעבד
The negation preceding the כי clause is לא.

Judg 15:13

οὐχί, ἀλλὰ δεσμῷ δήσομέν – לא כִּי אסר נאסרך ונתנוך בידם
σε καὶ παραδώσομέν σε εἰς χεῖρας αὐτῶν

The negation preceding the כי clause is לא.

Josh 22:26-27

נעשה נא לנו לבנות את המזבח לא לעולה ולא לזבח 27 כִּי עד
ποιῆσαι οὕτως τοῦ οἰκοδομῆσαι τὸν βωμὸν – הוא בינינו וביניכם
τοῦτον οὐχ ἕνεκεν καρπωμάτων οὐδὲ ἕνεκεν θυσιῶν, 27 ἀλλ' ἵνα
ᾖ τοῦτο μαρτύριον ἀνὰ μέσον ἡμῶν καὶ ὑμῶν

---

[129] For a כי clause expressing a positive alternative see Aejmelaeus 1993, 175-176.

Here the conjunction ἀλλά is taken to be an equivalent of the Hebrew כִּי alone. The negations preceding the כִּי clause are לֹא and וְלֹא. The case is close to the aforementioned verse Josh 22:28.

3.5.2 Free rendering

On one occasion the translator of Judges freely rendered the passage including כִּי indicating a positive alternative.

Judg 11:15-16

לֹא לָקַח יִשְׂרָאֵל אֶת אֶרֶץ מוֹאָב וְאֶת אֶרֶץ בְּנֵי עַמּוֹן [16] כִּי בַּעֲלוֹתָם
מִמִּצְרַיִם וַיֵּלֶךְ יִשְׂרָאֵל בַּמִּדְבָּר – οὐκ ἔλαβεν Ἰσραὴλ τὴν γῆν
Μωὰβ καὶ τὴν γῆν υἱῶν Ἀμμών [16]__ ἐν τῇ ἀναβάσει αὐτῶν ἐξ
Αἰγύπτου, ἀλλ᾽ ἐπορεύθη Ἰσραὴλ ἐν τῇ ἐρήμῳ
Here the Hebrew כִּי clause starts with the embedded infinitive construction בַּעֲלוֹתָם מִמִּצְרַיִם. The translator employed the prepositional phrase to render the Hebrew infinitive בַּעֲלוֹתָם.[130] While he connected the prepositional phrase with the negative alternative, he omitted the visible counterpart for כִּי, but the Hebrew ו connecting the infinitive construction with the main body of the כִּי clause is rendered by ἀλλά instead.

3.5.3 Translation-technical evaluation

The translation technique of the translators of Joshua and Judges may be explained mainly in terms of three contributory factors: the narrow segmentation, the natural, "easy" choice of equivalents, and the requirements of the target language, Greek. The easy choice of equivalents is based on an idea introduced by Barr. He claims that the LXX translators worked in an *ad hoc* manner when translating.

---

[130] The Hebrew בּ + inf. is often rendered by ἐν τῷ with the infinitive in Judges (and in the LXX in general). The prepositional phrase is seldom used as a rendering of בּ + inf; see Soisalon-Soininen 1965, 82-83.

They opted for usual equivalents without making an exhaustive study of the context.[131]

The first two factors influenced the literary product, the word-for-word outlook of the translation. The narrow segmentation occasionally made it difficult to consider the context. Should we then expect the translators to have employed ὅτι as a rendering of כי expressing the positive counterpart? The translators of Joshua and Judges never employed ὅτι in instances where כי expresses a positive alternative.

By using the conjunction ἀλλά the translators demonstrated their ability to note the context of the parent text when executing their task. The use of ὅτι to render the Hebrew כי expressing a positive alternative would definitely be a wrong solution. Not only would the Greek reader gain the wrong idea, but often ὅτι would be very difficult to interpret. The use of ἀλλά, on the other hand, results in idiomatic Greek expressions that are easy to understand.

My conclusion is, therefore, a natural one: the translators of the LXX, even very literal ones, were not numbskulls. They knew what they were doing. May I quote James Barr, who puts this very nicely:

> Word-for-word expression did not necessary exhaust the literal translator's appreciation of the meaning of the text: rather, it was his *choice* that he should express himself so in the versional language. It is therefore not necessarily true that the literal translator was stupid or unintelligent, as has often been implied.[132]

---

[131] See Barr 1979, 7. For the term "easy technique" see *ibid.*, 26.
[132] Barr 1979, 23.

4 Conclusions regarding the translation technique

For the evaluation of the translation technique of the LXX some criteria applicable to the use of וand כי are more useful than others. The most important criteria concerning the possibility of setting the translation technique of Joshua and Judges into a broader perspective are the renderings of ו at the beginning of an ordinary main clause (pp. 24-82), the renderings of ו in an apodosis (pp. 109-129) and the renderings of כי in a causal clause (pp. 142-168). These aspects make it possible to compare the translations of Joshua and Judges with each other and with the translations of the books of the Pentateuch.

4.1 The renderings of ו at the beginning of an ordinary main clause

Obviously the use of καί in renderings of the main clause initial ו is a powerful indicator of the translation technique of any book of the LXX. It describes the literalness of a translator and makes it possible to compare different translators and their translation techniques.

The extensive use of καί in renderings of Hebrew co-ordinate main clauses is a typical feature of the LXX. Thus, it is not a surprise that in the Greek Joshua καί is employed very often and in Judges practically always in renderings of the main clause initial Hebrew ו. Even though καί is employed more often in Judges than in Joshua, both translators used καί often and one may describe them as literal.

The literalness of Joshua and Judges may be set in a wider perspective by comparing the use of καί in Joshua and Judges with the
use of καί in the books of the Pentateuch. Here the study by Aejmelaeus offers the materials needed for the comparison. Since I have
organized my material differently, I must also introduce some minor
changes into my statistics.[1] The ratio for καί of all the main clauses
including the formulas is 87.8% in Joshua and 97.8% in Judges. The
similar ratios for καί in the books of the Pentateuch can be divided
into two. In Genesis the ratio is 62.2% and in Exodus 69.0%. The
translators of these two books employed καί less often than the
translators of the other three books. In Leviticus the ratio is 89.4%,
in Numbers 89.0% and in Deuteronomy 83.3%. Statistically the
translation of Joshua comes close to those of Leviticus, Numbers and
Deuteronomy. The translation of Judges, for its part, deviates from
the translations of the Pentateuch, being more literal than they are.

There are good reasons why the translators of the LXX, those of
Joshua and Judges included, employed καί as often as they did. In
its immediate context καί was a suitable rendering. It is a fitting
counterpart for ז, if one does not wish to consider the wider context
and the stylistic impression given by the translation. The translators
hardly allowed for the context or the style. Their work does not illustrate deep stylistic concerns, but merely the so-called easy technique.[2] That is, the translator rendered without exhaustive contem-
plation of the broad context and meaning of the parent text and employed the equivalents in an *ad hoc* manner.

καί was not, however, the only possibility used when rendering
the main clause-initial Hebrew ז. Aejmelaeus showed that the use of
the Greek conjunction δέ describes the translation technique very
well in the Pentateuch.[3] Similarly, the use of δέ describes the translation technique in Joshua and Judges. In Joshua the ratio for δέ is
5.7% and in Judges 0.9%. These figures also suggest the difference

---

[1]   For Aejmelaeus' statistics for the renderings of ז at the beginning of an ordinary main clause see Aejmelaeus 1982, 123. Her statistics include the renderings of the formulas which I have separated from the other co-ordinate main
clauses.

[2]   For the term "easy technique" see Barr 1979, 26 and 50 and the present
study p. 79; especially note 163.

[3]   Aejmelaeus 1982, 42-43, and 179-181.

in translation technique between Joshua and Judges. The translator of Judges used δέ very seldom, but the translator of Joshua more often, and more idiomatically, though there are some signs of mechanical usage.

Overall, the rare use of δέ influences the style, since in genuine Greek δέ is used more often than in the LXX. The most important reason for the rare use of δέ must lie in the extensive use of καί.

When compared with the Pentateuch, the translations of Joshua and Judges are again set in perspective. The figures for δέ in the Pentateuch are the following: Genesis 25.2%, Exodus 15.7%, Leviticus 2.4%, Numbers 2.1%, and Deuteronomy 2.7%.[4] Thus, Judges is more literal than the translations of the Pentateuch. Joshua, on the other hand, comes close to Leviticus, Numbers, and Deuteronomy. Here I believe that the conclusions drawn from the stylistic considerations are needed to support the statistics. The translator of Joshua used δέ almost idiomatically and thus Joshua is different from Leviticus, Numbers, and Deuteronomy.

Aejmelaeus saw the use of the *participium coniunctum* as important for the understanding of the translation technique employed.[5] I have added a minor improvement to the use of the *part.coni.* by counting the use of the *part.coni.* and the use of the *genetivus absolutus* together.

It is surprising how seldom the translators of Joshua and Judges employed the *part.coni.* and the *gen.abs.* while compared with genuine Greek. In Joshua the ratio of these two participle constructions is 3.5% and in Judges 0.7%. Again, one may see the difference between Joshua and Judges as translations. The difference is not limited to the statistics alone. The translator of Joshua employed the *gen.abs.* more seldom than the *part.coni.*, but in the translation of Judges they appear equally often in renderings of the main clause-initial ו. Also, the translator of Judges did not separate the embedded *part.coni.* from the rest of the clause by using καί, but the translator of Joshua occasionally employed καί if the parent text contained ו.

In the Pentateuch the same ratios concerning the use of the *part. coni.* and the *gen. abs.* are 7.0% for Genesis, 4.7% for Exodus, 1.9%

---

[4] The figures are based on Aejmelaeus 1982, 36 with modifications; cf. footnote no. 1 on p. 194.

[5] Aejmelaeus 1982, 108-109, and 179-181.

for Leviticus, 3.5% for Numbers, and 6.2% for Deuteronomy.[6] One can instantly see that the difference between various books of the Pentateuch in the use of participles is not as wide as it is in the use of καί or δέ. Joshua now comes closest to Leviticus though, the differences between the books of the Pentateuch are very small. Judges, again, is different from Joshua or the books of the Pentateuch.

If these three criteria are put together, a more general classification of Joshua and Judges is achieved. The translation of Joshua lies between the freer books of the Pentateuch, Genesis and Exodus, and the more literal Leviticus, Numbers and Deuteronomy. This conclusion is reached if the use of δέ is counted as more weighty a criterion than the other two; an interpretation I firmly believe. Judges, for its part, is a very literal translation and sharply deviates from the translations of the Pentateuch and Joshua.

4.2 The use of καί as a rendering of ו in an apodosis

After Aejmelaeus published her study on the co-ordinate clauses in the Pentateuch, the importance of the ו opening an apodosis as an indicator of the translation technique employed has been generally recognized. This being the case, let us next discuss the apodoses in Joshua and Judges.[7] In Joshua the translator used καί in 52.3% of the cases where ו opens an apodosis in Hebrew. In Judges the ratio is, again, higher, being 82.7%.

The basic reason for καί opening an apodosis lies in the fact that the Hebrew *Vorlage* included ו. When employing καί the translator probably regarded the apodosis as a normal co-ordinate main clause, which it in fact looks like. It is also possible that he simply did not care to avoid καί at the beginning of an apodosis. After all, employing καί with the apodosis was not totally wrong, because genuine

---

[6]   Based on Aejmelaeus 1982, 89 and 110.

[7]   While discussing the clause construction in the Greek Joshua den Hertog 1996, 172-180 almost entirely focuses on the use of the apodotic καί.

Greek authors also used the apodotic καί, albeit only occasionally. We do not know whether the translator noted the stylistic problem involved in employing the apodotic καί or not, but the narrow segmentation provides a very good explanation for the use of καί. Because the segment was very narrow, the translators did not note the apodosis and employed καί as if the clause were an ordinary main clause.[8]

TABLE 17 The use of καί in the renderings of an ordinary main clause and in an apodosis

%	Ordinary main clause	Apodosis
Joshua	88.6	52
Judges	97.6	83

In this table the ordinary main clauses do *not* include the formulas and thus the ratio differs from that given when discussing main clauses. The difference between this table and the ratios given earlier is very small and insignificant however.

If compared with the use of καί in renderings of an ordinary main clause, the use of καί in apodosis is less extensive. Thus, the translators of Joshua and Judges did at least occasionally notice the apodosis and left the Hebrew ו without any visible counterpart. The difference between the use of καί in renderings of an ordinary main clause and those of the apodosis is especially noteworthy in Joshua. καί is used in only one half of the apodoses (52%) whereas the translators nearly always employed it when dealing with ordinary co-ordinate main clauses. In Judges καί is the main rendering of ו at the

---

[8]   In some instances the tense or mood in the apodosis differs from that of the protasis (cf. examples of the conditional apodosis and the apodotic καί on p. 114). This fact does not indicate that the translator did not regard the apodosis as a normal co-ordinate main clause, because the apodosis contains the tense and mood of an ordinary main clause. The tense or mood shift does not, then, indicate that the use of the apodotic καί was intentional or that the translator noticed the problem in using the apodotic καί, but helps us to determine the presence of apodoses.

beginning of an apodosis (83%), but the ratio is a little lower than the ratio of καί for ordinary main clauses.

When the translations of the Pentateuch are taken into consideration, Joshua again seems to lie between Genesis-Exodus and the more literal translations of Leviticus, Numbers and Deuteronomy. Judges, on the other hand, shows its very literal nature here, too. Not one translation of the Pentateuch matches the ratio for Judges. The ratios for the books of the Pentateuch are in ascending order: Exodus 21.9%, Genesis 41.6%, Leviticus 59.5%, Numbers 64.1% and Deuteronomy 69.7%.[9]

4.3 The use of ὅτι and γάρ as renderings of the causal כי

By studying the renderings of causal clauses in Hebrew Aejmelaeus showed that the use of ὅτι as compared with the use of γάρ is an indicator of the translation technique employed and that the ratios for these Greek conjunctions in the renderings of the causal כי are significant for translation technique.[10] This is especially true for the ratio for γάρ calculated from the so-called "potential cases" that refer to כי clauses, where γάρ would have been the correct rendering, but ὅτι not.[11] If these כי clauses are used as a criterion for the translation employed, the difference between the two translations is seen very clearly. In Joshua the ratio for γάρ of all the potential causal כי cases is 65%, but in Judges as low as 2%.

The low ratio of γάρ in Judges becomes understandable when the use of ὅτι as a rendering of causal כי is taken into account. The translator of Judges employed ὅτι as the equivalent of causal כי, because ὅτι is often suitable in renderings of כי. The literalness of the translation and the narrow segmentation in the translation technique are also seen in the rare use of γάρ. Because the ratio for

---

[9]   Aejmelaeus 1982, 128 gives the statistics for the Pentateuch.
[10]   Aejmelaeus 1993, 26-27.
[11]   See Aejmelaeus 1993, 26 and my discussion on pp. 157-158.

γάρ in Joshua is remarkably higher than in Judges, the translation of Joshua is not as literal as that of Judges.

The comparison with the translations of the Pentateuch verifies the conclusion. The translators of Genesis and Exodus used γάρ frequently. The ratio of γάρ for Genesis is 78% and for Exodus 96% respectively. The translator of Joshua, then, almost achieves their standard. The rest of the books of the Pentateuch show more limited use of γάρ, the ratios being 45% for Leviticus, 40% for Numbers, and 32% for Deuteronomy.[12] Judges is indeed very different as a translation from the books of the Pentateuch or Joshua.

The general picture is clear. The Greek Judges is more literal than the Greek Joshua or any books of the LXX of the Pentateuch as a translation. Its translator used a small selection of equivalents to render a conjunction in the cases discussed. For the Hebrew ו it was καί and for the Hebrew כי it was ὅτι. The translator of Joshua seems to have rendered more freely. He even surpasses the more literal translators of the Pentateuch, the translators of Leviticus, Numbers and Deuteronomy. This does not, however, make his translation as free as the translations of Genesis or Exodus. Joshua evidently lies between the free and literal translations of the Pentateuch, if the renderings of ו and כי are considered as criteria of the translation technique.

4.4 The classifications compared

Next, this general classification needs to be set alongside the results and classifications by other scholars who have studied the translation technique of Joshua and Judges. The studies by Thackeray, Wifstrand, Soisalon-Soininen and Sollamo mentioned in the introduction to the present study (pp. 1-3) offer the classifications analogous to the classification reached in the present study, and next I shall compare my results with theirs.

---

[12] See Aejmelaeus 1993, 26 for the statistics.

Thackeray bases his classification on the impression that the translations gave him.[13] Nevertheless, the classification has turned out to be fairly trustworthy. According to Thackeray, the LXX books can be classified into four groups reflecting translation technique and style. These groups are good translations, indifferent translations, literal or unintelligent translations and paraphrases. Pentateuch and Joshua are included in the first group but Judges in the third.[14] Thus, my analysis fits Thackeray's interpretation.

Wifstrand's classification is based on the position of the enclitic personal pronoun in the LXX. Because Hebrew uses pronominal suffixes to mark possession, the translators often placed the Greek pronoun right after its substantive, but in Classical Greek writers did not favour that word order. Instead, the pronoun is often separated from the substantive and only seldom follows it.[15]

The translators of Joshua and Judges nearly always followed the Hebrew word order, placing the pronoun immediately after its substantive. Wifstrand detects only 2 cases out of 210 in Judges where the pronoun was not used immediately following the substantive. In Joshua there occur, according to him, 2 cases out of more than 80.[16] Accordingly, Wifstrand classifies these books in the same group of the more literal translations. In the books of the Pentateuch the position of the pronoun more often follows the Classical usage.[17]

Thus, the difference between the translations of Joshua and Judges is not visible in Wifstrand's material and the translation of Joshua is more literal according to Wifstrand's analysis than according to mine. Consequently, my analysis corresponds better with Thackeray's conclusions than with Wifstrand's analysis.[18]

---

[13] Thackeray 1909, 12 mentions the "point of view of style" as the basis of the classification, but seemingly there is more than that; see Sollamo 1975, 775 and Barr 1979, 9.

[14] Thackeray 1909, 13.

[15] Wifstrand 1950, 44.

[16] Wifstrand 1950, 45.

[17] Wifstrand 1950, 52-55.

[18] See also Wifstrand's discussion concerning Thackeray's classification; Wifstrand 1950, 67-68.

TABLE 18 The grouping of the Pentateuch, Joshua and Judges according to Soisalon-Soininen

	Part.coni.	τοῦ with the inf.	ב + inf.
Gen	I (1)	I (8)	I (6)
Ex	I (4)	I (1)	I (4)
Lev	II (12)	II (9)	I (10)
Num	I (8)	I (6)	I (8)
Dtn	I (5)	I (2)	I (5)
Josh	**I (7)**	**I (5)**	**I (7)**
Judg	**III (17)**	**III (16)**	**III (20)**

The table gives the position of the books of the Pentateuch, Joshua and Judges in Soisalon-Soininen's classification with the three criteria. The Roman numeral shows the group the book belongs in and the Arabic numeral in brackets shows the position of the book if listed in descending order.

Soisalon-Soininen's study on the infinitive and its use by the various translators of the LXX allows him to compare various translators and set them in relation to each other. For the comparison Soisalon-Soininen selects three different criteria and divides the books of the LXX into three different groups reflecting the freedom of the translation of the book.[19] These criteria are a) the use of the Greek participle in the construction *participium coniunctum*,[20] b) the use of τοῦ + the infinitive,[21] and c) the renderings of the constructions ב with the Hebrew construct infinitive.[22]

---

[19] Soisalon-Soininen also introduces a fourth criterion, the use of the Greek infinitive without a Hebrew counterpart (Soisalon-Soininen 1965, 190), but it is not important here and will not be taken into consideration.

[20] Soisalon-Soininen 1965, 177-178.

[21] Soisalon-Soininen 1965, 186-187.

[22] Soisalon-Soininen 1965, 188-190. From the discussion Lev has accidently been omitted, but its position can be deduced from the table given on page 188 and from Soisalon-Soininen's description of how the groups are formed. Lev belongs in group I.

By using Soisalon-Soininen's criteria one may set the books of the LXX in descending order and calculate the mean of the relative positions of various books. Interestingly enough, Exodus, Deuteronomy, Joshua, Numbers, Leviticus, and Judges appear in the same order no matter what criterion Soisalon-Soininen selects. Only the position of Genesis seems to vary, and Leviticus, of course, belongs either in group I or in group II. The Pentateuch, Joshua and Judges may be organized (by relying on the mean value) into the following sequence: Exodus (3.0), Deuteronomy (4.0), Genesis (5.0), Joshua (6.3), Numbers (7.3), Leviticus (10.3), Judges (17.7).

My classification matches that of Soisalon-Soininen, because in his classification Joshua comes after Genesis and Exodus but before Leviticus and Numbers. Judges differs from the translations of the Pentateuch and Joshua, being more literal than they.

Sollamo examines every occurrence of the semiprepositions in the MT, studying the way they are rendered in the LXX, but for the translation-technical discussion she includes only the renderings of the common semiprepositions, classifying them as free, literal, and slavish.[23]

Sollamo's classification of the books of the LXX is based on three criteria.[24] She calculates a ratio for free renderings of the semipreposition by comparing the number of the free renderings to the total number of renderings in a book of the LXX.[25] The ratio for slavish renderings is calculated accordingly. Finally, Sollamo uses the stereotyping tendency as a criterion calculating the tendency as the ratio of the most common single Greek equivalent for a semipreposition against the total number of renderings.[26]

Sollamo concludes that it is possible to arrange the books of the LXX into four groups according to the position they occupy when

---

[23] The common semiprepositions are לְעֵינֵי ,בְּעֵינֵי ,עַל־פְּנֵי ,מִלִּפְנֵי ,מִפְּנֵי ,לִפְנֵי, בְּתוֹךְ ,מִקֶּרֶב ,בְּקֶרֶב ,עַל־פִּי ,עַל־יַד ,מִיַּד ,בְּיַד, and מִתּוֹךְ; Sollamo 1979, 280. She does not offer any discussion as to how the status of an equivalent is determined in her classification (see *ibid.*, 280 note 1.).

[24] Sollamo 1979, 281-283.

[25] Sollamo 1979, 280.

[26] Sollamo 1979, 283.

different criteria are used.[27] Among the most freely rendered books
is Exodus (4.3). In the second category belong such books as Leviticus (8), Genesis (9.3), Joshua (10), Numbers (10.7) and, Deuteronomy (10.7). Judges (22.6) turns out to be among the most slavish
translations in the LXX. The number in brackets is the mean value
of the relative position of the book when different criteria were used.

TABLE 19 The criteria used by Sollamo in the Pentateuch, Joshua,
and Judges

	Free	Slavish	Stereotyping tendency
Gen	27.2 (11)	29.2 (9)	50.0 (8)
Ex	46.0 (5)	20.1 (4)	43.1 (4)
Lev	35.9 (7)	9.9 (2)	64.1 (15)
Num	25.5 (12)	28.2 (7)	60.9 (13)
Dtn	28.2 (9)	42.1 (11)	54.5 (12)
Josh	32.2 (8)	43.6 (12)	52.3 (10)
Judg A	1.7 (24)	75.2 (24)	68.6 (20)

In the three columns on the right-hand side the ratios computed by Sollamo for
different criteria are given. The columns include the ratios for free renderings,
slavish renderings, and the stereotyping tendency, i.e. the medium of ratios for
the most common equivalent for each semipreposition. The number in brackets
indicates the relative position of a book in the classification.

The classification by Sollamo matches mine. In her classification
Joshua follows Genesis and Exodus, but comes before Numbers and
Deuteronomy. Judges, on the other hand, is more literal than any
translations of the Pentateuch.

The classifications reached in various studies mainly match with
each other, but occasionally the picture given of the translations is
less homogeneous. In her study Sollamo proposed that the trans-

---

[27] Sollamo 1979, 284-286.

lators were probably "fairly consistent" in their translation technique, translating most cases of very different types freely or slavishly according to the normal practice.[28] This is not obvious, however, and the different phenomena probably triggered variant translation techniques.[29] Despite this, my study and the discussion in the present chapter support Sollamo's suggestion, even if some variation is seen in the classifications.[30] The variation is probably based on the different demands the different phenomena made of the translators. For instance, the ability to deviate from the word order of the parent text (Wifstrand's main question) is probably a different issue from the selection of a suitable conjunction (my main question).

4.5 Other aspects in the translation technique

The renderings of various formulas (pp. 82-109), the renderings of circumstantial clauses (pp. 168-180), and the renderings of clauses expressing the positive alternative after a negative statement (pp. 189-192) reveal *different things* about the translation technique than the ordinary main clauses, apodoses and causal clauses discussed above.

With these aspects one may study how far the translators could take the special character of the Hebrew expression into account while translating.

The formulas ויהי, והיה, ועתה, and והנה posed a problem for the translators. The translators of Joshua and Judges mostly employed very literal or even slavish equivalents for the Hebrew formulas, resulting in questionable consequences: either the Greek expression is clumsy or simply gives a wrong idea about the Hebrew text.

---

[28] Sollamo 1979, 289.

[29] Soisalon-Soininen 1965, 187 proposes that the translation-technical classifications probably vary depending on the phenomenon under study.

[30] Sollamo's own material is not completely homogeneous, but according to her explanation the deviations are not as surprising as one might think; see Sollamo 1979, 284.

For the formula ויהי the most often used equivalent in the LXX is καὶ ἐγένετο (or sometimes καὶ ἐγενήθη). The translator of Judges always employed this slavish counterpart, but the translator of Joshua also used either literal or free alternatives that mainly consist of the conjunctions καί and δέ without any counterpart for the verb היה.[31]

The translators of Joshua and Judges mainly rendered the formula והיה by the slavish καὶ ἔσται. In Joshua this happens in seven out of the total of eleven cases and in Judges in five out of the total of nine.[32]

The formula והנה is frequently rendered as καὶ ἰδού. The slavish rendering appears in every instance of והנה in the translation of Judges, but in the translation of Joshua only once. Five times the translator of Joshua produced a less slavish rendering for the formula. Clearly the formula והנה was less problematic for him than the other formulas.[33]

The formula ועתה is translated very mechanically, employing καὶ νῦν, a slavish counterpart poorly reflecting the function of the Hebrew formula. The translator of Joshua only four times abandoned the slavish counterpart, and the translator of Judges did so only once.[34]

The literal translation technique employed by the translator of Judges is seen in the limited number of Greek counterparts – frequently slavish in character – for the Hebrew formula. The translator of Joshua employed several equivalents for the formulas and could occasionally produce correct and free renderings of the Hebrew. However, most of his renderings are slavish, such as those employed by the translator of Judges. This suits the picture about the translator of Joshua as being literal, although he is not as literal as the translator of Judges.

---

[31] For the evaluation of the renderings of the formula ויהי see pp. 90-91.

[32] The discussion about the formula is to be found on pp. 96-97.

[33] For conclusions regarding the translations of the formula והנה see pp. 101-102.

[34] For the treatment of the formula ועתה by the translators of Joshua and Judges see pp. 106-107.

The circumstantial clauses and the clauses expressing a positive alternative after a negative statement did not pose insurmountable problems for the translators, because they are fairly easy to recognize. The circumstantial כי clause always precedes the clause expressing the main event and the positive alternative always follows a negative statement. Thus, the special nature of these כי clauses is clearly marked in the Hebrew text.

The most often used Greek equivalents for the circumstantial כי are ὅτε and ὅταν. These are employed only in seven cases out of the total twenty. Especially noteworthy is the fact that the translator of Joshua never used ὅτι to render כי at the beginning of a circumstantial clause and that the translator of Judges used ὅτι only in four instances out of the total eleven cases.[35]

When כי marks the positive alternative after a negative statement, the translators of Joshua and Judges employed ἀλλά as the rendering of כי.[36] Only once the rule is not followed (Judg 11:15-16),[37] but even in that particular instance the translator of Judges marked the change from a negative statement to a positive one by using the conjunction ἀλλά!

Because the special כי clauses were easy to recognize, it comes as no surprise that the translators could compose correct Greek counterparts for them during the translation process. The special treatment accorded these clauses by the translators shows, on the other hand, that they were occasionally well aware of the context of the segment they were concentrating on.

There is a tension between the translations of the formulas and the translations of the special כי clauses. This is because the formulas were more difficult for the translators than the special כי clauses. The problem with the formulas is that they often look like normal co-ordinate clauses. The similarity to an ordinary co-ordinate clause made the formulas difficult to recognize. Only concentration on the text could reveal the formula. For the translator translating word for word the proper handling of formulas seems to have been a task too difficult to master totally.

---

[35] The renderings of the circumstantial clauses are discussed on pp. 168-180.
[36] See pp. 189-192.
[37] See p. 191.

4.6 The basic elements of the translation technique of the conjunctions ו and כי

The most important result of my study is not linked with the classification of Joshua and Judges as translations, as important as it is. More important is that we may now confidently explain the nature of the translation technique of the clause linkage. Consequently, the nature of the translation may be better understood. It is a result of narrow segmentation, interplay with Hebrew and Greek grammar or similarity and dissimilarity in the functions of conjunctions.

The first factor, **the narrow segmentation**, influenced the literary product, the word-for-word outlook of the translation. Obviously considering the context and the problems involved was difficult to do. Because of these problems the translations include stylistic and even grammatical problems, if not even errors. The use of the apodotic καί or the use of ὅτι to express motivation are examples of the problems.

A certain tolerance towards clumsy, otiose, or unidiomatic use of Greek is a part of the natural selection of Greek renderings. The ability to tolerate problematic language is of course a gift which varies from one person to another. Some people are more open to employ expressions that are unnatural or do not belong to the normal usage of a language. The tolerance may be seen in the translations of the apodotic ו by καί or in the translations of the motivational כי by ὅτι. The translator of Judges employed καί and ὅτι more often than the translator of Joshua. Therefore, he was more tolerant towards the unidiomatic use of these conjunctions.

Understandably, the degree of tolerance depends on the commonness of the expression. With a common conjunction, such as ו, the translators very probably became accustomed to rendering the conjunction in a certain way. The habit of acting in a certain way is closely related to the easy technique, too. Thus, I suggest that habit, the tolerance depending on the habit, and narrow segmentation laid the path to the actual translation technique now detectable in Joshua and in Judges.

The tolerance had its limits, too. Seldom did the translators make a true mistake, that is hardly ever does the translation contradict the formal usage of Greek or not suit the context. In cases where absolute literalism would result in clear error, the translators were apt to abandon the normal equivalent or literal renderings and employ correct, idiomatic ways of rendering the Hebrew idiom. Here the renderings for the circumstantial כי or כי expressing the positive alternative are very illustrative.

I would welcome a medium to measure the width of the segmentation or the limits of toleration. Expressions such as "very" or "fairly" tend to be equivocal until someone discovers a way to describe the segmentation or tolerance precisely. The only meaningful way of speaking about them available for the present study is to compare the translations of Joshua and Judges with other translations of the LXX. Since the available material is limited to the Pentateuch, the Pentateuch has been used in comparison.

The narrow segmentation does not alone explain the translation technique used in renderings of the conjunctions. The **grammatical functions** of various conjunctions had a role, too. The grammatical function of a Greek conjunction could probably provide support for the narrow segmentation. If the equivalent that naturally occurred to the translator seemed to suit the segment it was used without any further thought. In some instances this caused problems, but not at all always. Let us consider the use of καί as a rendering of the main clause initial ו. Since the function of καί in Greek is very similar to that of the main clause initial ו in Hebrew, the need for alternative renderings was not immense. The natural selection tends to limit the equivalents occurring to the translator to a minimum.

The outcome of the factors may be seen in the translations of Joshua and Judges. That the translations differ each other and from those of the books of the Pentateuch is only due to the human nature of the translation process. The personal gifts and contribution of the translator also played a significant role during the translation process.

What was important was the translators' ability to use free renderings or vary the equivalent if necessary. This is very clearly seen if one studies the renderings of the circumstantial כי. The literal nature of the translation does not automatically imply an incompetent translator.

The validity of the results depends, naturally, on the material selected as the basis. Not only is the material limited, but by using it one may describe only a narrow angle of the translation process: the way many clauses are linked together. By adding material concerning the translation of the verbal forms or lexicalisation of nouns one might gain a wider perspective.

4.7 Individual characteristics of the translators

The true fingerprints of the translator cannot be detected by using general characterisations or statistics. On the contrary, the personal traces of a translator are only to be seen if we regard rare and unique renderings. Despite the narrow segmentation, tolerance and the habit of using only certain Greek equivalents, the translators were occasionally capable of producing renderings displaying imagination and a clear understanding of the possibilities of the target language, Greek. To illustrate this I will set out some examples of these free and inventive insights on part of the translators mentioned during the detailed discussion.

In Josh 23:5-6 (p. 51) οὖν serves as a rendering of the Hebrew co-ordinator ו.
In Josh 6:17-18 (p. 52) ἀλλά serves as a rendering of the Hebrew co-ordinator ו.
In Josh 8:6 (p. 176) καί acts as the counterpart of the circumstantial כי.
In Judg 3:12 (p. 160) διὰ τό with the infinitive serves as a rendering of the Hebrew causal כי.
In Judg 8:1 (p. 161) ὅτε serves as a rendering of the Hebrew causal כי.

By bearing in mind these examples and the abilities of the translators one may hear a familiar tone in the words of Hollenberg, written over a century ago:

Wer diese Beispiele sorgfältig vergleicht, wird leicht erkennen, daß sie nicht leichtsinnige Zusätze eines oberflächlichen Uebers. enthalten, sondern daß sie nur der leichteren Auffassung des Lesers da zu Hülfe kommen wollen, wo der Sinn bei wörtlicher Wiedergabe nicht klar hervortrat. Kein Uebersetzer wird sich derartigen Zusätzen entziehen können.[38]

However, the material allows even more. The detailed study of the translations and their comparison with each other and with the translations of the Pentateuch brought to light individual ways of using Greek. The question is not solely one of single fine inventions but of more general ways of employing the language. These are not numerous, but very interesting.

The translator of Joshua differs from the translator of Judges and those of the Pentateuch in three ways. He often used either καί or δέ as renderings of the formula ויהי and left the verbal element of the formula without any counterpart. Similar translations do not occur in Judges, and in the Pentateuch they are very rare. He occasionally employed the supplementary participle when rendering the formula והנה. The construction is not used by the translator of Judges at all and in the Pentateuch it is very rare. Also, he once used the apodotic δέ, a very rare phenomenon in the LXX as a whole.

The translator of Judges had his own idiosyncrasies too. He occasionally rendered the co-ordinate main clauses by using subordinate causal clauses, especially introduced either with ὅτι or with διὰ τοῦτο. He also employed the *genetivus absolutus* in renderings of the co-ordinate main clauses more often than the translators of the Pentateuch and Joshua. Yet typical of him is the avoidance of καί to separate the embedded *part.coni.* from the rest of the clause. He never used it, but the translators of the Pentateuch and Joshua occasionally did. Finally, the translator of Judges employed ὅτε in renderings of the circumstantial clauses introduced by כי.

Finally it is time to describe the translations of Joshua and Judges in the light of my analysis and discussion.

---

[38] Hollenberg 1876, 7.

Joshua

Segmentation was narrow, toleration fairly high

The translation of Joshua is a literal one. Since almost every book of the LXX is literal, the general description is hardly helpful. According to my analyses, Joshua is freer than the most literal books of the Pentateuch, but Genesis and Exodus are clearly freer than Joshua. Joshua resembles Leviticus, Numbers and Deuteronomy as a translation. This is hardly surprising, since earlier studies point in the same direction.

As I mentioned in my introduction, Joshua has often been described as a translation standing somewhere between literalism and freedom. This description is justified if one bears in mind the fact that hardly any translation of the LXX is *not* literal. The continuum literalism versus freedom has to be understood within the framework set by the LXX books themselves. Joshua clearly is not the most literal translation of the LXX. In my study Judges turned out to be far more literal than Joshua. At the same time Joshua is not among the freest of the LXX books. We could say that the description "between literal and free" suits many books of the LXX and it has been used to describe, e.g. Numbers too.[39] Since Joshua is, I would now conclude, freer than Numbers, the description does offer only limited help in understanding the translations. It is more helpful to set the various translations on the same line and compare them.

Judges

Segmentation was very narrow, toleration high

As a translation Judges is more literal than Joshua or any book of the Pentateuch. This is not a new observation at all, since the conclusion could be based on earlier studies. If the translation of Judges deviates from Joshua or the books of the Pentateuch in the direction of literalism, can we still maintain Soisalon-Soininen's judgement that Judges is the weakest of all the translations of the LXX?[40] The

---

[39] See Voitila 1997, 108-109, and esp. his note no. 1.
[40] Soisalon-Soininen 1951, 60.

question is, of course, one concerning a value judgement. That the translation is literal and contains many instances of Hebraisms, does not necessarily mean that it is *weak*. Besides, speaking about weakness may give the wrong idea about the translator. Admittedly, Judges is a very literal translation. Yet even it contains some very clever and inventive renderings demonstrating the competence of the translator.

5 Abbreviations

For the abbreviations used in this work, see the style sheet for *JBL* available at http://www.sbl-site.org/scripts/SBL/Publications/SBL-pubs-JBL-inst.html. For abbreviations of the biblical manuscripts, see BrM.

AASF	Annales Academiae Scientiarum Fennicae
BDB	= Brown-Driver-Briggs 1907
BHK	= *Biblia Hebraica.* Edidit R. Kittel. Ed. tertiam 1937
BHS	= *Biblia Hebraica Stuttgartensia*
Blass-Debrunner-Rehkopf	= Blass-Debrunner 1984
BrM	= Brooke-McLean 1906-1917
Diss.	dissertatio
Einheitsübersetzung	= *Einheitsübersetzung der Heiligen Schrift* 1988
GNB	= *Good News Bible. Today's English Version* 1976
GesK	= Gesenius 1910
IOSCS	International Organization for Septuagint and Cognate Studies
Joüon-Muraoka	= Joüon 1991
Kühner-Gerth II:1	= Kühner 1898
Kühner-Gerth II:2	= Kühner 1904
LSJ	= Liddell-Scott 1996
LXX	Septuagint
Margolis	= Margolis 1931-1992
Mayser	= Mayser 1926-1970
MS(S)	manuscript(s)
MSU	Mitteilungen des Septuaginta-Unternehmens
MT	Masoretic Text
NEB	= *The New English Bible* 1970
NJB	= *The New Jerusalem Bible* 1985
NRSV	= *The Holy Bible. New Revised Standard Version* 1989
OG	Old Greek
OT	Old Testament
Rahlfs	= Rahlfs 1935
s.a.	sine anno
s.l.	sine loco
SBL	Society for Biblical Literature
SCS	Septuagint and Cognate Studies
SLCS	Studies in Language Companion Series.
TA	Teologinen Aikakauskirja
TOB	= *Traduction œcuménique de la Bible* 1975
ZVS	Zeitschrift für vergleichende Sprachforschung auf dem Gebiete der indogermanischen Sprachen

6 Bibliography of works cited

A. Sources and reference works

Aristotle
> *The "Art" of Rhetoric*. With an English translation by J.H.Freese. Aristotle in twenty-three volumes 22. LCL. Cambridge, MA.-London 1982.
> *Historia Animalium 2*. Books IV-VI. With an English translation by A.L.Beck. LCL 438. Cambridge, MA.-London 1970.

Barthélemy, Dominique
1955 "6. Juges" *Qumran Cave 1*. Ed. by D. Barthélemy and J.T.Milik. DJD 1. Oxford. pp. 62-64 and Pl. 9.

Bauer, Walther
1988 *Griechisch-deutsches Wörterbuch zu den Schriften des Neuen Testaments und der frühchristlichen Literatur*. 6., völlig neu bearbeitete Aufl. Hrsg. von K. Aland und B. Aland. Berlin-New York.

Biblia Hebraica. Edidit R. Kittel. Textum masoreticum curavit P. Kahle. Ed. tertiam denuo elaboratam ad finem perduxerunt A. Alt et O. Eissfeldt. Stuttgart 1937.

Biblia Hebraica Stuttgartensia. Editio funditus renovata, ed. K.Elliger et W.Rudolph. Editio quarta emendata, opera H.P.Rüger. Stuttgart 1990.

Brown, Francis - Driver, S. R. - Briggs, Charles A.
1907 *A Hebrew and English Lexicon of the Old Testament*. With an Appendix containing the Biblical Aramaic. Oxford. [Reprint 1972]

Brooke, Alan England - McLean, Norman
1906-1917 *The Old Testament in Greek according to the Text of Codex Vaticanus*, Supplemented from Other Uncial Manuscripts, with a Critical Apparatus containing the Variants of the Chief Ancient Authorities for the Text of the Septuagint. Vol. I: The Octateuch. Cambridge.

Clines, David J.A.
> *The Dictionary of Classical Hebrew*.
1993 1. א. Sheffield.
1995 2. ב-ו. Sheffield.
1998 4. ל-י. Sheffield.

Einheitsübersetzung der Heiligen Schrift. Die Bibel. Gesamtausgabe. 5. Aufl. 1988.

Good News Bible. Today's English Version. London 1976.

Harlé, Paul
1999 *Les Juges*. Traduction des textes grecs de la Septante, introduction et notes. La Bible d'Alexandrie 7. Paris.

Herodotus
Historiae 1-2. Recognovit C.Hude. Editio tertia. Oxonii 1927.

The Holy Bible. New Revised Standard Version. New York - Oxford 1989.

Jastrow, Marcus
s.a.　*A Dictionary of the Targumim, the Talmud Babli and Yerushalmi, and the Midrashic Literature*. With an Index of Scriptural Quotations. [Repr. New York 1985]

Liddell, Henry George - Scott, Robert
1996 *A Greek-English Lexicon*. New Edition. Revised and augmented throughout by H.S. Jones with the assistance of R. McKenzie and with the cooperation of many scholars. With a revised supplement ed. by P.G.W. Glare. Oxford.

Lust, J. - Eynikel, E. - Hauspie, K.
A Greek - English Lexicon of the Septuagint.
1992 Part I: A-I. Stuttgart.
1996 Part II: K-Ω. Stuttgart.

Margolis, Max L.
1931 *The Book of Joshua in Greek according to the Critically Restored Text with an Apparatus Containing the Variants of the Principal Recensions and of the Individual Witnesses*. Part 1-4. Paris.
1992 *The Book of Joshua in Greek according to the Critically Restored Text with an Apparatus Containing the Variants of the Principal Recensions and of the Individual Witnesses*. Part 5. Preface by. E.Tov. Annenberg Research Institute Monograph Series. Philadelphia.

Moatti-Fine, Jacqueline
1996 *Jésus (Josué)*. Traduction du texte grec de la Septante, introduction et notes. La Bible d'Alexandrie 6. Paris.

The New English Bible. 1970.

The New Jerusalem Bible. 1985.

Novum Testamentum Graece post Eberhard et Erwin Nestle editio vicesima septima revisa communiter ed. B. et K. Aland, J. Karavidopoulos, C. M. Martini et B. M. Metzger. Stuttgart 1993.

Philo

De Specialibus Legibus III et IV. Introduction, traduction et notes par A. Mosès. Les œuvres de Philon d'Alexandrie 25. Paris 1970.

Plato

Introduction - Hippias Mineur - Alcipiade - Apologie de Socrate - Euthyphron - Criton. Texte établi et traduit par M.Croiset. Platon œuvres completes 1. Collection des Universités de France. Paris 1949. *Gorgias - Ménon.* Texte établi et traduit par A.Croiset. Platon œuvres completes 3:2. Collection des Universités de France. Paris 1949.

Rahlfs, Alfred

1935   *Septuaginta.* Id est Vetus Testamentum graece iuxta LXX interpretes 1-2. Stuttgart .

Septuaginta. Vetus Testamentum Graecum Auctoritate Scientiarum Gottingensis editum

I   *Genesis.* Edidit J.W.Wevers. Göttingen 1974.

II,1   *Exodus.* Edidit J.W.Wevers, adiuvante U. Quast. Göttingen 1991.

II,2   *Leviticus.* Edidit J.W.Wevers, adiuvante U. Quast. Göttingen 1986.

III,1 *Numeri.* Edidit J. W. Wevers, adiuvante U. Quast. Göttingen 1982.

III,2 *Deuteronomium.* Edidit J.W.Wevers, adiuvante U. Quast. Göttingen 1977.

X   *Psalmi cum Odis.* Edidir A. Rahlfs. 3., unveränderte Aufl. Göttingen 1979.

XIII   *Duodecim Prophetae.* Edidit J. Ziegler. 3., durchges. Aufl. Göttingen 1984.

XIV   *Isaias.* Edidit J. Ziegler. 3. Aufl. Göttingen 1983.

XV   *Ieremias, Baruch, Threni, Epistula Ieremias.* Edidit J. Ziegler. 2., durchges. Aufl. Göttingen 1976.

Thucydides

Historiae 1-2. Recognovit H.S.Jones. Apparatum criticum correxit et auxit J.E.Powell. Oxonii 1942.

Tov, Emanuel
1992   "4QJosh^b." *Intertestamental Essays in Honour of Józef Tadeusz Milik*.
       Ed. by Z.J.Kapera. Qumranica Mogilanensia 6. Kraków, 205-212.
1995   "48. 4QJosh^b." *Qumran Cave 4. Vol 9. Deuteronomy, Joshua, Judges,
       Kings*. Ed. by E. Ulrich et alii. DJD 14. Oxford, 153-160 and Pl. 35.

Traduction œcuménique de la Bible. Édition intégrale. 1975.

Trebolle Barrera, Julio
1989   "Textual variants in 4QJudg^a and the textual and editorial history of the
       book of Judges (1)." *RevQ* 14, 229-245.
1992   "Édition preliminaire de 4QJuges^b. Contribution des manuscrits
       qumrâniens des Juges à l'étude textuelle et littéraire du livre." *RevQ* 15,
       79-100.
1995a "49. 4QJudg^a." *Qumran Cave 4. Vol 9. Deuteronomy, Joshua, Judges,
       Kings*. Ed. by E. Ulrich et alii. DJD 14. Oxford, 161-164 and Pl. 36.
1995b "49. 4QJudg^b." *Qumran Cave 4. Vol 9. Deuteronomy, Joshua, Judges,
       Kings*. Ed. by E. Ulrich et alii. DJD 14. Oxford, 165-169 and Pl. 36.

Ulrich, Eugene
1994   "4QJoshua^a and Joshua's first Altar in the Promised Land." *New
       Qumran Texts and Studies*. Ed. by G.J.Brooke with F. García Martínez.
       Leiden - New York - Köln, 89-104.
1995   "47. 4QJosh^a." *Qumran Cave 4. Vol 9. Deuteronomy, Joshua, Judges,
       Kings*. Ed. by E. Ulrich et alii. DJD 14. Oxford, 143-152 and Pl. 32-34.

Urkunden der Ptolemäerzeit (Ältere Funde) 1. Papyri aus Unterägypten. Hrsg.
von U. Wilcken. Berlin-Leipzig 1927.

Xenophon
       Hellenica. Recognovit E.C.Marchant. Xenophontis opera omnia 1.
       Oxonii 1900.
       Hellenica. Books I-V. With an English Translation by C.L. Brownson.
       LCL 88. London-Cambringe, MA. 1918.
       Institutio Cyri. Recognovit E.C.Marchant. Xenophontis opera omnia 4.
       Oxonii 1910.

B. Works consulted

Abel, F. M
1927   Grammaire du grec biblique suivie d'un choix de papyrus. Paris.

Aejmelaeus, Anneli
1982   *Parataxis in the Septuagint.* A Study of the Renderings of the Hebrew Coordinate Clauses in the Greek Pentateuch. AASF Dissertationes humanarum litterarum 31. Helsinki.
1982a   *"Participium coniunctum* as a Criterion of Translation Technique." *VT* 32, 385-393.
1985   "OTI causale in Septuagintal Greek." *La Septuaginta en la investigacion contemporanea* (V Congreso de la IOSCS) Ed. por N. Fernández Marcos. Textos y estudios *"Cardenal Cisneros"* 34. Madrid, 115-132
1986   "Function and Interpretation of כי in Biblical Hebrew." *JBL* 105,193-209.
1993   *On the Trail of the Septuagint Translators.* Collected Essays. Kampen.

Andersen, Francis I.
1974   *The Sentence in Biblical Hebrew.* Janua Linguarum. Series Practica 231. The Hague-Paris.

Auld, A. Graeme
1975   "Judges 1 and History: A Reconsideration." *VT* 25, 261-285.

Bandstra, Barry Louis
1982   *The Syntax of Particle 'ky' in Biblical Hebrew and Ugaritic.* Diss. Yale. New Haven, CT.

Barr, James
1979   *The Typology of Literalism in ancient biblical translations.* MSU 15. Nachrichten der Akademie der Wissenschaften in Göttingen. Philologisch-historische Klasse Jahrgang 1979 Nr. 11. Göttingen.

Barthélemy, Dominique
1963   *Les devanciers d'Aquila.* Première publication intégrale du texte des fragments du Dodécaprophéton trouvés dans le Désert de Juda, précédée d'une étude sur les traductions et recensions grecques de la Bible réalisées au premier siècle de notre ère sous l'influence du rabbinat palestinien. VTSup 10. Leiden.

Benjamin, Charles Dow
1921   *The Variations between the Hebrew and Greek Texts of Joshua:* Chapters 1-12. s.l. [Diss. University of Pennsylvania. Philadelphia]

Beyer, Klaus
1968   *Semitische Syntax im Neuen Testament* I. Satzlehre 1. Studien zur Umwelt des Neuen Testaments 1. Zweite, Verbesserte Aufl. Göttingen.

Bieberstein, Klaus
1995   *Josua —Jordan —Jericho.* Archäologie, Geschichte and Theologie der Landnahmeerzählungen Josua 1-6. OBO 143. Freiburg-Göttingen.

Blass, Friedrich - Debrunner, Albert
1976   *Grammatik des neutestamentlichen Griechisch.* Bearbeitet von F. Rehkopf. 14. Auflage. Göttingen.
1984   *Grammatik des neutestamentlichen Griechisch.* Bearbeitet von F. Rehkopf. 16. Auflage. Göttingen.

Blomqvist, Jerker
1969   *Greek Particles in Hellenistic Prose.* [Diss]. Lund.
1982   "Translation Greek in the trilingual inscription of Xanthus." *Opuscula Atheniensia 14.* Acta instituti atheniensis regni sueciae, Series in 4, 29. Stockholm 1982, 11-20.

Bodine, Walter Ray
1980   *The Greek Text of Judges. Recencional Developments.* HSM 23. Chico, CA.

Boling, Robert G.
1982   *Joshua.* A New Translation with Notes and Commentary. Introduction by G.E. Wright. AB 6. New York-London-Toronto-Sydney-Auckland.

Brandt, Willi
1908   *Griechische Temporalpartikeln vornehmlich im ionischen und dorischen Dialekt.* [Diss.] Göttingen.

Brockelmann, Carl
1956   *Hebräische Syntax.* Neukirchen.

Butler, Trent C.
1983   *Joshua.* WBC 7. Waco, TX.

Buzón, Rodolfo
1984   *Die Briefe der Ptolemäerzeit. Ihre Struktur und ihre Formeln.* [Diss.] Heidelberg.

Conybeare, F. C. - Stock, St. G.
1905   *Selections from the Septuagint,* according to the text of Swete. Boston, MA. [repr. in part as *A Grammar of Septuagint Greek.* Boston, MA. 1980]

Deissmann, Adolf
1923   *Licht vom Osten.* Das Neue Testament und die neuendeckten Texte der hellenistisch-römischer Welt. 4. völlig neubearb. Aufl. Tübingen.

Denniston, J.D.
1954   *The Greek Particles.* Oxford.

Dillmann, August
1886   *Die Bücher Numeri, Deuteronomium und Josua.* Zweite Aufl. Kurzgefasstes exegetisches Handbuch zum Alten Testament 13. Leipzig.

Frankel, Z.
1841   *Vorstudien zu Septuaginta.* Historisch-kritische Studien zu der Septuaginta 1:1. Leipzig. [repr. Hants 1972]

Fritz, Volkmar
1994   Das Buch Josua. HAT I/7. Tübingen.

Gesenius, W, - Kautzsch, E.
1910   *Gesenius' Hebrew Grammar* as Edited and Enlarged by the Late E. Kautzsch. 2nd English Ed. Revised in accordance with the 28th German Edition (1909) by A.E.Cowley. Oxford.

Givón, Talmy
1990   *Syntax.* A Functional-typological Introduction. Volume II. Amsterdem-Philadelphia.

Greenbaum, Sidney & Quirk, Randolph
1990   *A Student's Grammar of the English Language.* Harlow.

Greenspoon, Leonard J.
1983   *Textual Studies in the Book of Joshua.* HSM 28. Chico, CA.
1992   "The Qumran Fragments of Joshua: Which Puzzle are They Part of and Where do They Fit?" *Septuagint, Scrolls and Cognate Writings.* Papers Presented to the International Symposium on the Septuagint and Its Relation to the Dead Sea Scrolls and Other Writings (Manchester, 1990). Ed. by G.J. Brooke and B. Lindars. SBLSCS 33. Atlanta, GA, 159-194.

Gärtner, Hans
1964   "Andokides." *Der Kleine Pauly* 1, 344-345.

Haumann, Dagmar
1997   *The Syntax of Subordination.* Linguistische Arbeiten 373. Tübingen.

Helbing, Robert
1920 *Kasussyntax der Verba bei den Septuaginta.* Ein Beitrag zur Hebraismenfrage und zur Syntax der κοινή. Göttingen.

Hentschel, Elke
1989 "Kausale Koordination. Die Konjunktion *denn* und einige ihrer Entsprechungen in anderen Sprachen." *Sprechen mit Partikeln.* Hrsg. von H. Weyndt. Berlin-New York. pp. 675-690.

Hertog, Cornelis Gijsbert den
1996 *Studien zur griechischen Übersetzung des Buches Josua.* [Diss.] Gießen.
1996a "Drei Studien zur Übersetzungstechnik des griechischen Josuabuches." *BIOSCS* 29, 22-52.

Hollenberg, Joh.
1876 *Der Charakter der alexandrinischen Uebersetzung des Buches Josua und ihr textkritischer Werth.* Wissenschaftliche Beilage zu dem Osterprogramm des Gymnasiums zu Moers. Moers.

Holmes, S.
1914 *Joshua. The Hebrew and Greek Texts.* Oxford.

Humbert, Jean
1960 *Syntaxe greque.* 3ᵉ édition, revue et augmentée. Tradition de l'humanisme 8. Paris.

Jellicoe, Sidney
1968 *The Septuagint and Modern Study.* Oxford.

Jobes, Karen H.
1996 *The Alpha-text of Esther.* Its Character and Relationship of the Masoretic Text. SBL Dissertation Series 153. Atlanta, GA.

Johannessohn, Martin
1925 "Das biblische καὶ ἐγένετο und seine Geschichte." *ZVS* 53, 161-212.
1937 "Der Wahrnehmungssatz bei den Verben des Sehens in der hebräischen und griechischen Bibel." *ZVS* 64, 145-260.
1939 "Das biblische καὶ ἰδού in der Erzählung samt seiner hebräischen Vorlage." *ZVS* 66, 145-195.
1942 "Das biblische καὶ ἰδού in der Erzählung samt seiner hebräischen Vorlage." *ZVS* 67, 30-84.
1943 "Das biblische Einführungsformel καὶ ἔσται." *ZAW* 59, 129-184.

Joüon, Paul
1923 *Grammaire de l'hébreu biblique.* Rome.

Joüon, Paul
1991   *A Grammar of Biblical Hebrew.* Translated and Revised by T. Muraoka. Part 3: Syntax. Subsidia biblica 14/II. Rome.

Kaddari, Menahem Zevi
1997   "The Syntax of כִּי in the Language of Ben Sira." *The Hebrew of the Dead Sea Scrolls and Ben Sira.* Proceedings of a Symposium held at Leiden University 11-14 December 1995. Ed. by T. Muraoka and J.F. Elwolde. Studies on the Texts of the Desert of Judah 26, 87-91.

Korhonen, Riitta
1993   *Buts about conjunctions.* A syntactic study of conjunction expressions in Finnish. [Diss.] Studia Fennica Linguistica 4. Helsinki.

Kortmann, Bernd
1997   *Adverbial Subordination. A Typology and History of Adverbial Subordinators Based on European Languages.* Empirical Approaches to Language Typology 18. Berlin-New York.

Kühner, Raphael
        Ausführliche Grammatik der Griechischen Sprache. 3. Aufl. in neuer Bearbeitung besorgt von B. Gerth.
1898   2er Teil: Satzlehre 1. Hannover-Leipzig.
1904   2er Teil: Satzlehre 2. Hannover-Leipzig.

König, Ed.
1899   "Syntactische Excurse zum Alten Testament." *ZAW* 19, 259-287.

Lang, Ewald
1977   *Semantik der koordinativen Verknüpfung.* Studia grammatica 14. Berlin.
1984   *The sematics of coordination.* SLCS 9. Amsterdam.

MacDowell, D.
1962   Andocides, *On the Mysteries.* The Text edited with Introduction, Commentary and Appendixes. Oxford 1962.

Macintosh, A. A.
1985   "The Meaning of *mlkym* in Judges XVIII 7" *VT* 35, 68-77.

Mandilaras, Basil G.
1973   *The Verb in the Greek Non-Literary Papyri.* Athens.

Martin, Raymond A.
1964 "Syntactical Evidence of Aramaic Sources in Acts i-xv." *New Testament Studies* 11, 38-59.
1974 *Syntactical Evidence of Semitic Sources in Greek Documents.* SCS 3. Cambridge, MA.

Mayser, Edwin
Grammatik der Griechischen Papyri aus der Ptolemäerzeit mit Einschluss der gleichzeitigen Ostraka und der in Ägypten verfassten Inschriften.
1970 I:1 Laut- und Wortlehre. Teil 1. 2. Aufl. bearb. H. von Schmoll. Berlin.
1926 II:1 Satzlehre. Analytischer Teil 1. Berlin-Leipzig.
1933 II:2.1 Satzlehre. Analytischer Teil 2.1. Berlin-Leipzig.
1934 II:2.2 Satzlehre. Analytischer Teil 2.2. Berlin-Leipzig.
1934 II:3 Satzlehre. Synthetischer Teil. Berlin-Leipzig.

Mazor, Lea
1994a *The Septuagint Translation of the Book of Joshua - Its Contribution to the Understanding of the Textual Transmission of the Book and Its Literary and Ideological Development.* [Diss.] Jesusalem.
1994b "The Septuagint Translation of the Book of Joshua (Abstract)." *BIOSCS* 27, 29-38.

Metzger, Henri
1979 "L'inscription grecque." *La stèle trilingue du Létôon.* Fouilles de Xantos 6. Paris 1979, 29-48.

Moatti-Fine, Jacqueline
1995 "La 'Tâche du traducteur' de Josué / Jésus." KATA TOYΣ O' *Selon les Septante.* Trente études sur la Bible grecque des Septante. En hommage à Marguerite Harl. Sous la direction de G. Dorival et O. Munnich. Paris 1995. pp. 321-330.

Moulton, James Hope
1906 *A Grammar of New Testament Greek* 1. Prolegomena. Edinburgh.

Muraoka, Takamitsu
1964 "The Use of ΩΣ in the Biblical Greek." NT 7, 51-72.
1985 *Emphatic Words and Structures in Biblical Hebrew.* [Diss.] Jerusalem-Leiden.
1993 "A Septuagint Greek Grammar, but of which Text-Form or -Forms?" *EstBib* 51, 433-458.
1997 "The Alleged Final Function of the Biblical Hebrew Syntagm <waw + a volitive verb form>." *Narrative Syntax and the Hebrew Bible. Papers of the Tilburg Conference 1996.* Ed. E. van Wolde. Biblical Interpretation Series 29. Leiden-New York- Köln, pp. 229-241.

Nelson, Richard D.
1997 *Joshua. A Commentary.* OTL. Louisville, KY.

Niccacci, Alviero
1986 *Sintassi del verbo ebraico nella prosa biblica classica.* Studium Biblicum Franciscanum Analecta 23. Jerusalem.
1990 *The Syntax of the Verb in Classical Hebrew Prose.* Transl. from Italian by W.G.E.Watson. JSOTSup 86. Sheffield.

Nilson, Martin P.
1907 *Die Kausalsätze im Griechischen bis Aristoteles 1.* Die Poesie. Beiträge zur historischen Syntax der griechischen Sprache 18. Würzburg.

Noort, Ed[ward]
1998 *Das Buch Josua. Forschungsgeschichte und Problemfelder.* Erträge der Forschung 292. Darmstadt.

Noth, Martin
1938 *Das Buch Josua.* HAT 7. Tübingen. [2. Aufl. 1953]

Olofsson, Staffan
1990 *The LXX Version.* A Guide to the Translation Technique of the Septuagint. ConBOT 30. Stockholm.

Radermacher, Ludwig
1911 *Neutestamentliche Grammatik.* Das Griechisch des Neuen Testaments in zusammenhang mit der Volksprache. Handbuch zum Neuen Testament I:1. Tübingen.
1925 *Neutestamentliche Grammatik.* Das Griechisch des Neuen Testaments in zusammenhang mit der Volksprache. 2., erweiterte Aufl. Handbuch zum Neuen Testament I. Tübingen.

Rijksbaron, Albert
1976 *Temporal and Causal Conjunctions in Ancient Greek.* With special reference to the use of ἐπεί and ὡς in Herodotus. [Diss.] Amsterdam.
1984 *The Syntax and Semantics of the Verb in Classical Greek.* An Introduction. Amsterdam.

Rofé, Alexander
1985 "Joshua 20: Historico-Literary Criticism Illustrated." *Empirical Models for Biblical Criticism.* Ed. by J. H. Tigay. Philadelphia.

Ruijgh, C.J.
1971 *Autour de "τε épique".* Études sur la syntaxe grecque. Amsterdam.

Rørdam, Thomas Skat
1859   *Libri Judicum et Ruth secundum versionem syraico-hexaplarem ex codice muisei britannici nunc primum editi graece translati notisque illustrati.* Fasc. I, lib. Jud. cap. I-V. Havniae.

Schneider, Wolfgang
1974   *Grammatik des biblischen Hebräisch.* Völlig neue Bearbeitung der "Hebräischen Grammatik für den akademischen Unterricht" von Oskar Grether. Ein Lehrbuch. München.

Schoors, A.
1981   "The Particle כי." *Remembering All the Way...* A Collection of Old Testament Studies Published on the Occasion of the Fortieth Anniversary of the Oudtestamentisch Werkgezelschap in Nederland. *Oudtestamentische Studiën* 21, 240-276.

Schreiner, Joseph
1957   *Septuaginta-Massora des Buches der Richter.* [Diss.] Analecta Biblica 7. Roma.

Sickling, C.M.J
1993   "Devices for Text Articulation in Lysias I and XII." *Two Studies in Attic Particle Usage: Lysias and Plato.* By C.M.J.Sickling and J.M.van Ophuijsen. Mnemosyne Suppl. 129. Leiden-New York-Köln. pp. 1-66.

Sipilä, Seppo
1993   "A Note to the Users of Margolis' Joshua Edition." *BIOSCS* 26, 17-21.
1995   The Renderings of ויהי and והיה as Formulas in the LXX of Joshua. *VIII Congess of the International Organization for Septuagint and Cognate Studies. Paris 1992.* Ed. by L. Greenspoon and O. Munnich. SBLSCS 41, 273-289.

Smyth, Herbert Weir
1956   *Greek Grammar.* Revised by G.M. Messing. Cambridge, MA.

Soisalon-Soininen, Ilmari
1951   *Die Textformen der Septuaginta-Übersetzung des Ricterbuches.* [Diss.] AASF B 72,1. Helsinki.
1963   "Septuagintan lauseopin tutkimuksen periaatteista." *TA* 68, 216-231.
1965   *Die Infinitive in der Septuaginta.* AASF B 132,1. Helsinki
1987   *Studien zur Septuaginta-Syntax.* Zu seinem 70. Geburtstag am 4. Juni 1987. Hrsg. von A. Aejmelaeus und R. Sollamo. AASF 237. Helsinki.
1990   "Zurück zur Hebraismenfrage." *Studien zur Septuaginta - Robert Hanhart zu Ehren.* MSU 20. Göttingen. pp. 35-51.

Sollamo, Raija
1975   "Some 'improper' prepositions, such as ΕΝΩΠΙΟΝ, ΕΝΑΝΤΙΟΝ, ΕΝΑΝΤΙ, etc., in the Septuagint and early Koine Greek." *VT* 25, 773-782.
1979   *Renderings of the Hebrew Semiprepositions in the Septuagint.* AASF Dissertationes humanarum litterarum 19. Helsinki.
1987   "Joosuan kirjan Septuaginta-käännöksen luonteesta." *TA* 92, 191-198.
1995   *Repetition of the Possessive Pronouns in the Septuagint.* SBLSCS 40. Atlanta, GE.

Steuernagel, Carl
1900   *Übersetzung und Erklärung der Bücher Deuteronomium und Josua und Allgemeine Einleitung in den Hexateuch.* HAT I.3. Göttingen.

Thackeray, Henry St. John
1908   "The Infinitive Absolute in the LXX." *JTS* 9, 597-601.
1909   *A Grammar of the Old Testament in Greek according to the Septuagint.* Vol. 1: Introduction, Orthography and Accidence. Cambridge. [Repr. Hildesheim - New York 1978]

Thumb, Albert
1901   *Die griechische Sprache im Zeitalter des Hellenismus.* Strassburg.

Tov, Emmanuel
1978   "Midrash-Type Exegesis in the LXX of Joshua." *RB* 85, 50-61.
1981   *The Text-critical Use of the Septuagint in Biblical Research.* Jerusalem Bible Studies 3. Jerusalem.
1997   *The Text-critical Use of the Septuagint in Biblical Research.* 2nd Ed., Revised and Enlarged. Jerusalem Bible Studies 8. Jerusalem.

Trebolle Barrera, Julio
1998   *The Jewish Bible and the Christian Bible.* An introduction to the history of the Bible. Translated by W.G.E.Watson. Leiden-New York-Köln.

Trenkner, Sophie
1960   *Le style KAI dans le récit attique oral.* Bibliotheca classica vangorcumiana 9. Assen.

Turner, Nigel
1955   "The Relation of Luke i and ii to Hebraic Sources and to the Rest of Luke-Acts." *New Testament Studies* 2, 100-109.
1963   *A Grammar of New Testament Greek* by *J.H. Moulton.* Volume III: Syntax. Edinburgh.

Waltke, Bruce K. - O'Connor, M.
1990   *An Introduction to Biblical Hebrew Syntax.* Winona Lake, IN.

van der Meer, Michaël
1998   *Textual Criticism and Literary Criticism in Joshua 1:7.* An unpublished paper presented in the XII Meeting of the IOSCS, Oslo.

Van Wolde, Ellen
1995   "Who Guides Whom? Embeddedness and Perspective in Biblical Hebrew and in 1 Kings 3:16-28." *JBL* 114, 623-642.

Wifstrand, Albert
1947   "Ett nytestamentlig ordföljdsproblem." *SEÅ* 12, 367-341.
1950   *Die Stellung der enklitischen Personalpronomina bei den Septuaginta.* Kungl. humanistiska vetenskapssamfundets i Lund årsberättelse 1949-1950 II. Lund.

Williams, Ronald J.
1976   *Herbew Syntax.* An Outline. 2nd. Edition. Toronto-Buffalo-London.

Viteau, Joseph
1893   *Étude sur le grec du Nouveau Testament.* Le verbe. Paris.

Voitila, Anssi
1995   *Verbimuodot Septuagintassa.* Qatal-, wayyiqtol-, yiqtol-, weqatal-muotojen kääntäminen Septuagintan Pentateukissa. Unpublished licenciate thesis. University of Helsinki.
1997   "The Translator of the Greek Numbers." *IX Congress of the International Organization of Septuagint and Cognate Studies. Cambridge 1995.* Ed. by B.Taylor. SBLSCS 45, 109-121.

Yeivin, Israel
1980   מבוא למסורה הטברנית. *Introduction to the Tiberian Masorah.* Translated and ed. by E. J. Revell. SBL Masoretic Studies 5. s.l.

7 Indices

References throughout are to pages. The letter n indicates that the source is cited only in the footnote(s) on that page.

7.1 Index of Scriptural References

Joshua

2:14	95	7:15	95, 131-132, 147, 164
2:15	142n	7:20	71-72
2:18	37	7:20-21	72
2:19	92	7:21	98
2:19-20	134-135	7:22	99
2:20	120, 130n	7:25-26	29
2:24	187	8:1	47
3:2	5	8:3	38, 43
3:3	122	8:5	93, 174-175
3:5	146	8:6	90, 162, 176-177, 179, 209
3:6	26, 28		
3:7	185	8:8	96
3:8	103, 112n	8:14	183
3:13	92-93	8:20	101, 127
3:14	37, 86	8:21	131, 182
3:14-15	38	8:22-23	27
3:15	115	8:24	86
4:1	5, 86	8:28	72
4:2-3	58	8:29	66n
4:6	170-171, 178	9:1	88
4:6-7	113, 119	9:4-5	63
4:8	127n	9:5	105
4:16	67	9:7	120n
4:21-22	119	9:12	105
4:23	66n	9:13	99
4:24	54n, 182	9:16	133, 183
5:1	5	9:18	145
5:5	142n	9:22	37
5:7	142n, 160	9:22,24	164-165
5:8	89	9:24	59
5:13	5, 57, 115	10:1	88, 131-132, 182
5:14	164-165	10:2	155
5:15	154	10:4	153n
6:1	46	10:6	146
6:5	65	10:8	154
6:7	73	10:11	88, 116
6:10	47	10:19	127n
6:15	86	10:24	86
6:17	142n	10:25	47
6:17-18	52, 209	10:27	84
6:20	5, 88	10:37	122
6:25	159	10:38-39	58
7:5	29	11:1	88, 122
7:13	164	11:6	147, 154

7.2 Index of Ancient Authors and Works

7.3 Index of Modern Authors